The Future of North America

2025

Significant Issues Series

Timely books presenting current CSIS research and analysis of interest to the academic, business, government, and policy communities.

Managing Editor: Roberta Howard Fauriol

About CSIS

In an era of ever-changing global opportunities and challenges, the Center for Strategic and International Studies (CSIS) provides strategic insights and practical policy solutions to decisionmakers. CSIS conducts research and analysis and develops policy initiatives that look into the future and anticipate change.

Founded by David M. Abshire and Admiral Arleigh Burke at the height of the Cold War, CSIS was dedicated to the simple but urgent goal of finding ways for America to survive as a nation and prosper as a people. Since 1962, CSIS has grown to become one of the world's preeminent public policy institutions.

Today, CSIS is a bipartisan, nonprofit organization headquartered in Washington, D.C. More than 220 full-time staff and a large network of affiliated scholars focus their expertise on defense and security; on the world's regions and the unique challenges inherent to them; and on the issues that know no boundary in an increasingly connected world.

Former U.S. senator Sam Nunn became chairman of the CSIS Board of Trustees in 1999, and John J. Hamre has led CSIS as its president and chief executive officer since 2000.

CSIS does not take specific policy positions; accordingly, all views expressed herein should be understood to be solely those of the author(s).

The CSIS Press

Center for Strategic and International Studies
1800 K Street, N.W., Washington, D.C. 20006
Tel: (202) 775-3119   Fax: (202) 775-3199
E-mail: books@csis.org   Web: www.csis.org

The Future of North America

2025

Outlook and Recommendations

EDITED BY ARMAND B. PESCHARD-SVERDRUP

Published in collaboration with the
Centro de Investigación y Docencia Económicas
and the
Conference Board of Canada

THE CSIS PRESS

Center for Strategic
and International Studies
Washington, D.C.

Significant Issues Series, Volume 30, Number 4
Cover design by Robert L. Wiser, Silver Spring, Md.
Cover photograph: © Corbis

11 10 09 08 07   5 4 3 2 1

ISSN 0736-7136
ISBN 978-0-89206-520-2

Library of Congress Cataloging-in-publication Data
The future of North America, 2025 : outlook and recommendations / edited by
Armand B. Peschard-Sverdrup.
     p. cm. — (Significant issue series ; v. 30, no. 4)
  Includes index.
  ISBN 978-0-89206-520-2 (pbk. : alk. paper) 1. Economic forecasting—North
America. 2. Business forecasting—North America. 3. Environmental policy—North
America. 4. National security—North America. 5. North America—Economic
policy 6. Canada—Economic policy—1991– 7. United States—Economic policy—
1981– 8. Mexico—Economic policy—1994– I. Peschard-Sverdrup, Armand B.
II. Center for Strategic and International Studies (Washington, D.C.) III. Centro de
Investigación y Docencia Económicas. IV. Conference Board of Canada. V. Title.
VI. Series.
  HC95.F88 2007
  330.97—dc22   2007047188

In memory of

Anne Armstrong

*who as chairman of the CSIS Board of Trustees
spurred the United States toward constructive diplomacy
with its neighbors and beyond.*

CONTENTS

PREFACE

This volume is the product of a multiyear research project conducted by the Center for Strategic and International Studies in collaboration with the Centro de Investigación y Docencia Económicas and the Conference Board of Canada. The project was designed to examine the strategic issues that North America will face in the year 2025.

In light of the hectic daily lives led by decisionmakers in each of the three North American nations, who, more often than not, are forced to put out policy or political fires that erupt on an almost daily basis or whose average citizens are trying to juggle family, work, and a host of competing priorities, scholars at the three institutions felt that policymakers, legislators, and the citizens of the three North American nations would benefit from thinking about what lies ahead. More important, we recognized the importance of examining how the three governments can best position themselves to hand future generations a better world—be it as a nation, as a region, as a hemisphere, or as part of the global community.

The objective of the project was to provide reliable information that would enable the leaders of all three nations to create sounder policy and enact needed legislation related to six areas of critical strategic importance to each of the three nations, to the region as a whole, and to the trilateral relationship: energy, the environment, labor mobility, competitiveness, infrastructure, and security. Specifically, the project focused on a detailed examination of current trends in each of these sectors and projected future scenarios based on these trends. Limiting our focus to these six areas by no means indicates that these are the only issues of vital importance to the future of all three nations; rather, our decision was based on the need to limit the study's already ambitious scope.

As part of the project, representatives from all three nations met in roundtable sessions to assess current and future trends in each of the areas that had been identified at the outset. The sessions—designed as analytical exercises—were conducted in a closed-door format purely in an effort to facilitate a candid and manageable discussion; by no means was there any intent to exclude differing perspectives or to advance a preconceived political agenda. To ensure a free-flowing and balanced discussion as well as a trilateral approach to assessments and viable recommendations resulting from the sessions, we invited an equal number of representatives from Canada, Mexico, and the United States to participate in the roundtable addressing each critical sector. Each session included a mix of representatives from relevant agencies or committees in the executive and legislative branches of all three governments who could contribute a practical, policy, or legislative perspective to the discussion and its results; relevant stakeholders from the private sector and nonprofit organizations; and highly specialized and multidisciplinary academics, analysts, and experts from all three countries who have solid experience in assessing current global and North American trends and in projecting scenarios. In this way, these trilateral brainstorming sessions were able to capture not only the very best thinking on the issues but also wide-ranging practical perspectives, thereby strengthening the capacity of Canadian, U.S., and Mexican government officials—in the executive branch as well as the legislative branch—to analyze, comprehend, and anticipate the challenges facing North America as well as the coordination and harmonization that are needed to prepare for them.

The chapters in this volume encapsulate the results of each of the roundtables—including the discussion, analysis, and recommendations—as well the additional research conducted by the authors of each chapter. The order in which the chapters appear is intended to provide a logical progression for the reader—particularly because some of the issues are clearly interconnected—rather than to place any priority whatsoever on any of the six issues. Although each chapter focuses on a specific issue, the discussions that are reported took into account the way shifts in one area would have repercussions on areas that were the topics of other roundtables. The chapters reflect this overlap, but the recommendations included in each chapter are presented from the perspective of the particular issue that was under analysis.

The project's underlying objective was to produce a well-researched analytical document that would assist the leaders of all three North American nations to formulate sound public policy and implement legislative decisions that anticipate future trends, based on today's facts and figures, projected out to the year 2025 and beyond. Although aimed at the policymaking and legislative community, the book's analysis also serves the average citizen of Canada, the United States, and Mexico through its ability to raise public awareness of the issues. It can help create the political will needed either to implement public policies or to pass legislation with necessary foresight—thereby empowering us all to work proactively toward the type of future that next generations will enjoy.

The project by no means presumed to predict what the future will be for North America in 2025. After all, many unknown variables can emerge and have a major impact—either favorable or adverse—on the projected future. If anything, we hope that this book does a sound enough job of articulating what the data tell us today about the need to anticipate various scenarios and, more important, helping to broaden the analytical horizon of decisionmakers and legislators in the United States, Canada, and Mexico.

It is apparent that the different stakeholders in all three nations have varying perspectives on the further integration of North America as well as on ways to move forward. It is therefore worth noting that this volume is not intended merely to prescribe the further integration of North America; rather, each of the chapters takes factual stock of the integration that has already taken place, anticipates future developments, and identifies the areas that warrant the formulation of a complementary set of trilateral public policies to more effectively address the transnational challenges and opportunities that lie ahead.

Clearly, the respective governments of North America will continue to make policy decisions that leaders consider necessary to pursue unilaterally and other policies that they will prefer to pursue bilaterally. Nonetheless, there will surely continue to be transnational challenges or opportunities facing the three nations that will necessitate a trilateral approach—if not a multilateral one—but these approaches are not mutually exclusive. If anything, by working trilaterally on transnational challenges and opportunities, North America can demonstrate true global leadership. After all, if the three North American governments cannot work together in harmonizing policies when such cooperation best suits the needs of their respective citizens, what does this failure say about the prospects for a global consensus or multilateral progress on many of these daunting issues?

All project participants hope that this volume will help the peoples of Mexico, Canada, and the United States develop a greater appreciation for the strategic importance of their North American neighbors for their own individual futures as well as for their collective future. This is particularly relevant when considering the major transformations that we are likely to experience between now and 2025 and beyond. Simply reflecting on the developments—both positive and negative—that we have witnessed in North America and throughout the world since 1990 leads one to conclude that the twenty-first century is likely to bring a quantum sea change in both the challenges and the opportunities facing the region and the world.

Reluctance to accept change is an inherent part of human nature, as is the longing to keep things as they have always been. Nevertheless, as the following chapters illustrate, a changing global environment is imminent. An effective response to the consequences of these changes will call on the people of North America—as well as the entire world—to spearhead the necessary action if civilization is to adapt and prosper.

Governments will undoubtedly have to be much more nimble in responding to changing conditions—be they challenges or opportunities—by making policy formulation flexible and its implementation more expeditious so that governments can adapt to evolving circumstances and conditions swiftly and effectively. The same holds true for the U.S. and Mexican Congresses and the Canadian Parliament. Given the interconnection—or cause-and-effect relationship—between many of the challenges that loom on the horizon, governments will also be called upon to build up the level of collaboration between the different government agencies that are responsible for overseeing seemingly distinct yet interrelated portfolios.

It is also important to recognize that developments on the international stage will have an ever-increasing impact on whatever forces are in play within and between Mexico, the United States, and Canada. These global forces will emerge in an environment that does not respect political borders or national sovereignty when it comes to pandemics, demographic changes and mobility, financial shocks, natural disasters, the scarcity of natural resources, and the advent of nonstate actors. These are just some of the developments that are capable of having significant ramifications on all the world's societies.

If it is true that the world is getting smaller with the onset of globalization, it is even more remarkable to see the increasing interdependence of the three North American nations. Although this development may not be an earth-shattering revelation to those residing along the borders of all three nations who regularly cross the border into the neighboring nation, it may be less apparent to someone living far away from the border.

North America will undoubtedly face both opportunities and daunting challenges in the years to come. How we capitalize on these opportunities or tackle these challenges will help determine the kind of future that lies ahead for North America.

ACKNOWLEDGMENTS

This volume is the result of a major research project on the future of North America in 2025. Countless individuals from Mexico, Canada, and the United States contributed their ideas, expertise, and time to this undertaking. Among them are the authors who took on the challenge of thinking analytically out to the year 2025 and then wrote the chapters in this book.

The two cosponsoring institutions—Mexico's Centro de Investigación y Docencia Económicas (CIDE) and the Conference Board of Canada—believed in the policy relevance of this project. Both institutions made substantive contributions during the research phase and also oversaw the peer review process of the reports published in this book to make sure that the six issue areas examined in this project were approached in a balanced manner and that they reflect the perspectives of Mexico and Canada, respectively, to the extent possible.

I am especially indebted to Enrique Cabrero, Jorge Schiavon, Jorge Chabat, Víctor Carreon, Juan Rosellón, and Alejandro Villagómez—all from the CIDE—for participating in the various roundtables and for carrying out the peer review process for the chapters. Although not with the CIDE, Miguel Molina and Luis Herrera-Lasso, who reviewed the chapter on infrastructure, and Isabel Studer, who reviewed the chapters on labor mobility and the environment, also deserve my gratitude. I also thank Alejandra Aguilar Lanz for her invaluable support in organizing the two roundtable sessions that were held on the CIDE campus.

I am grateful to the following individuals from the Conference Board of Canada for participating in the various roundtables and for carrying out the peer review process of all six chapters: Glen Hodgson, Louis Theriault, Mario Iacobacci, Len Coad, and Trefor Munn-Venn. I am also grateful to Yvette Diepenbrock, Brent Dowdall, and Yvonne Squires—members of the Communications Department at the Conference Board—for handling the Canadian media's interest during the research phase of the project.

Numerous colleagues at the Center for Strategic and International Studies offered valuable support, particularly Peter DeShazo, director of the Americas Program. Kristin Wedding, the research associate for the Mexico Project at the time, should be singled out for her close work with me throughout various phases to ensure the project's success. Danilo Contreras, the former coordinator of the Americas Program, pitched in with the logistically difficult task of organizing six roundtable sessions in three separate countries, and Chris Sands of the Americas Program reviewed the chapter on security to ascertain that the facts and analysis related to Canada were sound. A special acknowledgment goes to Sidney Weintraub, William E. Simon Chair for Political Economy at CSIS, not only for authoring one of the chapters but also—and more important—for serving as my unsuspecting mentor during my tenure at CSIS.

James Dunton, director of the CSIS Press, and his colleagues Donna Spitler and Roberta Howard Fauriol kept the publication production trains running on time and ensured that this publication upholds the high standards of the CSIS Press. I am grateful to freelancer and CSIS alumna, Mary Marik, who took on the tedious task of doing the desktop publishing of the many charts contained in the book. Along these lines, my deepest gratitude goes to freelance copy editor Bita Lanys Wicart, with whom I have worked over the years, for her painstaking review of each chapter to make sure that the very specialized text would be readily understandable to the lay reader.

In the spirit of adhering to a truly trilateral approach, each of the three nations hosted two of the six roundtables convened to study the topics examined in these pages. Needless to say, I am indebted to all the individuals who found the time to travel and attend these sessions—let alone share their ideas and expertise during the day-long discussions. There were too many participants in the sessions to mention in the acknowledgments; their names are listed elsewhere in this volume.

It goes without saying that this ambitious research undertaking would not have been possible without the generous financial support of the U.S. National Intelligence Council (NIC), the North American Development Bank (NADBANK), Mexico's Foreign Ministry, and Mexico's National Science and Technology Council (CONACYT).

I am grateful for the support that this project received from the NIC chairman, Dr. Thomas Fingar, as well as from Patrick Maher, the NIC's national intelligence officer for the Western Hemisphere. Clearly, this project coincides with the kind of "over the horizon" thinking about broader trends that the NIC usually produces in order to assist in the policymaking process. The fact that both this research project and its deliverable have been completely open to the public speaks to the ability of representatives of all three nations to work together to address issues that are of a trilateral nature and also underscores the need to continue such collaboration.

My thanks go to Jorge Garcés, managing director of NADBANK, as well as Juan Antonio Flores, NADBANK's associate director of public affairs, for recognizing the importance of thinking about the future—something that undoubtedly has a direct impact on NADBANK, whose mandate puts it at the axis of the U.S.-Mexican bilateral relationship.

This project had the support of many individuals from the Mexican Foreign Ministry under the administration of President Vicente Fox, including Gerónimo Gutiérrez, the undersecretary for North American affairs, and Juan Bosco Martí, the director general for North American affairs. The project overlapped two different Mexican presidential administrations, and I am grateful for the support from the administration of President Felipe Calderón, particularly from Arturo Sarukhan, Mexico's ambassador to the United States (whose support dates back to his time as adviser to the then president-elect during the transition between administrations); Patricia Espinosa, secretary of foreign relations; Carlos Rico, undersecretary for North American affairs; Alejandro Estivill, director general for North American affairs; and Enrique Rojo, Undersecretary Rico's chief of staff.

I also appreciate the support that this project received over time from successive general directors of CONACYT: Jaime Parada, Gustavo Chappela, and Juan Carlos Romero Hicks. A special acknowledgment also goes to Efraín Aceves Pina, CONACYT's director of international affairs, who is resolute in seeking to transform the bilateral agenda into one that will better meet the challenges of the twenty-first century by taking advantage of advances in science and technology.

Thanks go to the Commission for Environmental Cooperation of North America (CEC) and the executive director of its Secretariat, Adrián Vázquez-Gálvez, for their in-kind support to this project—support that came in the form of offering the CEC's renowned biodiversity experts to research and then write the biodiversity section of chapter 2.

Over and above the financial and in-kind support, the project also received the moral support of a number of "big thinkers" within the U.S. and Mexican governments, who recognized the value of a totally independent assessment—in particular, Tom Shannon, the special assistant to the president of the United States and senior director for Western Hemisphere affairs at the National Security Council prior to becoming assistant secretary of state for the Western Hemisphere; Dan Fisk, the current special assistant to the president and senior director for Western Hemisphere affairs at the National Security Council; and Kim Breier, former director for North America at the National Security Council. In Mexico, the project received moral support from Eduardo Sojo, the special adviser to President Fox before being appointed secretary of the economy by President Felipe Calderón, and Alberto Ortega Venzor, special adviser to President Fox and current chief of staff to Secretary Sojo.

Armand B. Peschard-Sverdrup
August 2008

OUTLOOK FOR ENERGY

SARAH O. LADISLAW

Over the coming decades, energy will continue to play a crucial role in ensuring greater security and prosperity within North America. Energy trends both inside North America and within the broader global community will present challenges and opportunities for governments and businesses to provide sufficient, affordable, and reliable energy to meet society's growing demands. This chapter will present a view of energy production and use in North America out to 2025 and seek to analyze the factors that may have an impact on the development of energy markets and resource adequacy in Canada, Mexico, and the United States.

The baseline projections for this outlook are taken from the *International Energy Outlook 2007* produced by the U.S. Energy Information Administration (EIA),[1] with some changes where views in Canada and Mexico differ from the EIA's projections. It is important to note that the baseline projections represent a view of the future in a policy-static context; significant shifts in energy policies could bring about a range of trends in resources, production, and use in the future that differ from the ones provided in the baseline view.

Author's note: Energy is a dynamic field in which policies and pricing are constantly changing in response to global events. The unavoidable time lapse between writing and publication of this report may mean that some data may not be current and do not reflect the dramatic rise in oil prices; therefore some implications of recent changes may need to be updated. Nevertheless, the general trends, most of the data, and the recommendations included in this chapter are directionally relevant.

Over the next 17 years, conventional production of oil and natural gas in North America is expected to decline as demand for these resources increases. Unconventional resources such as oil sands, oil shale, coal bed methane, coal-to-liquids, and biofuels are expected to help make up for the decline in conventional production, but these resources will require massive investment, sustained high prices, and additional infrastructure. Production of unconventional resources will—and in fact already does—face mounting criticism over its questionable environmental viability, increased cost, and long-term sustainability.[2] Despite the increase in production from unconventional resources, the North American continent is still expected to increase its reliance on imported oil and natural gas resources. Because global demand for these resources is also projected to increase at the same time that production of oil and natural gas resources are expected to come from a diminishing number of countries outside North America, this dependence on imports could have financial and security implications for the three neighboring countries.[3]

For the most part, the economies of North America were built on inexpensive fuel obtained from readily available supply sources. The infrastructure (mostly pipelines and transmission lines) within and between the countries was built to accommodate trade among major demand and supply centers. However, the infrastructure that is currently in place is no longer adequate to meet energy delivery needs and must be modernized and expanded to accommodate newly developed sources of supply and the growing needs of society. The companies expected to develop and deliver new resources face a future in which many factors—including rising costs (resulting from the increased cost of materials like steel, iron, cement, and so forth), a shortage of skilled labor, public opposition to infrastructure or resource development projects, and growing uncertainty over the future policy and regulatory environments within and across jurisdictional boundaries—may pose challenges to bringing adequate resources online in a timely, affordable, and reliable manner.[4]

Moreover, concerns over global climate change and the emergence of carbon-constrained environments introduce a significant degree of uncertainty into "business as usual" projections. Decisions to limit the amount of climate change causing greenhouse gases (GHGs) are being implemented at the international, national, state, and local levels. This patchwork of carbon constraints is the source of increasing uncertainty over the investment and operational choices of energy companies operating around the world. In an attempt to resolve some of this uncertainty, many companies have joined forces with environmental advocacy groups to call for sustained, long-term, and transparent policies designed to mitigate GHGs in order to create a more stable investment climate and inspire greater certainty in the future.

The major challenge over the next 17 years is to achieve adequate growth in energy resources and infrastructure in order to meet increasing demand while making the transition to a low-carbon energy future in line with emerging climate change policies. Current policy frameworks are not conducive either to addressing our energy security concerns adequately or to determining the path to a low-carbon energy future. Energy security, within the context of this report, will be defined as "a condition in which a nation and all or most of its citizens and businesses have access to sufficient energy resources at reasonable prices for the foreseeable future, free from serious risk of a major disruption of service."[5] According to this definition, the inability to develop major projects and resources in a timely and cost-effective manner is as much a threat to energy security as is a potential disruption in the supply. This chapter will examine the major trends that North America's energy stakeholders (including governments, companies, and the public) will need to consider in order to balance the economic, security, and environmental implications of our production and use of energy.

COMPLEXITY OF NORTH AMERICA'S ENERGY SECTOR

It is difficult to convey the complexity of the energy sectors in North America and the forces that affect the production, distribution, and use of energy in our everyday lives.[6] Energy is used to fuel vehicles, power homes, and run factories. The energy that is used for these purposes comes from oil, natural gas, coal, nuclear power, and a variety of renewable sources like wind, solar power, biomass, and hydropower. Many of these resources are produced domestically; others are imported. Each fuel varies in terms of energy content and quality, processing techniques and technologies, environmental impact, economic value, level of importance in different regions, and the number of companies involved along its value chain. Each sector—broadly divided into power generation and transportation—and fuel is subject to different regulations, receives different subsidies and tax treatment, and has a unique set of associated stakeholders. One expert has aptly described the continuing evolution of the energy sectors in North America as a "geopolitico-economic mosaic" made up of—and at the same time driven by—various regional, economic, and political motivations.[7] Developing the infrastructure and markets for this mosaic took over a century and the investment of trillions of dollars.

This complexity makes it even more difficult to predict in any great level of detail how the sector will evolve into the future. It is also important to note that the EIA projections examined in this report do not represent a prediction of the future. The projections are based on existing policies and therefore project the future in a policy-static context. The projections also include a range of economic growth and oil price scenarios in order to illustrate how those factors may alter the business as usual projected view. The EIA's outlook also includes discussion of policies and business decisions that must occur to enable projects and resources to come to fruition. This is only to say that the projected future is neither preordained nor is it necessarily the most desired outcome. The EIA's business as usual projections for North America show the following:

- a greater demand for roughly the same mix of energy resources used today (fossil fuels);

- declining production of conventional oil and natural gas resources;

- an increase in the production of unconventional resources (oil, natural gas, biofuels, coal-to-liquids, and so forth);

- greater reliance on imported sources of oil and natural gas;

- strong growth in the demand for coal in the United States;

- strong growth in the demand for natural gas in Canada and Mexico and declining production of natural gas in Canada and possibly in Mexico;

- the need for an investment of nearly US$4 trillion to modernize and build new infrastructure; and

- an overall increase—28 percent—in carbon dioxide emissions.

Between 2004 and 2025, energy demand is projected to increase in North America by 27 percent, with the fastest rate of growth in Mexico and the highest level of absolute growth in the United States. Energy demand in North America is projected to grow at a slower rate than the world average, which will be driven by strong growth in economies that are not part of the Organization of Economic Cooperation and Development (OECD).[8] Demand for liquids (mostly petroleum) is likely to continue to occupy the largest share of the continent's consumption because of the strong demand growth in the transportation sector (although natural gas will surpass liquids in the overall mix in Canada and Mexico). As the supply of conventional liquids declines, the demand for liquids will increasingly be met by the production of unconventional resources, such as heavy oil, biofuels, and coal-to-liquids; their production will be driven by a combination of higher prices and policy incentives. Coal and natural gas are expected to be the fastest growing shares of North American energy demand—at an average growth rate of 2.1 percent and 1.5 percent per year, respectively—and production of these resources are driven by strong demand growth for electric power and industrial needs. As figure 1.1 illustrates, the fuel mix differs considerably in each country and, under a business as usual scenario, is projected to remain relatively constant over the forecast period.

The United States is by far the largest energy consumer in North America, accounting for nearly 83 percent of North American demand in 2004 (23 percent of world consumption) and projected to account for 81 percent of demand in 2025 (19 percent of world consumption). The projected demand for energy is driven by population growth and gross domestic product (GDP), levels of which are expected to grow in each country over the forecast period, with the fastest rate of growth expected in Mexico and the highest level of absolute growth expected in the United States.[9] At the same time, economies in the region are expected to become less energy-intensive (that is, they will rely on less energy to produce a given unit of GDP). A major source of uncertainty in the projections is how energy intensity trends will change over time and within individual economies.

INTERDEPENDENCE AND TRADE

Energy trade is an important part of meeting energy needs in various regions within North America and is expected to remain strong to the

Figure 1.1. Energy Mix in North America, Actual and Projected, 2004 and 2025

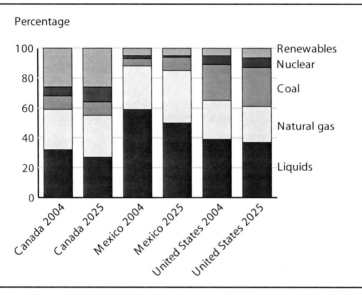

Source: U.S. Energy Information Administration, "International Energy Outlook 2007," http://www
.eia.doe.gov/oiaf/ieo/index.html.

extent that new resources are located and produced and the infrastructure necessary to get them to market is made available. Inter-regional energy trade flows are detailed in box 1.1.

Canada and Mexico are consistently among the top five sources of oil imports for the United States (along with Saudi Arabia, Venezuela, and Nigeria); together, the two neighboring countries provide 19 percent of the overall U.S. supply. Canada also provides 16 percent of U.S. natural gas needs (84 percent of U.S. gross imports in 2004). The United States provides Mexico and Canada with electricity, natural gas, petroleum products, and coal. Electricity trade across the Canadian-U.S. border is extremely integrated, whereas the linkages on the U.S.-Mexican border are less developed. Between 2007 and 2025, the entire continent is projected to grow more dependent on natural gas and petroleum imports, and the overall level of integration is expected to increasingly depend on the ability to build new cross-border infrastructure—oil and natural gas pipelines, transmission lines, facilities for liquefied natural gas imports, refineries, and so forth. U.S. imports of liquefied natural gas are expected to outpace

---

Box 1.1. Energy Trade in North America in 2004: Facts and Figures

---

Oil

- Canada and Mexico are among the top five suppliers of oil imports to the United States.

- Canada provided 16 percent of U.S. oil imports (2.138 million barrels per day of crude and products).

- Mexico provided 13 percent of U.S. oil imports (1.665 million barrels per day of crude and products).

- Canada imported 158,000 barrels of oil per day from the United States (mostly refined products).

- Mexico imported 209,000 barrels of oil per day from the United States (all refined products).

Natural Gas

- Canada exported 3,606 billion cubic feet of natural gas to the United States (85 percent of total imports and 16 percent of total consumption).

- The United States exported 394.6 billion cubic feet of natural gas to Canada.

- The United States exported 765 billion cubic feet of natural gas to Mexico.

Electricity

- Canada imported 22.4 million megawatt hours (MWh) and exported 33 million MWh of electricity from the United States.

- Mexico imported 415,715 MWh and exported 1.2 million MWh to the United States.

Coal

- The United States exported 19.4 million short tons (Mst) of coal to Canada and 1.0 Mst to Mexico.

- The United States imported 2.0 Mst of coal from Canada and 1,340 Mst from Mexico.

Sources: U.S. Energy Information Administration, "Mexico: Country Analysis Brief," January 2007, http://www.eia.doe.gov/emeu/cabs/Mexico/Oil.html, and "Canada: Country Analysis Brief," January 2007, http://www.eia.doe.gov/emeu/cabs/Canada/Oil.html.

imports of pipelined natural gas from Canada. The high level of integration between the three countries indicates that the energy sectors in all three countries are relatively interdependent and that energy policies and investment decisions in one country will inevitably have some impact on the energy sectors of the others.

FUTURE CHALLENGES
CONTINUED RELIANCE ON OIL

Despite the projected continuation of high oil prices, demand for liquids in all three countries—largely driven by the transportation sector—remains strong. According to the U.S. Energy Information Administration, demand for liquids is predominantly a demand for petroleum-derived products but also includes biofuels, coal-to-liquids, and gas-to-liquids. The EIA projects that the demand for liquids will rise in all three countries. At the same time, conventional oil production in all three countries is set to decline. Thus, demand for liquids will increasingly be met by a variety of unconventional sources and imports from outside North America.

The Challenge for Canada

According to the EIA's projections, Canada's demand for liquids is expected to grow from 2.1 million barrels of oil per day (MMBD) in 2004 to 2.2 MMBD in 2025, representing an average annual increase of 0.2 percent per year change over the forecast period.[10] In Canada, massive investment in the production of oil sands in Alberta is expected to make up for the shortfall in production of conventional oil. Overall Canadian production is projected to increase from 3.1 MMBD in 2004 to 4.8 MMBD in 2025. Oil sands are expected to account for 3.2 MMBD of total production in 2025, but production and delivery will require massive amounts of investment, infrastructure, and other resources (as detailed in box 1.2). Much of the oil sands output is destined to be exported to the United States, but there is a great deal of uncertainty and market speculation over not only the best location for upgrading, expanding, and constructing new pipeline infrastructure but also the most opportune market for the oil sands. In recent years, given the sustained increase in oil prices and advances in technology, production of oil sands has become economically viable.[11] However, the enormous amount of natural gas and water used to produce the labor-intensive and energy-intensive oil sands has driven up costs in Alberta and threatens the environmental and resource stability of the industry. Oil sands producers and the government of Alberta are working to resolve some of the concerns over the environmental and social impacts of producing oil sands. However, as Canadian citizens continue to express increasing concern over the ramifications of the industry not only on the citizens of Alberta but also on the ability of

---

Box 1.2. Canada's Oil Sands

Production of oil sands will make up an increasing share of Canada's overall oil production over the forecast period. Canada's oil sands are considered cost-competitive—at an oil price that ranges between US$30 and US$40 per barrel. The high price of oil over the last few years has spurred a flurry of activity to develop these resources, but, going forward, development of Canada's oil sands will continue to face a number of economic and environmental challenges.

Canada has nearly 175 billion barrels of economically recoverable oil sands—a figure that ranks Canada second only to Saudi Arabia in terms of global oil reserves. Oil sands are produced by extracting bitumen from the oil sands either through mining or in situ techniques. Currently, open-pit mining accounts for more than half the total production of oil sands. Future production is likely to use in situ processes, because nearly 80 percent of oil sand deposits are too deep to be developed through the use of traditional open-pit mining methods. Once extracted, the oil sands must be diluted (either with natural gas liquids or synthetic crude oil), transported, and upgraded. Extraction and upgrading require large amounts of water and natural gas. Increased prices of natural gas could significantly slow the pace of developing oil sands and also increase the cost of development. Thus, the industry is developing a number of new methods—those that do not rely as much on natural gas—to extract and upgrade this resource. According to a National Energy Board report entitled Canada's Oil Sands:Opportunities and Challenges to 2015, released in June 2006, Canada's production of oil sands could require 2.1 billion cubic feet of gas per day to produce 3 million barrels per day by 2015. The same report stated that between 2 and 4.5 barrels of water are withdrawn to produce each barrel of synthetic crude oil in a mining operation and that planned oil sands projects could use up to 3.3 billion barrels of water per year. Much of this water comes from the Athabasca River, and, even though some is recycled, most is stored in tailing ponds.

The oil sands projects are also a major source of carbon dioxide emissions. Federal and provincial authorities are working to promote the development of carbon dioxide capture and storage for enhanced oil recovery options in order to facilitate the production of oil sands in a carbon-constrained environment. Issues of increased cost, the need to transport carbon dioxide to injection sites through pipelines, and a variety of legal and regulatory issues still present obstacles, however.

The oil sands boom in Canada is driving up the cost of labor and materials in Alberta, leading to revised cost estimates for projects and a potential slowdown in the rate of growth in production. Citizens of Alberta have recently expressed growing concern over the social, economic, and resource impact of oil sands production. Moreover, the provincial government of Alberta has been conducting a strategic review of the royalties and tax structure associated with oil sands production—as well as a number of other reviews related to the regulatory regime and stakeholders' issues—to ensure that the province will be fairly compensated for its resources and to limit the adverse environmental and social impact of oil sands development.

Canadians to meet their GHG mitigation goals, oil sands production has come to represent a pivotal issue in Canadian politics.

One of the biggest policy challenges Canada faces is reconciling its aspirations to develop policies related to climate change with its position as a major energy exporter. The production of oil sands is at the heart of this debate. Under the Kyoto Protocol, Canada is obligated to reduce carbon dioxide emissions to 6 percent below 1990 levels during the 2008–2012 commitment period, but currently Canada is not on track to meet these commitments. Each barrel of oil produced from the Canadian oil sands yields approximately three times more greenhouse gas emissions than a barrel of conventional oil yields. Oil sands production represents the largest contributor to the increase in GHG emissions in Canada. Despite the public's concerns about the impact of oil sands production, the enterprise has contributed $3.7 billion (in Canadian dollars) in royalties and lease sales to the provincial government in 2006 and is responsible for much of the economic development and job growth in the region.[12] The high price of energy and the rush to develop Alberta's oil sands resources has spurred a more general debate about how quickly Canadians should develop their energy resources and at what cost to local communities.

The political environment surrounding Canada's energy policy is particularly complex because of the relationship between the federal and provincial governments. Different strategies for developing energy resources have traditionally differed by province, with the provinces in the west being the largest holders of natural resources. Incidentally, this difference is also the source of divergent views on strategies to mitigate GHG emissions; certain provinces would be disproportionately affected by mandatory limits to GHG emissions because of the nature of their industrial base. A major unanswered question for the future is whether provinces that produce and export energy will want to control the pace of future development as rapid growth continues to strain communities and resources and undermine long-term considerations related to climate change.

The Challenge for Mexico

Over the forecast period, the demand for liquids in Mexico is expected to increase by approximately 27 percent—from 1.8 MMBD in 2004 to 2.5 MMBD in 2025—driven by demand for transportation fuels. Oil production in Mexico is expected to decline as a result of a lack of new investment aimed at bringing additional resources online. Mexico's state-run oil company, Petroleos Mexicanos (PEMEX), does not have sufficient resources to produce its most promising fields in the deepwater Gulf of Mexico and is counting on nitrogen injection plans in fields that are already producing oil to make up for the 14 percent annual decline in its major producing field, Cantarell. The EIA's projections show Mexico's production falling from 3.8 MMBD in 2004 to 3 MMBD in 2015, but EIA also assumes that a decline in government revenue will encourage reform within Mexico's hydrocarbons sector and will allow investment to take place. With Mexico's ample proven reserves (nearly 12.4 billion barrels), EIA anticipates that Mexico will eventually reverse this trend but not until it can attract technology and capital.[13]

Mexico's main policy challenge is to find new capital and the expertise to develop its domestic energy resources and deliver them cost-effectively to its growing and developing population. Mexico's ability to alter its current energy policy environment significantly is critical to the future of the country's development as well as to North American energy integration. With the decline in production at Mexico's mammoth oil-producing field, Cantarell, the constitutional prohibition against private sector involvement in upstream oil and natural gas enterprises, combined with the dismal fiscal situation in which PEMEX finds itself, leaves Mexico in a difficult position. Without private capital, expertise, and greater financial freedom for PEMEX, it will be nearly impossible for Mexico to maintain its status as a major oil exporter. The information in box 1.3 provides greater detail.

In addition, in light of the growing need to import refined petroleum products at higher prices, it will become increasingly difficult for the government to guarantee the affordability of oil and natural gas resources to the Mexican population. During his campaign for presidency, the current Mexican president, Felipe Calderón announced his commitment to improve the energy sector when he proposed fiscal, labor, structural, and investment reforms. However, the closeness of the election and the subsequent need to build consensus with other major political parties has tempered the current administration's aspirations to pursue energy reform.

It is important to note that energy reform in Mexico, particularly in the oil and gas sector, remains an area of great political sensitivity. Polling still indicates that the vast majority of the Mexican citizenry still supports state control of the country's oil and natural gas resources. Consequently, absent a major domestic energy crisis, the likelihood of any sweeping reforms—especially opening up the oil sector to private investment—is minimal at best. Indeed, any changes that are made will have to be introduced incrementally and will have to be creative for the policy discussion to move forward in Mexico. Energy

---

Box 1.3. Facts about Mexico's Oil Sector

The Mexican Constitution prohibits private sector involvement in the hydrocarbons sector and places all responsibility for developing oil and natural gas resources under the state-run oil company, PEMEX. Throughout the 1980s and 1990s, PEMEX relied on its major oil-producing field, Cantarell, for the major part of its oil production. In turn, the Mexican government has relied on PEMEX to fund a large percentage of government spending (between 30 and 40 percent of the government's budgetary needs in 2005).[1] As government expenditures grow and production from Cantarell is expected to decline at a rate of 14 percent per year, the outlook for Mexico's ability to maintain current production levels looks ominous. The vast majority of the Mexican citizenry still opposes private sector involvement in exploration and development of hydrocarbons. Nationalization of the hydrocarbons sector in 1938 occurred at a very passionate and nationalistic time in the country's history, and that era is still a great source of pride to the Mexican people.

Because of the state's fiscal dependence on PEMEX revenues to fund government spending, PEMEX is heavily indebted—according to one report, in 2005, PEMEX had US$46 billion in long-term debt and an additional US$34 billion in liabilities. The increasing level of debt makes it harder for PEMEX to borrow the money it needs to increase its operational capacity.[2] The government takes approximately 60 percent of the company's net revenues each year. Adequate investments to fund exploration and production have not been made, and thus new fields to replace production from Cantarell have not been found and developed because the budget for PEMEX expenditures must be approved by the Mexican government—a process that has often left PEMEX underfunded. PEMEX plans to focus its development activities on increasing production at fields that are already producing oil through nitrogen injection (a process that proved to be very successful in Cantarell), but PEMEX lacks the resources necessary to go after its most promising deepwater oil reserves. Given the lack of experience in deepwater reserves, PEMEX is also at a technological disadvantage when it comes to developing its promising deepwater resources in the Gulf of Mexico.

Mexico is exploring ways to gain technological expertise via partnerships with foreign companies (primarily national oil companies like Norway's Statoil and Brazil's Petrobras) but, to date, has made little progress on creating new mechanisms for establishing partnerships. Without greater investment in the production of hydrocarbons, Mexico stands to lose not only its status as a major oil exporter but also a major source of government revenue.

---

1. Sidney Weintraub, "Mexico," in *Energy Cooperation in the Western Hemisphere,* ed. Sidney Weintraub (Washington D.C.: CSIS Press, 2007), p. 109.

2. U.S. Energy Information Administration, "Mexico: Country Analysis Brief," January 2007, http://www.eia.doe.gov/emeu/cabs/Mexico/Oil.html.

---

experts at Mexican institutions appear to be aware of the extent of the difficulty the country faces in its efforts to maintain needed levels of oil and natural gas production and to provide enough electricity to enable economic growth and development in Mexico. The last administration introduced a number of creative policy initiatives in an attempt to circumvent some of the obstacles introduced by the constitutional prohibition on private investment; these measures were met with some resistance and with limited success.[14] However, it appears that a larger segment of Mexico's political establishment is now arriving at a better understanding and appreciation of the country's energy problems— such as declining production, insufficiency of natural gas resources, imports of refined products, issues related to the electricity market, and the financial viability of PEMEX. A broader cross-section of Mexican politicians is now committed to finding ways to pass fiscal reforms that will enable PEMEX to improve its operations.

The Challenge for the United States

Over the forecast period, demand for liquids in the United States is projected to grow from approximately 21 MMBD in 2006 to 25 MMBD in 2025; this demand is overwhelmingly driven by a marked increase in transportation demand. In 2005, the nearly 14 MMBD of liquids consumed in the U.S. transportation sector made up 66 percent of U.S. demand for liquids; in 2025, transportation is expected to account for 73 percent of the demand for liquids[15] Production of crude oil in the United States is expected to remain relatively flat over the forecast period because of declining production in mature fields. Production in the onshore regions in the lower 48 states is projected to remain relatively constant as a result of high prices, enhanced oil recovery, and new oil shale discoveries. Production in the deepwater Gulf of Mexico is also expected to increase. EIA's projections assume that access to resources in the Arctic National Wildlife Refuge will not be granted. The contribution from unconventional resources (oil sands, ultra-heavy oil, biofuels, and coal-to-liquids) is expected to temper the overall production decline in the United States if oil prices remain high enough to encourage production. Production of unconventional resources is expected to come online starting in 2011—with 37,000 barrels per day in 2011 growing to 1.47 MMBD in 2025 in a high-price environment. However, over the forecast period, U.S. reliance on imported oil is expected to increase—from 60 percent of consumption in 2005 to a possible 63 percent in 2025.[16] Additional production could come online if the government decides to allow access to resources in the outer continental shelf, as the Minerals Management Service has recently proposed.[17] According to one estimate by that office, 18 billion barrels of crude oil and 77 trillion cubic feet of natural gas (technically recoverable resources) are currently off-limits in the lower outer continental shelf of the 48 contiguous states.[18]

Within U.S. policy circles there is on ongoing debate over whether to promote the increased production of domestically sourced fuels (via production of unconventional resources and increased access to areas that are currently off-limits) or to continue on the current trajectory of increasing the level of oil imports from abroad. Concern over the economic, security, and foreign policy consequences of continued dependence on foreign sources of oil has spurred a great deal of recent policy action. The twin goals of reducing U.S. dependence on foreign sources of oil and the emerging desire to address the impact of energy production and use on the earth's climate have led to a flurry of legislative activity within the U.S. Congress. In 2005, Congress and the administration worked to pass energy legislation that not only encouraged greater production and use of biofuels through a mandatory renewable fuels standard but also increased incentives for oil and gas companies to produce oil and gas resources that are harder to develop within the United States. Again, in 2007, the Congress passed energy legislation that was signed into law to increase the renewable fuels standard and increase vehicle fuel efficiency standards. Many legislative efforts in the 110th Congress have been geared toward removing incentives for oil and gas production and creating greater incentives for developing alternative and clean-energy technologies. This change reflects the overwhelming public sentiment that oil and natural gas companies are reaping disproportionately large profits and no longer deserve public support and also that the time to reinvest in fossil fuel resources has come to an end. At the same time, policymakers have started to pay attention to warnings about the potential negative environmental and economic trade-offs associated with production of unconventional resources—such as coal-to-liquids, biofuels, and oil shale. At a political level, the future of U.S. energy production and use is very much an open question. As the U.S. Congress continues to debate legislation dealing with energy security and climate change and as candidates for the presidency consider their stance on energy and climate issues, these trade-offs will become increasingly important.

AN INCREASING ROLE FOR LIQUEFIED NATURAL GAS

The demand for natural gas in North America is projected to increase over the forecast period, with the entire region expected to grow more dependent on imported liquefied natural gas (LNG). The United States is the largest producer and consumer of natural gas in North America and relies on Canada for 85 percent of its natural gas imports (approximately 16 percent of total consumption). Between 2007 and 2025, production of conventional natural gas in the United States and Canada is set to decline, with a growing share of production expected to come from unconventional natural gas sources like oil shale, tight sands, and coal bed methane. Today, LNG imports account for less than 3 percent of total U.S. consumption; by 2025, U.S. imports of LNG are projected to account for nearly 17 percent of total consumption. In fact, U.S. imports of LNG are set to surpass Canadian pipeline imports after 2015. Growing demand for natural gas in Canada (driven by the need for natural gas used for oil sands production and greater demand for natural gas for generating electricity) and the declining production in the Western Sedimentary Basin contribute to this trend. Going forward, the importation of LNG will have significant implications for pricing, infrastructure, and policy.

In 2004, Canada consumed 52 percent of its domestic natural gas production; in 2030, Canada is projected to consume 87 percent. Even though production of unconventional resources and LNG imports will make up for part of the decline in the production of conventional natural gas, Canadian demand for natural gas is expected to grow by nearly 44 percent. Both Canada and the United States await the completion of massive new infrastructure projects to bring additional natural gas resources to the market. The Mackenzie Delta pipeline is expected to come online by 2014—in time to offset the decline in conventional natural gas resources in Alberta and the increase in Canadian natural gas consumption. The Mackenzie Delta pipeline will bring natural gas from three fields in the Northwest Territories (inside the Arctic Circle) to northern Alberta, where the gas will be entered into a larger pipeline network. The three fields being developed to fill the Mackenzie Delta pipeline—Taglu, Parsons Field, and Niglintgak—can provide 800 million cubic feet of natural gas per day with a potential for 1.2 billion cubic feet per day to be provided from the region.[19] In addition, the Alaska natural gas pipeline, which is scheduled to come online in 2018, has the potential for adding nearly 2 trillion cubic feet of natural gas each year to the U.S. supply from Alaska's North Slope (the majority of the new supply projected). However, a number of issues—such as disputes over physical configuration of the ownership of the pipeline, taxes for production of oil and natural gas resources in Alaska, and changing trends in both construction costs and natural gas prices could threaten the time line and overall viability of the project if these concerns remain unresolved.[20]

The demand for natural gas in Mexico will be strong in all sectors, leading to more than double the current demand by 2025. Despite the existence of ample natural gas reserves—16 trillion cubic feet—Mexico's production of natural gas is not projected to keep pace with demand. Just like the oil sector, exploration and production in Mexico's natural gas sector is off-limits to private investment. However, private companies are allowed to participate in either the transportation, storage, or distribution of natural gas in Mexico. Without private capital, PEMEX is not projected to have enough capital to gain access to its domestic natural gas resources unless the government (which sets PEMEX's budget and collects much of its revenue) makes more investment possible. Mexico is therefore projected to continue its dependence on imported liquefied natural gas and pipeline imports from the United States. In 2003, in an effort to attract more interest in developing Mexico's nonassociated natural gas resources, PEMEX offered private companies the opportunity to become involved in nonassociated gas projects on a fee-for-service basis (according to which the private companies do not take ownership of the resources) through a multiple-service contract structure. The multiple-service contracts were not overwhelmingly successful and attracted only a handful of companies. However, PEMEX's experience with these types of contracts is a good example of the type of incremental changes and creative policy solutions that PEMEX and various members of the Mexican government are putting forth in an effort to increase natural gas production and overcome the constitutional prohibition on the involvement of private companies in the country's natural gas sector.

In the United States, the desirability of trading the country's dependence on oil imports for dependence on natural gas imports is a potential issue on the horizon, considering that many of the same countries with significant natural gas resources are the same ones that have oil resources. It is still an open question as to how global trading in natural gas will evolve over time and whether or not North America will attract sufficient natural gas resources. The evolution of LNG supply contracts, agreements, pricing structures, and trade flows will influence the projections relating to natural gas. All three governments in North America, especially in the United States, have worked to overcome public opposition to LNG import facilities. An adequate number of projects are expected to come online to meet import needs in the future. (Figure 1.2 presents the Federal Energy Regulatory Commission's map, which locates existing and proposed terminals for LNG.) Nearly all the proposed LNG projects for Canada are presumed to export surplus volumes to the United States.

All three countries are working to build adequate LNG import capacity to meet the projected demand. Another key unknown not included in the EIA's projections is the potential impact of climate policy on the increasing demand for natural gas. If some sort of cost for carbon is instituted through some kind of cap and trade program or carbon tax, coal would arguably become more expensive, and the demand for natural gas could increase as a result.

TRANSITION TO A LOW-CARBON ENERGY FUTURE

According to EIA's baseline projections, energy-related carbon dioxide emissions in North America will increase by 28 percent—from 6,893 million metric tons of carbon dioxide in 2004 to 8,791 million metric tons in 2025. In 2025, the United States is expected to account for 84 percent of these emissions, as compared with 86 percent in 2004. Canada and Mexico's carbon dioxide emissions come mostly from oil but will have the strongest increase from coal use in the United States. The United States is relatively evenly split between oil and coal as the largest sources of carbon dioxide but will experience the strongest growth in carbon dioxide emissions from coal. As stated above, efforts to constrain emissions of carbon dioxide could have a strong impact on these projections. According to projections from the Intergovernmental Panel on Climate Change, North American emissions of greenhouse gases will need to be significantly reduced in order to reach GHG atmospheric stabilization of 450–550 parts per million. (The discussion of climate change in the next chapter provides further details.)

The largest share of energy-related carbon dioxide emissions is projected to come from the power sector. Between 2004 and 2025, demand for electric power in North America is projected to increase by 34 percent, with the highest level of absolute growth in the United States and the fastest rate of growth in Mexico. The highest absolute growth in sources that generate electric power supply in the United States is in the demand for coal, even though coal's overall share of the electric power mix is expected to decline. Over the forecast period, in Mexico, natural gas will move from supplying 29 percent of electric

Figure 1.2. Existing and Proposed North American Liquefied Natural Gas Terminals

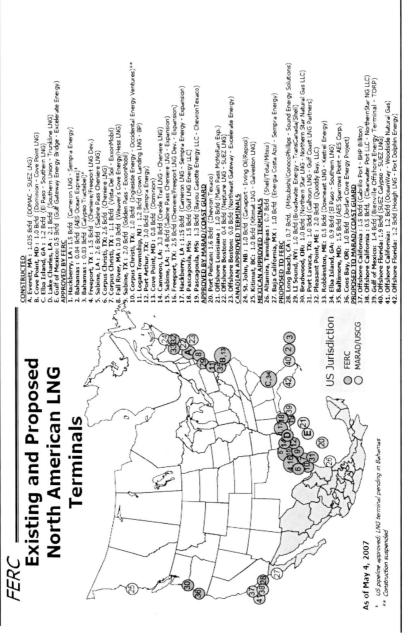

FERC

Existing and Proposed North American LNG Terminals

As of May 4, 2007

* US pipeline approved; LNG terminal pending in Bahamas
** Construction suspended

US Jurisdiction
- ● FERC
- ○ MARAD/USCG

CONSTRUCTED
A. Everett, MA : 1.035 Bcfd (DOMAC - SUEZ LNG)
B. Cove Point, MD : 1.0 Bcfd (Dominion - Cove Point LNG)
C. Elba Island, GA : 1.2 Bcfd (El Paso - Southern LNG)
D. Lake Charles, LA : 2.1 Bcfd (Southern Union - Trunkline LNG)
E. Gulf of Mexico: 0.5 Bcfd (Gulf Gateway Energy Bridge - Excelerate Energy)

APPROVED BY FERC
1. Hackberry, LA : 1.5 Bcfd (Cameron LNG - Sempra Energy)
2. Bahamas : 0.84 Bcfd (AES Ocean Express)*
3. Bahamas : 0.83 Bcfd (Calypso Tractebel)*
4. Freeport, TX : 1.5 Bcfd (Cheniere/Freeport LNG Dev.)
5. Sabine, LA : 2.6 Bcfd (Sabine Pass Cheniere LNG)
6. Corpus Christi, TX: 2.6 Bcfd (Cheniere LNG)
7. Corpus Christi, TX : 1.1 Bcfd (Vista Del Sol - ExxonMobil)
8. Fall River, MA : 0.9 Bcfd (Weaver's Cove Energy/Hess LNG)
9. Sabine, TX : 2.0 Bcfd (Golden Pass - ExxonMobil)
10. Corpus Christi, TX : 1.0 Bcfd (Ingleside Energy - Occidental Energy Ventures)**
11. Logan Township, NJ : 1.2 Bcfd (Crown Landing LNG - BP)
12. Port Arthur, TX: 3.0 Bcfd (Sempra Energy)
13. Cove Point, MD : 0.8 Bcfd (Dominion)
14. Cameron, LA : 3.3 Bcfd (Creole Trail LNG - Cheniere LNG)
15. Sabine, LA : 1.4 Bcfd (Sabine Pass Cheniere LNG - Expansion)
16. Freeport, TX : 2.5 Bcfd (Cheniere/Freeport LNG Dev. - Expansion)
17. Hackberry, LA : 1.15 Bcfd (Cameron LNG - Sempra Energy - Expansion)
18. Pascagoula, MS: 1.5 Bcfd (Gulf LNG Energy LLC)
19. Pascagoula, MS: 1.3 Bcfd (Bayou Casotte Energy LLC - ChevronTexaco)

APPROVED BY MARAD/COAST GUARD
20. Port Pelican: 1.6 Bcfd (Chevron Texaco)
21. Offshore Louisiana : 1.0 Bcfd (Main Pass McMoRan Exp.)
22. Offshore Boston : 0.4 Bcfd (Neptune LNG - SUEZ LNG)
23. Offshore Boston : 0.8 Bcfd (Northeast Gateway - Excelerate Energy)

CANADIAN APPROVED TERMINALS
24. St. John, NB : 1.0 Bcfd (Canaport - Irving Oil/Repsol)
25. Kitimat, BC : 1.0 Bcfd (Kitimat LNG - Galveston LNG)

MEXICAN APPROVED TERMINALS
26. Altamira, Tamulipas : 0.7 Bcfd (Shell/Total/Mitsu)
27. Baja California, MX : 1.0 Bcfd (Energia Costa Azul - Sempra Energy)

PROPOSED TO FERC
28. Long Beach, CA : 0.7 Bcfd, (Mitsubishi/ConocoPhillips - Sound Energy Solutions)
29. LI Sound, NY : 1.0 Bcfd (Broadwater Energy - TransCanada/Shell)
30. Bradwood, OR: 1.0 Bcfd (Northern Star LNG - Northern Star Natural Gas LLC)
31. Port Lavaca, TX: 1.0 Bcfd (Calhoun LNG - Gulf Coast LNG Partners)
32. Pleasant Point, ME : 2.0 Bcfd (Quoddy Bay, LLC)
33. Robbinston, ME: 0.5 Bcfd (Downeast LNG - Kestrel Energy)
34. Elba Island, GA: 0.9 Bcfd (El Paso - Southern LNG)
35. Baltimore, MD: 1.5 Bcfd (AES Sparrows Point - AES Corp.)
36. Coos Bay, OR: 1.0 Bcfd (Jordan Cove Energy Project)

PROPOSED TO MARAD/COAST GUARD
37. Offshore California : 1.5 Bcfd (Cabrillo Port - BHP Billiton)
38. Offshore California : 0.5 Bcfd. (Clearwater Pot LLC - Northern Star NG LLC)
39. Gulf of Mexico: 1.4 Bcfd (Bienville Offshore Energy Terminal - TORP)
40. Offshore Florida: 1.9 Bcfd (SUEZ Calypso - SUEZ LNG)
41. Offshore California: 1.2 Bcfd (OceanWay - Woodside Natural Gas)
42. Offshore Florida: 1.2 Bcfd (Hoegh LNG - Port Dolphin Energy)

Source: Federal Energy Regulatory Commission, Office of Energy Projects, May 4, 2007, http://www.ferc.gov/industries/lng/indus-act/terminals/horizon-lng.pdf.

power needs to 36 percent, displacing fuel oil, which will drop from 58 percent to 49 percent of the electric power fuel mix. Mexico's demand for electric power is expected to almost double over the forecast period, and projections indicate that Mexico will need US$51 billion of investment in 28 gigawatts of additional generation capacity over the next decade in order to meet rising demand.[21] Canada's fuel mix remains relatively static over the forecast period, with the largest increases to be found in natural gas and a substantial increase in renewable energy in the form of additional hydropower capacity. Approximately 60 percent of Canada's electric power needs come from renewable energy. (Figure 1.3 presents a graphic depiction of these details.)

The emergence of a carbon-constrained environment appears more likely with each passing day. A patchwork of policies aimed at managing carbon dioxide emissions has emerged and is made up of initiatives undertaken by international, national, and regional governments as well as the private sector. At the international level, Canada and Mexico have signed the Kyoto Protocol, although Mexico is an Annex II country and therefore is not obligated to cut emissions at this point. The United States, which signed the Kyoto Protocol but did not ratify it, has established voluntary targets for limiting the intensity of greenhouse gas emissions. The U.S. federal government has, thus far, preferred to invest in clean-energy technology alternatives (like carbon capture and sequestration as well as wind, solar power, hydrogen, and biomass energy) instead of establishing mandatory emission caps. However, a number of U.S. states have formed regional partnerships through which they plan to institute cap and trade programs. Private companies have joined with environmental organizations to call for significant reductions in greenhouse gas emissions as part of the U.S. Climate Action Partnership and several other initiatives. In addition, major energy companies are working to reduce their own carbon footprint and investing in carbon sequestration and other clean-energy technologies. Strategies for managing carbon emissions will be a crucial component of energy planning for governments and companies alike. A key question in the near future is: What should companies and governments do to ensure that carbon management strategies evolve to bring greater efficiency and a competitive edge to industry and the economy as a whole?

The Canadian government released an action plan detailing measures designed to deal with climate change and air pollution. The plan

Figure 1.3. Projected Increase in and Sources of North America's Electricity Mix, 2004 and 2025

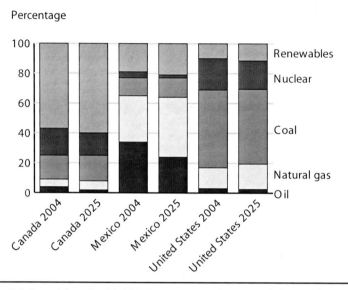

Source: U.S. Energy Information Administration, "International Energy Outlook 2007," http://www .eia.doe.gov/oiaf/ieo/index.html.

calls for limiting air pollution and greenhouse gas emissions by reducing vehicle fuel emissions, increasing the range of energy-efficient products available to consumers, and improving air quality. The plan includes mandatory reduction targets for all major industries that produce GHGs. Existing facilities will be required to cut greenhouse gas emissions per unit of production by 18 percent by 2010—an average reduction of 6 percent each year. After 2010, companies will have to cut an additional 2 percent of the intensity of emissions each year, resulting in an overall decrease in GHGs in Canada starting in 2010. The plan also establishes a climate change technology fund and a domestic trading scheme that will be linked to the Clean Development Mechanism (CDM). In addition, several Canadian provinces have announced their own proposals to mitigate the emission of greenhouse gases. For example, in late June 2007, Alberta announced that all facilities emitting more than 100,000 tons of greenhouse gases will be required to reduce the intensity of these emissions by 12 percent. British Columbia, on the other hand, has announced that starting in July 2008 it will begin to phase in a revenue neutral carbon tax on virtually all fossil fuels.

Under the Kyoto Protocol, Mexico is not subject to emissions reduction targets. However, Mexico, has sought to undertake climate change programs in anticipation of the time when the country's GHG emissions may be curtailed. In late 2006, Mexico released its first ever inventory of GHG emissions—a crucial step in monitoring and verifying emissions reductions under a cap and trade scheme and in tracking pollution. Mexico is also taking advantage of low-carbon energy technology financing that is available through the Clean Development Mechanism. With 20 registered CDM projects begun in 2006, Mexico is second only to Brazil in the number of CDM projects in Latin America.

The pillars of U.S. policy related to climate change have been voluntary emissions reductions and a focus on developing and deploying clean-energy technologies. Along with these strategies, the U.S. government has also taken steps to increase efficiency and other standards in an effort to reduce overall emissions. However, recent developments within states, regions, and cities—as well as reactions to rulings by the U.S. Supreme Court—seem to indicate that the U.S. public wants the government and the private sector to take more aggressive steps to limit GHG emissions. Indeed, efforts to establish mandatory caps on GHG emissions have taken on legislative form in the 110th Congress, where there are rumors that climate-related legislation would be brought up during the current session. Thus far, state and local governments have taken more aggressive steps to limit GHG emissions than the steps taken by the federal government. Even though leadership on this issue at the local level is admirable, there is evidence that companies require greater continuity in emissions reduction policies across state and national borders in order to make the investment that this effort needs. Making the transition to a low-carbon energy future will require a great deal of coordination and communication between the public and private sectors as well as within and across national boundaries.

To the extent that policymakers decide to limit the emission of greenhouse gases into the atmosphere in an attempt to avoid the most negative potential impact of climate change, the energy sector will need to undergo a fundamental transformation that will include carbon management strategies. Efforts to limit GHG emissions will have a profound effect on the way citizens of North America produce and use energy. In fact, anticipation of potential limits in the future is driving greater amounts of investment into renewable energy and is stalling investment in major new energy infrastructure projects that may or may not be economically viable in a carbon-constrained world. It is important for governments to set clear long-term policy goals with regard to carbon constraints in order to enable companies to plan their investments accordingly. To some extent, a proactive approach to addressing energy strategies in a carbon-constrained world could increase the competitiveness of domestic industry, reduce the overall cost of managing emissions, and expedite the transition to a low-carbon energy future.[22] It is difficult to make predictions about the level and nature of future carbon constraints, but it is reasonable to suggest that, for the limits to have an impact on climate change, the cuts need to be significant and require a new approach to energy production and use. Two areas with the potential to have a significant impact on the trajectory of carbon dioxide emissions in the future are coal and nuclear energy.

Nuclear supply is projected to grow by 15 percent in North America between 2004 and 2025. All the growth is expected to take place in Canada and the United States, with the highest level of absolute growth in the United States. Canada is the world's largest natural producer of uranium, with 25 percent of the world's production coming from mines in Saskatchewan. No new production of nuclear power is projected for Mexico. The generation of nuclear power has experienced a bit of a rebirth in U.S. policy circles as a result of the provisions of the Energy Policy Act of 2005 as well as strong support from the current presidential administration. Generating nuclear power still faces significant obstacles—including waste disposal, security, cost overruns, and permitting—but it is being heralded as a future source of low-carbon energy. A number of recent studies have highlighted nuclear power as a necessary major component of any strategy to significantly reduce greenhouse gas emissions on a global scale. The nuclear power industry has implemented a number processes and has standardized designs and operational procedures in an attempt to overcome the potential for cost overruns and permitting delays. According to the Nuclear Energy Institute, approximately 30 new combined construction and operating license applications are expected to be submitted for new nuclear power plants by the end of 2008. One of the biggest obstacles associated with nuclear energy in North America is overall acceptance by the public. Policymaking communities continue to be divided about the potential trade-offs associated with promoting nuclear power.

Over the years, coal consumption in the United States has been driven by the existence of cheap and plentiful supplies. The United States is projected to continue to be the largest consumer of coal in North America. In 2004, the United States consumed 1.08 billion short tons of coal—approximately 94 percent of total coal consumption in North America. The vast majority of coal consumption in the United States is used for generating electricity. In 2025, the demand for coal in North America is still projected to be overwhelmingly centered in the United States, where it is expected to account for nearly 92 percent of consumption. Coal use in Mexico and Canada is limited and occurs only in the electricity and industrial sectors. By 2025, U.S. demand for coal is expected to increase from 1.1 billion short tons to 1.3 billion short tons. The United States' net exports of coal to Canada equal approximately 18 million short tons per year and 0.569 million short tons to Mexico. The United States has vast amounts of coal reserves (nearly 19 billion short tons in 2005), and coal is increasingly considered a reliable indigenous source of energy by many U.S. policymakers who seek solutions to our growing dependence on imported oil. The projections indicate that coal-to-liquids consumption in the United States will come online by 2015, reaching 318,000 barrels per day by 2025. The legislative and executive branches have undertaken a number of initiatives designed to develop and promote environmentally friendly ways to utilize these indigenous coal resources for power generation and transportation in the form of coal-to-liquids. However, if efforts to limit carbon dioxide emissions continue at the state and federal level, increased coal use will be hampered by the increasing costs associated with mitigating carbon dioxide emissions from the production and use of coal (one of the sources of fuel that has the highest intensity of greenhouse gases).

Both the industry and the government are looking for technological solutions to this dilemma in the form of technologies for large-scale carbon capture and sequestration (CCS)—a process by which carbon dioxide is captured from a power generation facility and sequestered underground in liquid form—and efficient, cleaner-burning coal power plants. Two important efforts to enable CCS are FutureGen and the Weyburn Project. FutureGen is a US$1.5 billion public-private partnership to design, build, and operate the world's first coal-fueled power plant that has a near-zero level of emissions. The Weyburn Project, which involves carbon dioxide sequestration, is a bilateral effort between the United States and Canada designed to prove the viability of carbon sequestration. Similar projects are being examined in countries like China and India, where indigenous coal resources provide an easily accessible resource for power generation as well as for the fuel that a growing and developing population needs for transportation. However, severe pollution issues and, to some extent, concerns over climate change may cause those countries to rethink the long-term viability of traditional use of coal. Coal is perhaps one of the most pertinent examples of the conflict over near-term concerns about energy security and long-term climate considerations. How policymakers and the energy industry proceed will have significant ramifications on both issues.

PROMOTION OF RENEWABLE ENERGY AND ENERGY EFFICIENCY

Promoting renewable energy and energy efficiency will continue to be an important part of meeting future energy demand and of supporting the technologies and practices that will eventually enable a low-carbon energy future. For decades, environmental groups have espoused renewable energy, energy efficiency, and conservation as cleaner and more environmentally sound forms of energy. Over the next 17 years, renewable energy and energy efficiency are likely to be promoted not only because of their environmental attributes—particularly with regard to concerns about climate change—but also for their potential implications for energy security and industrial competitiveness. A recent study completed by the National Petroleum Council concluded that projected global demand for energy (North America included) will be strong enough over the next 25 years to necessitate the development of "all economic, environmentally responsible energy sources available to support and sustain future growth."[23]

Of the three North American countries, Canada has the largest portion of renewable energy in the national fuel mix, with nearly 25 percent of its energy mix coming from renewable energy sources, compared with 6 percent in the United States and 6 percent in Mexico.[24] Much of Canada's renewable energy comes from hydropower in British Columbia, Manitoba, Quebec, Newfoundland, and Labrador. Over the forecast period, the contribution of renewable energy sources to the overall fuel mix is expected to grow by close to 1.4 percent per year in the United States and Canada and 2.3 percent per year in Mexico (from a much smaller base).

Table 1.1. Cumulative Demand for Renewable Electricity in North America Based on Regulatory Mandates, 2006–2017 (in megawatts)

Year	Canada	Mexico	United States
2006	395	1,271	14,381
2007	1,745	1,356	16,967
2008	2,406	1,356	19,520
2009	2,406	1,457	21,866
2010	4,006	1,559	24,143
2011	4,006	1,710	26,450
2012	4,079	1,812	28,761
2013	4,079	1,913	31,171
2014	8,760	1,913	32,949
2015	8,760	1,913	34,854
2016	9,140	NA	36,094
2017	9,140	NA	37,175

Source: Commission for Environmental Cooperation, "Fostering Renewable Electricity Markets in North America," April 2007, http://www.cec.org/files/pdf/ECONOMY/Fostering-RE-MarketsinNA_en.pdf.

In 2007, the Commission for Environmental Cooperation conducted a study of renewable electricity markets in North America that included projections of the continent's cumulative demand through 2017 (relevant figures are provided in table 1.1). The report also noted that scaling up renewable electricity is one of the priorities set forth by the Mexican Energy Secretariat's strategic planning efforts. In addition, a draft of the Law for the Use of Renewable Sources of Energy seeks to establish a minimum requirement of an 8 percent contribution of renewable energy to the overall power-generation mix by 2012. Mexico also has a number of programs sponsored by the development community to encourage the production and use of renewable energy throughout the country.[25]

In the United States, various incentives and programs exist at the federal and state level to encourage the production and use of renewable energy. In absolute terms, the United States has the highest renewable energy consumption, much of which takes the form of hydropower, wind, and biomass. A recent study conducted by the American Council on Renewable Energy has estimated a potential for 600 gigawatts of new electric-generating capacity from renewable energy sources—such as wind, solar power, hydropower, geothermal power, and biomass—

by 2025. For the most part, these are very optimistic projections, but they reflect the confidence and enthusiasm of the renewable energy industry for the future of renewable energy sources in the United States. For many of these industries, continued support—through tax incentives, subsidies, and a robust commitment to research and development efforts, for example—will remain essential to enabling a cleaner energy future. As a result of various policy initiatives, the United States has a rapidly expanding biofuels sector and expects to see rapid growth in biofuels production capacity and use over the forecast period. (See box 1.4.) In 2004, 221,000 barrels of biofuels per day were produced in the United States, and this number is expected to grow to 851,000 barrels per day by 2025—an increase of more than 280 percent. Even with mandates and other incentives, the potential contribution of biofuels is limited because of agricultural, economic, and infrastructure constraints. Biofuels will play an important role in reducing oil consumption at the margins, but their production also involves significant environmental and economic trade-offs.

The three governments of North America and an increasing number of companies are investing to develop new renewable energy technologies. In 2008, the U.S. government alone will spend US$2.7 billion to promote the development of clean-energy technologies. In 2006, venture capital investments in industrial and energy enterprises more than doubled—to US$1.8 billion—from the amount invested in 2005, with about 40 percent earmarked for developing alternative energy, like advanced solar power, wind, cellulosic ethanol, and plug-in hybrid vehicles.[26] Other major technological advances could unlock the potential for more sources of renewable energy in the form of wind, solar power, hydropower, and biomass. Advances in battery technologies, vehicle technologies, basic materials, and combinations of various technologies are also promising areas for greater investment. Indeed, the market for clean-energy technologies is expected to grow quite large over the coming decades.

Nevertheless, questions abound in regard to where and when the next major technological breakthrough will occur and whether competition or cooperation on scientific and technological research and development will yield the most promising results. Major challenges for policymakers include finding ways to deploy existing technologies and striking a balance between public sector and private sector research to develop next-generation energy technologies. These challenges are

---

Box 1.4. Biofuels in the United States

Biofuels (mainly ethanol and biodiesel) have received a great deal of attention in the United States over the last few years. Since 2000, ethanol production in the United States has increased 300 percent. Driven by high oil prices, concerns over increasing reliance on imported oil, climate change concerns, and the potential for rural development in the Midwest, policymakers enacted a renewable fuels standard (RFS), part of the Energy Policy Act of 2005, as a mandatory increase in the amount of renewable fuels (mostly biofuels) in the transportation fuel mix. The combination of the mandate and high oil price environment, in addition to the 51-cents-per-gallon blending credit and tariff protection that effectively blocked low-cost import competition, caused a flurry of growth in the biofuels industry. Ethanol production capacity expansion plans surpassed the EPACT 2005–mandated RFS level for 2012 of 7.5 billion gallons, and in late 2007 the U.S. ethanol industry was on track to produce 10.9 billion gallons of ethanol by 2010.

As part of the Energy Independence and Security Act of 2007 (EISA 2007), signed into law on December 19, 2007, the 110th Congress, starting in 2008, raised each annual RFS target beyond the volumes set forth in EPACT 2005, thus expanding the RFS to an ultimate goal of 36 billion gallons per year by 2022. In an attempt to address some of the environmental and food security issues of conventional biofuels, EISA 2007 mandates that starting in 2009 a certain portion of the RFS target must be met by "advanced biofuels" (eventually reaching 21 billion gallons out of the 36 billion gallons by 2022) and that all renewable fuels must yield at least a 20 percent reduction in greenhouse gas emission compared to conventional gasoline or diesel.

In the midst of all the excitement over biofuels, a range of potential trade-offs or unintended consequences of these policies has emerged. The first and perhaps the one most widely discussed is the potential for the production of biofuels to displace food production. Ethanol is made primarily from corn, and the increased demand for corn—combined with the diversion of farmland to produce more corn for ethanol production—has driven the cost of corn-based food products and other products that rely on corn, such as meat and dairy products. Policymakers view the food versus fuel dilemma as a short-term concern and envision a future in which cellulosic ethanol (ethanol derived from the nonedible portions of plants) will provide a growing share of the mandated biofuel production. Other criticisms of these aggressive biofuels policies include the questionable energy and GHG balance of biofuels, the long-term cost of providing incentives for biofuels, the fact that greater mandated levels of biofuels undermine the bottom line for refiners and are likely to dissuade refiners from increasing capacity (also a priority), the degradation and water use issues associated with biofuels, the potential for stranded assets in small farmer districts as technology moves beyond conventional ethanol production, and the inadequacy of the current transportation infrastructure to effectively utilize mandated levels of biofuels.

Biofuels are destined to play an important role in the United States and in the global energy sector even if they never account for more than a small percentage of the demand for liquids. However, it important for biofuels to be developed in a sustainable manner—one that minimizes the economic and environmental trade-offs and manages the unintended consequences.

---

particularly important to North America, because increased trade and use of clean-energy technologies could yield significant benefits for the entire continent. A number of reports highlight innovative ways to encourage and expedite market entry of new energy technologies as well as ways to help make existing energy technologies cost-competitive. The governments of North America recently signed an agreement to cooperate on research and development in science and technology and to expedite technology deployment where possible. However, a great deal more work could be done in this area so that the obstacles to energy technology deployment and the implications of various policy initiatives can be fully understood.

One of the largest potential gains from deploying energy technology is in the area of greater energy efficiency. It is difficult to overstate the potential impact of greater energy efficiency throughout North America's transportation, industrial, building, and power generation sectors. A number of recent studies have highlighted the potential significant energy and cost savings to be gained by implementing measures to increase energy efficiency. According to the International Energy Agency's Alternative Policy Scenario presented in *World Energy Outlook 2006,* savings in the cost of fuel over the lifetime of energy-efficient products more than make up for the initial extra expense of producing more costly energy-efficient appliances and other goods.[27] Another recent study conducted by the McKinsey Global Institute estimates that an increase in efficiency and "energy productivity" could reduce global energy demand by 15–20 percent by 2020. Both studies outline market barriers to realizing greater levels of efficiency. When implemented properly, improvements in energy efficiency have the potential to alleviate concerns about energy security as well as environmental and economic concerns. To the extent that North America can pursue aggressive energy efficiency standards and seek to make these standards compatible across borders, the market for energy-efficient goods in North America could be enormous. However, a better understanding of the impact of harmonized standards across various sectors must be achieved first.

When assessing the long-term viability of promoting renewable energy, it is important to take into consideration the basic resource base, economics, cost, advances in technology, integration with existing infrastructure, and potential trade-offs. Because many of these factors differ from region to region within each country, a mix of local and national incentives and programs is evolving. Between 2008 and 2025, innovative markets and financing mechanisms are also likely to come into play in ways that are difficult to predict. A key question going forward is whether or not national or continental standards for both the content of renewable energy projects and energy efficiency are viable and effective options for deploying renewable energy and energy-efficient technologies.

MOUNTING INFRASTRUCTURE NEEDS

Under a business as usual scenario, the International Energy Agency's *World Energy Outlook 2006* projects that North America will need investments amounting to US$4.104 trillion for energy supply infrastructure between 2008 and 2030. Table 1.2 shows a breakdown of the amounts each energy sector will require. Investments are needed to expand supply capacity and to replace the existing infrastructure that will need to be retired over the next 25 years. At the global level, nearly half of this investment will be needed simply to maintain current supply capacity.[28]

One of the most difficult challenges of moving to a low-carbon energy future is making the transition from the current infrastructure used for fossil fuels. Power generation facilities, pipelines, and transmission lines are all major capital investments that last for decades, require substantial investment, and take a great deal of lead time to construct and make operational. Uncertainty in the marketplace can cause delays and significant cost increases. Companies face a myriad of challenges when it comes to making costly investment decisions. Many of these challenges have to do with managing legal and regulatory processes while simultaneously conducting outreach to stakeholders within the time frames and deadlines set for projects. This is especially true when dealing with new technologies, highly populated areas, or environmentally sensitive regions. Cross-border infrastructure projects pose their own particular set of challenges because of the need for regulatory and legal coordination in multiple jurisdictions. However, as the population continues to grow and energy infrastructure projects affect wider segments of the population and require complex regulatory decisions, these challenges are likely persist far into the future and may cause significant delays in much needed investment.

Canada, Mexico, and the United States already share an impressive level of cross-border infrastructure, which is largely responsible for the integration of the North American energy market. As of 2005, the continent shared 35 cross-border natural gas pipelines, 22 cross-border oil and petroleum product pipelines, and 51 cross-border electricity transmission lines.[29] Greater natural gas pipeline capacity, cross-border electricity interconnections, and refinery and pipeline infrastructure

Table 1.2. Cumulative Investment Needs for Energy Supply Infrastructure, 2005–2030 (in billions of 2005 US dollars)

	Coal	Oil	Gas	Power	Total
OECD members	156	1,149	1,744	4,240	7,289
North America	80	856	1,189	1,979	4,104
Transitional economies	33	639	589	590	1,850
Developing countries	330	2,223	1,516	6,446	10,515
Inter-regional transport	45	256	76	NA	376
World	563	4,266	3,925	11,276	20,192

Source: International Energy Agency, *World Energy Outlook 2006*, p. 77.

associated with the production of oil sands will be required over the forecast period. Consequently, the construction of at least five cross-border pipelines has been proposed—three coming from Canada and two bidirectional pipelines between the United States and Mexico.[30] Major new pipelines will need to be developed in order to bring additional crude oil and products from the oil sands to various regions of the United States. The complexities of the regulatory and siting processes that enable these pipelines are often arduous, and coordinating them requires a great deal of effort. The same is true of transmission lines within and between countries. Public opposition to major new infrastructure projects has become a pressing issue for governments and companies over the last few years, leading the U.S. Congress to arm the federal government with the authority to use the right of eminent domain for siting infrastructure projects that are in the national interest.

In addition, each country has its own distinct infrastructure needs. In Canada, energy resources are controlled by the provinces, and energy infrastructure can be covered under either federal or provincial jurisdiction. Over the years, this structure—plus the ability to readily integrate infrastructure with the United States—has led to the development of infrastructure in Canada that is oriented from north to south to a great degree. Canada's plans for significant expansion of its energy infrastructure are under way. Major investments have been made for infrastructure projects in association with the production of the Alberta oil sands. Canada will need to find additional materials, human resources, and capital to sustain the pace of development and will also need to assess infrastructure projects, such as power generation plants, in the face of potential carbon constraints.

Between 2008 and 2025, Mexico will need to attract vast amounts of capital to add infrastructure to its refining and electricity generation and transmission capacity to import liquefied natural gas and the infrastructure necessary to develop its oil and natural gas resources. PEMEX owns and operates a great deal of the country's energy infrastructure, including 453 pipelines totaling nearly 2,900 miles, 6 refineries with a capacity of 1.68 MMBD (plus a 50 percent stake in Deer Park), 5,700 miles of natural gas pipeline, and 11 natural gas processing centers. PEMEX claims that the company will need US$19 billion over eight years to make up the domestic shortfall in gasoline.[31] The most important obstacle to increased development of Mexico's infrastructure is attracting the capital required for infrastructure projects. The cash-strapped, highly indebted PEMEX does not have enough capital to manage both its upstream and downstream investment needs. In recent years, Mexico has been exploring the possibility of using partnerships between the public and private sectors in the areas of nonassociated gas production, expansion of the domestic natural gas pipeline system, greater integration with the United States, and new infrastructure connections with Central America. Greater interconnection with Central America has the potential to divert resources from going north but, if done correctly, these efforts could help integrate the energy markets of Central America and lead to the development of market-based energy markets in that region.

The United States must modernize, protect, and build new energy infrastructure in order to provide reliable energy to consumers across the country. Over the forecast period, a number of infrastructure inadequacies will need to be addressed, including the following needs:

- greater domestic refining capacity to curtail dependence on imports;

- expansion of natural gas pipeline capacity;

- increased capacity of electric power transmission;

- additional rail capacity to transport coal and biofuels;

- protection of overly concentrated energy infrastructure, such as production and refinery facilities in the Gulf of Mexico; and

- modernization of energy infrastructure that is outdated.

However, public opposition to the development of energy infra-structure has risen over the years, making it increasingly difficult for companies to build the infrastructure that will guarantee reliable energy to their customers. The successful integration of energy in-frastructure into local communities is a key issue going forward and, given the magnitude of the investment that needs to take place and the important decisions about the future of how the energy that is inher-ent in these infrastructure projects is produced and used, it behooves policymakers and companies to continue to actively engage the public about infrastructure decisions and to enable the public to understand the significant trade-offs associated with these decisions.

POLICY RECOMMENDATIONS

Over the next 17 years, it is critical for the governments of Canada, Mexico, and the United States to implement policies that will lead to an increase in energy resources and the creation of the infrastructure needed to meet future demand and will make a smooth transition to a low-carbon energy future. In light of the impact of climate change as well as the extent of the changes required to produce energy and to alter consumption patterns, North America cannot afford to delay addressing today's energy concerns as well as those that loom in the future. The following recommendations are offered to assist the three governments in this crucial undertaking:

- The three governments of North America should enlist the assis-tance of all appropriate stakeholders to discuss a joint vision of North America's oil outlook that explores some of the potential implications and solutions for problems associated with the con-tinent's continued reliance on oil. It is important for policymak-ers to evaluate the potential impact of continued reliance on oil and to examine possible ways to alleviate some of the broader concerns discussed in this report.

- Policymakers in Canada, Mexico, and the United States need to include constraints on carbon emissions in their joint outlook for North America. The three countries are on three different paths when it comes to developing policies to limit greenhouse gas emissions. A patchwork of carbon-constrained environ-ments will make it difficult for energy companies to operate in multiple states in the United States as well as in certain provinces in Canada and still remain competitive. Much like the current situation with boutique fuels, greater complexity in the regulatory environment may lead to inefficiency in energy markets. Many regions of the United States are poised to institute GHG emission targets, and federal coordination at this juncture is advisable. Policymakers must consider potential climate policies and have a clear understanding of how carbon constraints will affect the relatively integrated energy sectors of North America. Because of the enormous impact that carbon constraints could have on energy production and use, it is crucial to arrive at a joint outlook that takes into account the repercussions of climate policy on energy patterns.

■ Because promoting renewable energy and energy efficiency will continue to be an important part of meeting future energy demand, policymakers should study the effectiveness of various local policies and the potential impact of renewable energy incentives and harmonized energy efficiency standards on the North American market. A patchwork of local and federal initiatives to promote increased energy efficiency and renewable energy in North America has emerged, and even though various studies have been conducted on different aspects of these initiatives, the impact of harmonized standards and policies in these areas and their potential impact are issues that should be explored further.

■ To meet increasing infrastructure needs and attract the investments required to expand supply capacity and to replace the existing infrastructure, North America's policymakers should work to raise the level of public discourse and engage the public on energy issues. No matter what happens in the course of the next 17 years, an honest and more fruitful public discourse is needed to encourage long-term public support and to raise consumer awareness. Public opinion, public education, and public opposition have all—at one time or another—been cited as obstacles to enacting policies or as reasons why certain energy reforms simply cannot succeed. In the energy world, public opinion is an increasingly powerful tool that can be used to influence energy development in a number of ways. On the one hand, environmental nongovernmental organizations and local communities can shape public opinion in an effort to stop major infrastructure projects or to put pressure on local governments to adopt and implement environmentally friendly energy policies. On the other hand, fear of potential negative public reaction is often cited as the major reason why it is not politically feasible to implement often prescribed demand-side management strategies (such as imposing a gasoline tax) or why lawmakers seek to impose windfall profits taxes as a way to quell public anger over high gasoline prices. It is important to find a way to convey the complexity of the challenges confronting North America honestly and to discover how the public can play a constructive role in the decisionmaking process.

The future of energy in North America is still uncertain. The projections discussed in this report represent what the future would look like if the three governments' policies do not change and prices stay on a consistent path. Given the dynamic nature of the current environment when it comes to energy and climate policy, it is unlikely that this future scenario will be realized, but the transition to a low-carbon energy future cannot and will not take place overnight. Governments, companies, and citizens will continue to be the parties most immediately concerned with meeting near-term energy security requirements. However, incorporating and enabling a transition to a low-carbon energy future will become an ever larger component of the decisionmaking process for setting energy policy. In energy terms, 2025 is not very far away and does not allow much time to make major changes in the way energy is produced and used. In climate terms, changes must begin today if the countries of North America expect to meet their future goals. Strategic planning, new technologies, and innovative market mechanisms will be increasingly important for meeting the region's goals for both energy security and climate change simultaneously. This report recommends a number of forward-looking studies and greater engagement with the public as ways to enable the kind of creative thinking and innovation that will be necessary to bring about a more promising energy future.

NOTES

1. U.S. Energy Information Administration (EIA), "International Energy Outlook 2007," http://www.eia.doe.gov/oiaf/ieo/index.html.

2. The term "unconventional" sometimes refers to a type of oil or natural gas that requires a different type of production and upgrading (oil sands, oil shale, coal bed methane, and others). In this report, "unconventional" will refer not only to these unconventional oil and natural gas resources but also to biofuels and coal-to-liquids, which the EIA categorizes as "unconventional" in its category of liquid fuels.

3. National Petroleum Council, "Facing the Hard Truths about Energy," June 2007, http://www.npc.org.

4. Ibid.

5. Barry Barton et al., *Energy Security: Managing Risk in A Dynamic Legal and Regulatory Environment* (Oxford: Oxford University Press, 2004), p. 5.

6. Unless noted otherwise, the data cited throughout this paper comes from the U.S. Energy Information Administration's "International Energy Outlook 2007" or from the author's calculations based on data from this publication.

7. Joe M. Dukert, "North America," in *Energy Cooperation in the Western Hemisphere*, ed. Sidney Weintraub (Washington D.C.: CSIS Press. 2007), p. 133.

8. EIA uses OECD and non-OECD to represent developed and developing economies.

9. The EIA projects annual GDP growth rates of 2.3 percent for Canada, 3.6 percent for Mexico, and 2.9 percent for the United States. Assumptions about the GDP differ in Canada and Mexico over the forecast period, but the difference is negligible.

10. Natural Resources Canada's projections are higher, because they estimate a much stronger rate of demand growth in the transportation sector (approximately 1.8 percent per year over the forecast period, compared to EIA's 0.3 percent per year) but still below the historical average.

11. EIA, "Annual Energy Outlook 2007.

12. Canadian Association of Petroleum Producers, "Oil Sands: Benefits to Alberta and Canada, Today and Tomorrow, Through a Fair, Stable and Competitive Fiscal Regime," http://www.capp.ca/raw.asp?x=1&dt=NTV&e=PDF&dn=121342.

13. PennWell Corporation, *Oil and Gas Journal*, no. 47 (December 18, 2006). Oil includes crude oil and condensate.

14. The reforms did not lead to additional investment, but the reform efforts in and of themselves were a valuable instrument for gauging Mexico's acceptance of change in this area.

15. EIA, "Annual Energy Outlook 2007."

16. Ibid.

17. Minerals Management Service, News Release, "Secretary Kempthorne Unveils Major Initiative to Expand Oil, Natural Gas Production on the Outer Continental Shelf," April 30, 2007, http://www.mms.gov/ooc/press/2007/pressdoi0430.htm.

18. EIA, "Annual Energy Outlook 2007," Issues in Focus section, http://www.eia.doe.gov/oiaf/aeo/issues.html.

19. Data found on the Mackenzie Gas Project Web site at http://www.mackenziegasproject.com/theProject/overview/index.html.

20. EIA, "Annual Energy Outlook 2007," Issues in Focus section.

21. EIA, "Mexico: Country Analysis Brief," January 2007, http://www.eia.doe.gov/emeu/cabs/Mexico/Oil.html.

22. Her Majesty's Treasury, "Stern Review Report on the Economics of Climate Change," http://www.hm-treasury.gov.uk/media/3/2/Summary_of_Conclusions.pdf.

23. National Petroleum Council, "Facing the Hard Truths about Energy: A Comprehensive View to 2030 of Global Oil and Natural Gas," p. 2, http://downloads.connectlive.com/events/npc071807/pdf-downloads/Facing_Hard_Truths-Executive_Summary.pdf, July 18, 2007.

24. The demand for renewable energy is projected to grow from 3.5 QBtu in 2004 to 5.1 QBtu in 2025 in Canada, and 0.4 QBtu in 2004 to 1.0 QBtu in 2025 in Mexico, with most of the growth in the electricity sector. In the United States, demand for renewable energy is projected to grow from 6.0 QBtu in 2004 to 9.3 QBtu in 2025 and to be fueled by growth in the electricity and industrial sectors.

25. Commission for Environmental Cooperation, "Fostering Renewable Electricity Markets in North America."

26. PricewaterhouseCoopers/National Venture Capital Association, "MoneyTree Report: Full Year and Q4 2006 Report," data provided by Thomson Financial, http://www.pwcmoneytree.com/MTPublic/ns/moneytree/filesource/exhibits/MoneyTree_4Q2006_Final.pdf.

27. International Energy Agency, *World Energy Outlook 2006* (Paris: Organization for Economic Cooperation and Development and International Energy Agency, 2007).

28. Ibid., p. 75.

29. Veronica R. Prado, "Energy Infrastructure in the Western Hemisphere," in *Energy Cooperation in the Western Hemisphere*, ed. Sidney Weintraub (Washington D.C.: CSIS Press, 2007), p. 409.

30. Ibid.

31. EIA, "Mexico: Country Analysis Brief."

OUTLOOK FOR THE ENVIRONMENT

CLIMATE CHANGE JAISEL VADGAMA
WATER MANAGEMENT WILLIAM A. NITZE
BIODIVERSITY HANS HERRMANN, JAMIE K. REASER, AND
JOSE CARLOS FERNANDEZ UGALDE

This chapter discusses the outlook for the North American environment in 2025, focusing on climate change, water management, and biodiversity. The discussion does not attempt to predict what the North American environment will be in 2025, because there are too many scientific, technological, economic, and political uncertainties to make such a prediction possible. The chapter will, however, identify trends, such as increasing greenhouse gas emissions, higher average temperatures and less snowmelt, reduced supplies of and increased demand for freshwater, destruction of natural habitat as a result of resource extraction, and accelerating loss of native species. Absent many of the changes in policy and behavior recommended in this chapter, continuation of these trends will result in a substantially degraded North American environment in 2025.

The negative impacts of such degradation could be severe. The expense of protecting coastal areas against salt water intrusion could become prohibitive, forcing abandonment of some of North America's most valuable real estate. Large parts of the western United States and northern Mexico could become uninhabitable as surface and groundwater disappears and the land dries out. Water scarcity and migration pressures could lead to conflict within and between North American countries. Extraction of oil and other resources in response to growing North American and foreign demand could irreparably damage some of North America's most beautiful ecosystems. Habitat degradation and loss of native species could leave our grandchildren with a much diminished natural inheritance.

These negative impacts would not be limited to North America it-self. Other countries, most notably China and India, face even more difficult environmental challenges over the next few decades, as their rapid economic growth and dependence on fossil energy deplete their scarce water and topsoil and pollute much of what is left. Absent leader-ship by example and active cooperation on the part of other nations—including the United States and its North American neighbors—these countries will find it difficult to address these challenges. On the over-arching issue of climate change, these countries will simply refuse to make the hard economic and political trade-offs necessary to put their economies on a more sustainable path if the United States does not lead by example. Failure to do so not only would foreclose the possibil-ity of an effective global response to climate change but also would un-dermine the moral authority underlying the already diminished U.S. capacity to lead.

This dire forecast does not necessarily have to come to pass. This chapter discusses many positive trends and examples in all North American countries, which, if they are strengthened and replicated, could bring about significant improvements in the North American environment in 2025. North America has the institutional, human, technological, and financial resources needed to put its economy on a sustainable path and to avoid or mitigate many of the impacts listed above. The real problem is cultural and political. North Americans have developed a culture of abundance, because they have exploited the region's natural resources to achieve an ever-improving standard of living. North America must now develop a culture of stewardship in which the governments seek to anticipate the future and make changes now that will avert the negative impacts discussed above. This chapter can only help identify what those changes might be.

CLIMATE CHANGE
OVERVIEW

Climate change, caused by the release of greenhouse gases (GHGs) into the atmosphere, is a major threat to ecosystems, human health, and the livelihoods of the world's population in the twenty-first cen-tury. Greenhouse gases contribute to an overall warming of the climate by reducing the amount of energy radiated outward from the earth. The effect is known as radiative forcing.[1] Without an equivalent reduc-tion in the amount of energy entering the atmosphere from the sun, the net result is an overall increase in energy—or warming—of the atmosphere.

This section addresses the role that North America can—and must—play as part of a global effort to minimize and mitigate climate change. Canada and the United States, in particular, have a special responsibility to tackle a problem that has historically been created by industrialized countries and currently requires mobilization of political and investment capital that is most readily found in the developed world.

The analysis explores some immediate and medium-term policy implications for North America—essentially looking ahead to where the continent should be in 2025—by establishing the mitigation targets necessary for climate protection and placing these in the context of existing trends. This discussion is followed by a selective overview of options for trilateral collaboration on climate change action as well as opportunities for North America to play a leadership role in global action on climate change.

GLOBAL TRENDS

The challenge of addressing climate change is truly global. On one hand, the location of GHG emissions is immaterial—emissions have the same effect, no matter where they originate. On the other hand, the impact of climate change is likely to be distributed in complex, unequal, and unpredictable ways, with no direct link to the geography of emissions. In general, tropical and polar regions—home to the world's most vulnerable populations—are expected to experience more immediate and more severe impacts. Effective measures to solve the problem will require a combination of mitigation, which involves reducing emissions dramatically in order to minimize the lasting impact of climate change, and adaptation, which involves responding to present and future impacts that cannot be averted.

Scientific investigation has established that the magnitude of the risks posed by global warming is severe. The third assessment report issued by the Intergovernmental Panel on Climate Change (IPCC) in 2001, which was based on extensive reviews of scholarly, peer-reviewed literature, concluded that, if actions are not taken to forestall today's GHG emissions trends, average temperatures on the surface of the globe are likely to rise by between 1.4°C and 5.8°C from 1990 to 2100.[2] To put this in context, the difference between the temperature during the last ice age and today's temperature is between 4°C and 6°C.

Figure 2.1. Projected Temperature Changes under Three Different
Emissions Scenarios

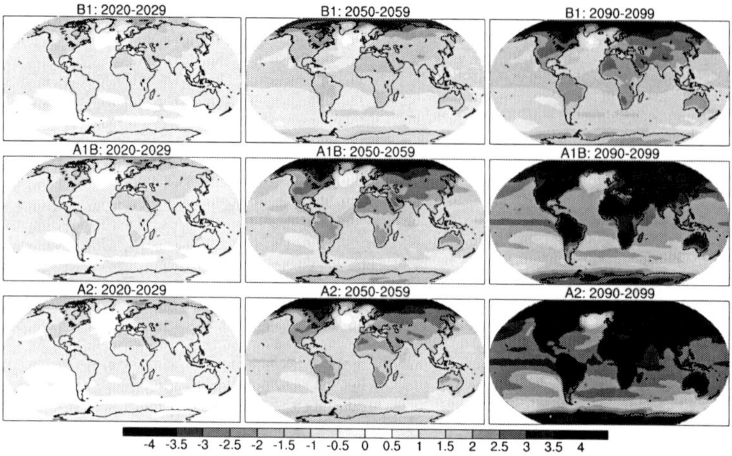

Source: G.A. Meehl and Thomas F. Stocker et al., "Global Climate Change Projections," Contribution of Working Group 1 to the Fourth Assessment Report, Intergovernmental Panel on Climate Change, in S. Solomon et al., *Climate Change 2007: The Physical Science Basis* (Cambridge: Cambridge University Press, 2007), p. 766, http://www.ipcc.ch/ipccreports/ar4-wg1.htm.

Figure 2.1 shows the distribution of projected temperature increases expected from three different emissions scenarios investigated by the IPCC. The predictions are based on an average of results obtained by testing scenarios in a wide range of models, yielding multimodel projections. The net effect is that the planet will get hotter, with more noticeable temperature increases over land, and in the Arctic. Table 2.1 outlines some of the most likely impacts of atmospheric warming under these and other emissions scenarios, as summarized by the IPCC.

In June 2005, the national science academies of the G-8 countries (including Canada and the United States) as well as those of China, India, and Brazil declared that—

The scientific understanding of climate change is now sufficiently clear to justify nations taking prompt action. It is vital that all nations identify cost-effective steps that they can take now to contribute to substantial and long-term reductions in net global greenhouse gas emissions . . . . Failure to implement significant reductions in net greenhouse gas emissions now will make the job much harder in the future . . . . We urge all nations . . . to take prompt action to reduce the causes of climate change, adapt to its impacts and ensure that the issue is included in all relevant national and international strategies.[3]

Table 2.1. Recent Trends and Projections of Extreme Climate Events

Phenomenon and direction of trend	Likelihood that the trend occurred in the late 20th century (typically post-1980)	Likelihood of future trends based on projections for the 21st century using SRES* scenarios
Warmer and fewer cold days and nights over most land areas	Very likely	Virtually certain
Warmer and more frequent hot days and nights over most land areas	Very likely	Virtually certain
Warm spells or heat waves, with frequency increasing over most land areas	Likely	Very likely
Heavy precipitation, with frequency (or proportion of total rainfall from heavy falls) increasing over most areas	Likely	Very likely
Increases in areas affected by droughts	Likely in many regions since 1970s	Likely
Increases in intense tropical cyclone activity	Likely in some regions since 1970	Likely
Increased incidence of extremely high sea levels (excluding the results of tsunamis)	Likely	Likely

Source: Adapted from Intergovernmental Panel on Climate Change, "Summary for Policymakers" (SPM-2) in Solomon et al., *Climate change 2007*, p. 8, http://www.ipcc.ch/pdf/assessment-report/ar4/wg1/ar4-wg1-spm.pdf.
* Special Report on Emissions Scenarios, http://www.grida.no/climate/ipcc/emission/.

Many government leaders and policymakers have responded to the call by making climate change a top priority for debate and discussion. However, actions taken by governments in North America and elsewhere in the world are not yet equal to the magnitude of the challenge.

ESTABLISHING MITIGATION TARGETS

Policy related to climate is necessarily driven by long-term projections of potential impacts on climate that result from GHG emissions. The difference between stabilizing emissions 10 years from now or 20 years from now will play out over time scales of a century or more, and the differences may limit the lower end of atmospheric GHG concentrations that can be achieved for several generations.

Figure 2.2 graphically depicts the logical flow by which decision-makers can use climate modeling and data to arrive at science-based targets for mitigating GHG emissions. Beginning with the best avail-

Figure 2.2. Logical Flow from Projected Impact of Climate to National Emissions Trajectories

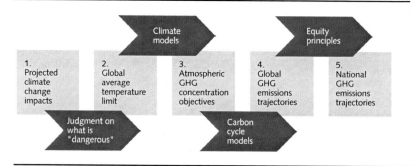

Source: Adapted from Matthew Bramley, *The Case for Deep Reductions: Canada's Role in Preventing Dangerous Climate Change* (Vancouver: David Suzuki Foundation, 2005), p. 19.

Figure 2.3. Projected Impact of Climate Change on Water, Health, Food, and Coastal Flooding (on millions of people)

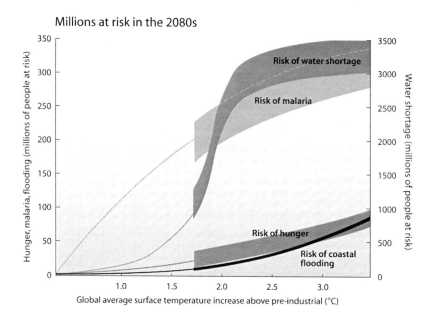

Source: Matthew Bramley, *The Case for Deep Reductions: Canada's Role in Preventing Dangerous Climate Change* (Vancouver: David Suzuki Foundation, 2005), 16. Based on a graph adapted by M. Meinshausen from M. Parry et al., "Millions at risk Defining Critical Climate Change Threat and Targets," *Global Environmental Change* 11 (2001): 181. See also http:mandela.inwent.org/ef/web02/parry.htm.

able scholarship about known and expected impacts, policymakers can assess what should be considered dangerous climate change. By setting impact thresholds, they can then establish a limit on the extent of increases in global temperature to which societies can adapt and are willing to "accept." Next, climate models can be used to estimate the atmospheric concentrations of greenhouse gases that will allow global temperatures to stay below derived limits. With a targeted concentration in place, policymakers can use carbon cycle models and equity principles to distribute responsibility for reducing emissions.

The answer to the question of "acceptable" limits for temperature increases relies on assessments of risk. In other words, for a given temperature increase, what is the likelihood that dangerous or irreversible changes to the climate and to ecosystems can be avoided? Figure 2.3 presents IPCC summary data (incorporating results from a wide range of models), which link temperature changes to the risks of selected impacts on human health and livelihoods. For example, an increase in temperature of 2°C above pre-industrial levels is expected to leave more than 2 billion people facing water shortages.

The IPCC takes no position on which impacts should be tolerated and which should not be tolerated; instead, the panel leaves it to policymakers to make their own assessments of acceptable versus dangerous climate change. One might expect this approach to lead to confusion, but, in practice, exhaustive reviews and analyses of available research have generated widespread support for establishing 2°C as the limit for an acceptable increase in global temperature.[4]

A number of scientific advisory bodies and governments share this assessment:

- In 2005, the European Council, which is made up of the heads of state of member countries of the European Union, reaffirmed the position it first endorsed in 1996, stating, ". . . with a view to achieving the ultimate objective of the UN Framework Convention on Climate Change, the global annual mean surface temperature increase should not exceed 2°C above pre-industrial levels."[5]

- The International Climate Change Taskforce, cochaired by Senator Olympia Snowe (R-Maine) and Steven Byers, a former UK minister for transport, made the following recommendation in 2005: "A long-term objective [should] be established to prevent global average temperature from rising more than 2°C above the pre-industrial level."[6]

- The German Advisory Council on Global Change conducted a detailed investigation of the meaning of "dangerous climate change" in 2003 and reported that increases of more than 2°C above pre-industrial levels would be "intolerable" with regard to impacts on the ecosystem, would be "dangerous" for food production and water availability, and "should not be exceeded" if sudden climate shifts are to be avoided.[7]

- A draft assessment of "dangerous" climate change conducted by the National Roundtable on the Environment and Economy in 2005 concluded that increases of 2°C may be too high from a Canadian perspective, given the greater than average vulnerability of Arctic ecosystems and communities.[8]

But what does stabilization at 2°C require in terms of objectives for acceptable levels of atmospheric concentration? Stabilization at GHG concentrations of 550 parts per million by volume (ppmv), expressed in terms of carbon dioxide equivalence (CO_2e) CO_2e has often been cited as a sufficient requirement.[9] However, more current evidence suggests that concentrations of GHGs must be as low as 400 or 450 ppmv CO_2e to avoid temperature increases of greater than 2°C, implying even lower concentrations of carbon dioxide itself—about 300 or 350 ppmv CO_2.[10] Although CO_2 concentrations reached 377 ppmv in 2004 and continue to increase by about 1.8 ppmv per year,[11] reabsorption of GHGs at sufficiently low emission levels would allow concentrations to stabilize below 350 ppmv over the course of a few decades. However, this trajectory requires immediate action to forestall and reverse the increased level of emissions.

Table 2.2 presents estimates of the reduction in total GHG emissions that would be required to achieve a range of stabilization scenarios from 350 ppmv CO_2e through 500 ppmv CO_2e, as assessed by the Potsdam Institute, the Netherlands Environmental Assessment Agency (MNP), and the Germany Federal Environmental Agency (UBA). The data suggest that stabilizing atmospheric GHG concentrations at levels of approximately 400 ppmv CO_2e—which is necessary in order to keep the risks of exceeding 2°C temperature rises acceptably low—will require reducing global emissions by more than 30 percent below 1990 benchmarks, or 45 percent below today's levels by 2050. A wide

Table 2.2. Summary of Stabilization Scenarios

	Potsdam Institute			MNP			UBA
Stabilized CO2e concentration (ppmv)	350	400	450	400	450	500	450*
Percent change in emissions from 1990 to 2020	-20 to+7	-10 to +11	+1 to+27	+15	+20 to +25	+25 to +35	+10
Percent change in emissions from 1990 to 2050	-51 to-22	-34 to-31	+0 to +20	-55 to -50	-40 to -30	-25 to -15	-60

*This is an approximate CO2e concentration based on the studies targeting CO2 concentration of 350–400 ppmv.

Sources: Potsdam Institute data derived from B. Hare and M. Meinhausen, "How Much Warming Are We Committed To and How Much Can Be Avoided?" PIK Report No. 93, 2004, http://www.pik-potsdam.de/pik_web/publications/pik_reports/reports/pr.93/pr93.pdf. Netherlands Environmental Assessment Agency (MNP) data are taken from M. Den Elzen and M. Meinhausen, "Meeting the EU 2 Climate Target: Global and Regional Emissions Implications," 2005, pp. 18–19, http://www.rivm.nl/bibliotheek/rapporten/728001031.pdf. Ger-man Federal Environment Agency (UBA) data are taken from N. Hoehne et al., Options for the Second Commitment Period of the Kyoto Protocol, Umweltbundesamt (2005), pp. 147 and 155, http://www.umweltbundesamt.org/fpdf-1/2847.pdf.

range of scientific and advisory institutions reinforce these estimates and generally converge around an overall global target of reducing emissions by 30–50 percent between 1990 and 2050 in order to prevent dangerous climate change.[12]

Figure 2.4 provides some more information by showing the range (solid swathes) of emissions trajectories that are the most likely to lead to a variety of long-term atmospheric concentrations of CO_2e. For example, stabilization at 450 ppmv requires a trajectory that peaks within the lightest green swathe at no more than about 45 Gt/yr around 2020, with rapid declines thereafter. The graph also shows that, the longer it takes to begin reducing total emissions, the more likely it will be that long-term concentrations will stabilize at unacceptable levels. In particular, if emissions do not begin to decline rapidly before 2050, achieving stabilization at any level below 550 ppmv CO_2e is unlikely. (The dotted lines in the figure indicate the lower uncertainty limits—that is, the most conservative emissions trajectory that could result in a given concentration.)

The final step in the process is political, rather than scientific, and depends on the answer to the following question: Given concentration objectives, how are global emission reductions to be distributed among nations? The United Nations Framework Convention on Climate Change (UNFCCC), which has been endorsed almost universally

Figure 2.4. Trajectories for Achieving a Range of CO2 Stabilization Scenarios

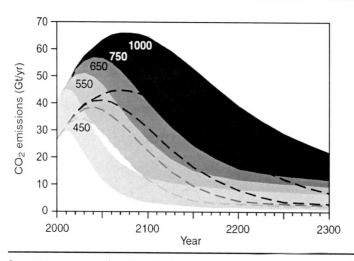

Source: Intergovernmental Panel on Climate Change, *Climate Change 2001: The Scientific Basis, Summary for Policymakers and Technical Summary of the Working Group* (Cambridge: Cambridge University Press, 2002), p. 76.

by the international community, provides important guidance—notably that "the largest share of historical and current global emissions of greenhouse gases has originated in developed countries, that per capita emissions in developing countries are still relatively low and that the share of global emissions originating in developing countries will grow to meet their social and development needs."[13]

Two series of data illustrate this point. Figure 2.5 shows Canadian, U.S., and Mexican shares of the 1,027 Gt in accumulated anthropogenic carbon dioxide emissions between 1900 and 2002—a total of 32.7 percent. It should be noted that all developed countries (including Canada and the United States, but not Mexico) have less than one-quarter of the world's population and account for just under 80 percent of total emissions over this same period.[14]

Table 2.3 provides a sampling of per capita emissions in developed and developing countries in 2000. When emissions resulting from changes in land use, such as deforestation, are excluded (the figures shown in column 1), Canada and the United States rank among the top 10 per capita emitters. Both countries are also among the top 10 total emitters. Mexico's per capita emissions are close to the world average, but Mexico ranks among the top 15 emitters in terms of total emis-

Table 2.3. Per Capita GHG Emissions, Selected Countries, 2000

	Total emissions excluding land use change (Mt/yr CO2e)	Rank	Total emissions including land use change (Mt/yr CO2e)	Rank
Qatar	54.7	1	54.7	2
Australia	25.6	5	25.9	9
United States	24.3	7	24.3	12
Canada	22.2	9	22.9	14
Netherlands	13.5	20	13.5	32
Japan	10.7	35	10.7	50
Sweden	7.5	58	7.5	76
Mexico	5.4	80	6.4	92
China	3.9	99	3.9	121
Indonesia	2.4	123	14.9	23
India	1.8	146	1.9	162
Uganda	1.1	169	2.7	137
World Average	5.6	—	6.8	—

Source: Climate Analysis Indicators Tool (CAIT), Version 3.0, World Resources Institute, Washington, D.C., http://cait.wri.org.

sions. (Mexico's exact ranking varies according to estimates related to land use, which are generally harder to quantify than those related to emissions resulting from energy use and industrial use. A few developing countries, such as Indonesia, have significant emissions associated with changes in land use.)

In responding to differences among nations, Article 3.1 of the UNFCCC includes the following recommendation: "The Parties should protect the climate system for the benefit of present and future generations of humankind, on the basis of equity and in accordance with their common but differentiated responsibilities and respective capabilities. Accordingly, the developed country Parties should take the lead in combating climate change and the negative effects thereof."[15] This text implicitly raises at least four key equity principles: the "polluter pays" approach (in the phrase "largest share of . . . current global emissions"), historical responsibility (also in the phrase "largest share of historical . . . emissions"), equal per capita rights to emit GHGs (that is, "per capita emissions . . . are still relatively low"), and ability to pay ("in

Figure 2.5. Share of Historical Global CO2 Emissions, 1900–2002

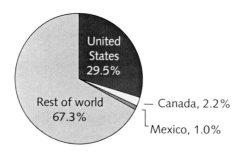

Source: Climate Analysis Indicators Tool (CAIT), version 3.0, World Resources Institute, Washington, D.C., http://cait.wri.org.

accordance with their . . . respective capabilities").[16] Every one of these principles points to the need for developed countries to bear a greater share of emissions reductions in the short and medium term.

Three major options have been identified for translating these principles into precise national emissions trajectories:

- a "multistage" approach, in which an increasing number of countries pass from having no targets, to having targets for the intensity of emissions, to having absolute targets; the transitions are triggered by a "capability-responsibility" index that responds to the key equity principles identified;

- a "contraction and convergence" approach, in which national per capita emissions begin to converge until they become equal in 2050; this approach tends to require significantly more stringent targets across the board in 2050 because early reductions are less significant;

- a "triptych" approach, in which targets are developed based on sectoral growth and efficiency requirements and are applied equally across countries.

In every case, industrialized countries must reduce emissions on the order of 75–90 percent below 1990 levels in order to achieve stabilization of the concentration levels at 400–450 ppmv CO_2e without shifting an undue burden to developing nations. This is roughly equivalent to reductions of 80–95 percent below current or 2010 emissions levels.

It should be noted that the variation among methods is relatively insignificant in comparison to the magnitude of the reductions required over this time frame. However, there is greater variation in the definition of interim targets for 2020. Existing nonbinding commitments and statements of intent range from reductions of 0 percent (made by California) to 30 percent (made by jurisdictions in the European Union) below 1990 levels.[17]

In general, the key principle is that the speed with which reductions are started is paramount. For example, a study conducted by the Netherlands Environmental Assessment Agency modeled a scenario in which the United States and developing countries take no measures during the two decades following 2012. In this scenario, other industrialized countries would have to reduce their emissions by 90 percent between 1990 and 2025 in order to achieve global emissions levels that would allow stabilization at 550 ppmv CO_2e.[18]

However, the 550 ppmv target is still likely to cause climate change at a dangerous level whereby the chances of overshooting the 2°C threshold exceed 70–100 percent.[19] Achieving stabilization at safer concentrations of 400 or 450 ppmv CO_2e would require these other industrialized countries to reduce their emissions by almost 100 percent by 2025. By contrast, early action by the heaviest emitters would substantially reduce the long-term burden for all countries.

EMISSIONS TRENDS IN NORTH AMERICA

Emissions of greenhouse gases in Canada, Mexico, and the United States have risen substantially since 1990, and "policy neutral" or "business as usual" projections suggest that this trend will continue in the absence of concerted action. Before looking at emissions figures, however, it is important to highlight some reporting conventions and definitions that can make comparison difficult. Notably, emissions are often separated into those related to energy (either combustion or fugitive emissions); those related to land use, land use change, and forestry (LULUCF); and those related to other sources, such as industrial processes.

Emissions related to energy are generally the easiest to estimate, and a wide range of data is available, especially given the existing databases of agencies such as the U.S. Energy Information Administration. Globally, energy-related GHG emissions account for about three-quarters of total emissions, but this proportion is greater than 80 percent in

Table 2.4. Projections of Energy-Related GHG Emissions, Canada, Mexico, and the United States, Selected Years, 1990–2025

ENERGY-RELATED GHG EMISSIONS (MT CO2e)

	Code	1990	1995	2000	2004	2010	2015	2020	2025
CANADA									
EIA International Energy Annual, 2004	Canada - EIA	479	505	568	588				
EIA International Energy Outlook, 2006 - Reference Case	Canada - IEO Ref	474			584	648	659	694	722
EIA International Energy Outlook, 2006 - Maximum Case	Canada - IEO Max	474			584	657	680	732	781
EIA International Energy Outlook, 2006 - Minimum Case	Canada - IEO Min	474			584	639	638	657	668
Environment Canada Emissions Inventory, 2004	Canada - EC	475	517	596	620				
MEXICO									
EIA International Energy Annual, 2004	Mexico - EIA	300	319	380	385				
EIA International Energy Outlook, 2006 - Reference Case	Mexico - IEO Ref	300			385	481	532	592	644
EIA International Energy Outlook, 2006 - Maximum Case	Mexico - IEO Max	300			385	489	553	628	700
EIA International Energy Outlook, 2006 - Minimum Case	Mexico - IEO Min	300			385	473	513	558	593
IEA World Energy Outlook 2004 - Reference Case	Mexico - IEA Ref					442	570	702	
Centro Molina	Mexico - Molina		292a		367		501b		
UNITED STATES									
EIA International Energy Annual, 2004	USA - EIA	5013	5480	5816	5912				
EIA International Energy Outlook, 2006 - Reference Case	USA - IEO Ref	4989			5923	6214	6589	6944	7425
EIA International Energy Outlook, 2006 - Maximum Case	USA - IEO Max	4989			5923	6304	6801	7322	7997
EIA International Energy Outlook, 2006 - Minimum Case	USA - IEO Min	4989			5923	6125	6363	6583	6842

Notes: (a) Data for 1994; (b) data for 2014.

Sources: U.S. Energy Information Administration, "International Energy Annual, 2004," http://www.eia.doe.gov/iea/; U.S. Energy Information Administration, "International Energy Outlook, 2006," http://www.eai.doe.gov/oiaf/archive/ieo06/index.html; Environment Canada, "National Inventory Report, 1990–2004: Greenhouse Gas Sources and Sinks in Canada," 2006, http://www.ec.gc.ca/pdb/ghg/inventory_report/2004_report/to=_e.cfm; International Energy Agency (Paris), "World Energy Outlook, 2004," http://www.worldenergyoutlook/2004.asp; Centro Mario Molina (Mexico City), "Hacia una Estrategia Nacional de Acción Climática para el Sector de Energía," http://www.centromariomolina.org/accion_climatica.html.

Figure 2.6. Net Emissions Profiles for Canada, Mexico, and the United States

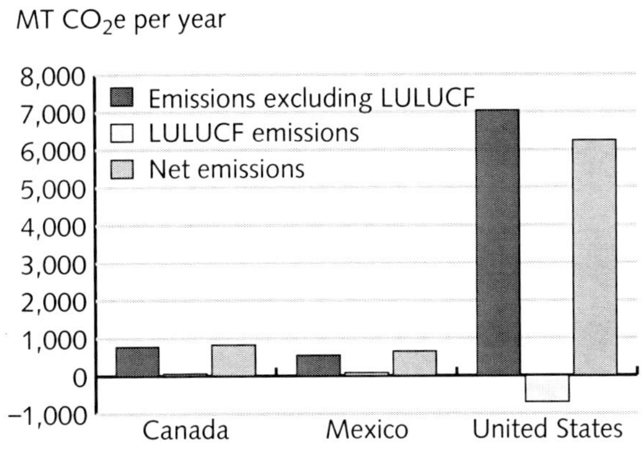

MT CO_2e per year

Legend:
- Emissions excluding LULUCF
- LULUCF emissions
- Net emissions

Categories: Canada, Mexico, United States

Sources: Data for Mexico: "Mexico: Third National Communication to the UNFCCC," Powerpoint presentation, http://regserver.unfccc.int/seors/file_storage/pluakyjv66tzwr5.pdf; Canada and the United States: "UNFCCC Emission Profiles for Annex I Parties," http://unfccc.int/ghg_emissions_data/items/3954.php.

Canada and the United States, where energy-related emissions trends are often reported as a proxy for trends as a whole. The proportion is much lower in Mexico, as it is in many developing countries.

On the other end of the spectrum, LULUCF emissions (or withdrawals) are generally difficult to estimate, and availability of data on these emissions is limited. Many sources explicitly exclude LULUCF emissions in their estimates. Figure 2.6 provides an overall snapshot of emissions trends in Canada, the United States, and Mexico and includes a comparison of LULUCF and non-LULUCF emissions. The data for Canada and the United States in the figure are for 2004; the data for Mexico are for 2002.

In 2004, Canadian GHG emissions, excluding those related to LULUCF were estimated at 758 Mt CO_2e, with LULUCF emissions contributing an additional 81 Mt, for a total of 839 megatons (Mt). U.S. emissions were estimated at 7068 Mt, with LULUCF withdrawals estimated at 773 Mt, for a total of 6294 Mt.[20] In Mexico, emissions in 2002 totaled 643 Mt, of which 90 Mt were attributable to LULUCF.[21] Figure 2.7 provides a breakdown of non-LULUCF emissions by UNFCCC sector in the three countries.

Projections of future GHG emissions vary by source and are even less directly comparable between countries. Moreover, a majority of

Figure 2.7. Sectoral Breakdown of Emissions for Canada, Mexico, and the United States

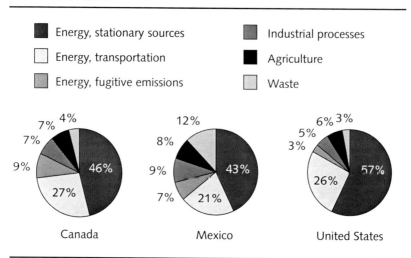

Sources: Data for Mexico: "Mexico: Third National Communication to the UNFCCC," Powerpoint presentation, http://regserver.unfccc.int/seors/file_storage/pluakyjv66tzwr5.pdf; Canada and the United States: "UNFCCC Emission Profiles for Annex I Parties," http://unfccc.int/ghg_emissions_data/items/3954.php.

projections is limited to those related to energy. Table 2.4 and figure 2.8 present a range of energy emissions scenarios from different sources (Environment Canada, the Centro Mario Molina, the International Energy Agency, and the Energy Information Administration). As the figure demonstrates, data values are different, but the trends reported by all these agencies are generally consistent. Between 2004 and 2025, Canadian and U.S. emissions are projected to increase by about 25 percent—at an annual rate of 1.0 percent and 1.1 percent, respectively. Mexican emissions are projected to increase by about 60 percent—at an annual rate of 2.3 percent.

As outlined in the previous subsection, industrialized nations should aim to reduce emissions by about 0–30 percent by 2020, compared with a 1990 baseline, and should be on the way to achieving reductions of 75–90 percent by 2050. The trends in Canada and the United States are clearly incompatible with these targets. However, some state-level and provincial governments have set targets that come close to these objectives. For example, California plans to reduce GHG emissions to the 1990 level by 2020, and a conference of New England governors and officials from eastern Canadian provinces, including Quebec, has

Figure 2.8. Projections of Energy-Related GHG Emissions, Canada, Mexico, and the United States, Selected Years, 1990–2025

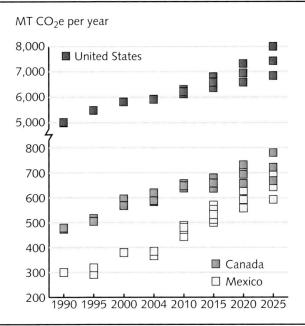

Source: See table 2.4.

adopted a regional goal of reducing GHG emissions to at least 10 percent below 1990 levels by 2020.[22]

POLICY RECOMMENDATIONS

Given that a majority of emissions are associated with energy use—especially in Canada and the United States—the emissions trajectories required to mitigate the danger are unlikely to be realized without dramatically transforming energy systems and adopting low-impact alternatives. The transition will require policy measures that encourage the transformation of energy infrastructure and direct new investments almost exclusively for the development of low-impact, renewable energy. Because Canada and Mexico aspire to reinforce their position as exporters of fossil fuel energy, the transition to low-impact, renewable energy will be a particular challenge for both countries.

As an example, Canada is currently focused on the tar sands (or oil sands) in Alberta's northern region, which is now the world's second largest proven oil reserve—only Saudi Arabia has more. Current production of the tar sands is about 1.3 million barrels per day (bpd), but there are plans to increase production to 5 million bpd by 2030. The difficulty arises because producing a barrel of oil in the tar sands generates about three times as many GHG emissions as producing a barrel of conventional oil (86 kg CO_2e/bbl versus 29 kg CO_2e/bbl).[23] Alberta's tar sands already represent Canada's fastest growing source of GHG emissions.

Canada is the only North American country to have ratified the Kyoto Protocol and to have accepted a legally binding emissions target—6 percent below 1990 levels—for the Kyoto Protocol's 2008–2012 commitment period. This agreement implies a total emissions target of 563 Mt (excluding LULUCF emissions). Business as usual projections compiled by the United Kingdom's Tyndall Centre project that the emissions from the production of the tar sands will be between 50 Mt and 105 Mt in 2012, representing 9–19 percent of Canada's allowable total.[24] In 2020, these emissions are projected to be between 70 Mt and 120 Mt.[25] If Canada accepts a target of 15 percent reductions below 1990 levels (halfway between the 0–30 percent options being considered in other jurisdictions), the tar sands would represent 15–25 percent of the country's allowable total. Other sectors and provinces would be forced to make drastic reductions to compensate for the increase in emissions attributable to the production of tar sands in Alberta.

Two potential solutions for Canada's "climate contradiction" are noteworthy, and both exemplify generally available policy options for various North American contexts. The first is the implementation of regulatory standards, or a sufficiently high polluter pays charge for carbon, which would make requisite investments in new technology economic. In the case of the tar sands, deployment of carbon capture and storage technology—coupled with offset purchases—can be used to reduce net emissions from oil production to zero. The costs would fall between US$2 and US$13 dollars per barrel, but they are likely to be closer to the lower end of the estimate—well within the normal range of fluctuations in the price of oil.[26] The same approaches—regulation and pricing—are appropriate for a wide range of opportunities to deploy technology across North America, including investments in clean coal and renewable energies, such as wind power and solar power.

A second policy option involves matching supply-side measures with demand-side efforts to reduce the need for fossil fuels in transportation. Fuel efficiency standards are a key element of this approach:

the difference between average fleet fuel efficiencies in North America and Europe is 3.4 liters per 100 kilometers, which represents clearly "irresponsible demand" or fuel waste in North America.[27] The development of efficiency standards for vehicles (as well as in other sectors) is a prime area for continental collaboration, given the integration of production chains and markets. Indeed, the competitiveness concerns associated with a wide range of opportunities to achieve efficiency and conservation (extending beyond the transportation sector to buildings, appliances, and industrial processes) may be effectively mitigated through North American collaboration.

North America can also seize important opportunities for specific virtuous cycles. For instance, California has proposed a low-carbon fuel standard whereby fuels that generate the lowest level of greenhouse gas emissions during production would be preferred. This could provide a prime market for carbon-neutral tar sands oil, especially given the minimal transportation emissions that would be generated in moving fuel from Alberta to California. This is an opportunity to match leadership in producer responsibility with leadership in consumer responsibility.

An overall framework for emissions reductions targets remains essential, however, in order to stimulate and realize the potential of such regional and sectoral initiatives. Targets are also essential for ensuring that North America takes on its "fair share" of global emissions reductions. Certainly, without leadership coming from developed countries, developing nations are unlikely to accept any form of mandated reductions. In this context, the United Nations Framework Convention on Climate Change remains the only forum in which most of the world's countries are represented and committed to advancing goals to deal with the problem of climate change. The UNFCCC is also the only forum in which the first victims of climate change—small island states and low-lying countries such as Bangladesh—are represented.

Effective North American action on climate change will require engagement with the UNFCCC process and a willingness to match targets for reducing emissions with the standards, regulatory frameworks, and carbon-pricing options that will bring about the necessary technology deployment and behavioral change. As industrialized nations, Canada and the United States have a special responsibility to act immediately and to take on targets of 75–90 percent reductions between 1990 and 2050, so that developing countries, such as Mexico,

can accept targets commensurate with their ability to pay, historical responsibility, and development objectives. In all three countries,
however, the solution lies in earnestly and purposefully *changing*, not
just reacting to emissions trends expected between today and 2025.

WATER MANAGEMENT

OVERVIEW

It is appropriate to discuss water management in North America after
a discussion of climate change and before a discussion of biodiversity,
because climate change will make the challenge of satisfying the demands for freshwater in North America even more difficult than it is
today, and the manner in which Canada, Mexico, and the United States
meet that challenge will have a significant impact on biodiversity. Climate models are not yet able to make detailed predictions regarding the
impact of climate change on specific regions in North America, but they
do predict that regions in the middle of the continent that are farthest
from the coasts will have less precipitation and that the runoff from the
Rocky Mountains on which the arid regions in the southwestern U.S.
and northern Mexico depend will be reduced and will come earlier.

In all three countries—and particularly in the arid regions referred to above—population growth, increased economic activity, and
changes in water availability are already forcing agencies responsible
for water management to reconsider long-standing agreements related
to allocation of surface water, such as the Colorado River Compact
or the 1944 Rio Grande/Rio Bravo Treaty. Increasing withdrawals of
groundwater are depleting aquifers at an unsustainable rate. As human demands for scarce water resources grow, the amounts left over
for ecosystems decline. Nonpoint source pollution remains a serious
problem in all three countries. All three face a significant backlog of
repairs and upgrades needed for their infrastructure for water distribution and for control of water pollution.

These problems are manageable if the United States, Canada, and
Mexico take appropriate steps to improve water management at all levels of government, including the following:

- improving the enforcement of existing laws and regulations;

- improving coordination among existing institutions responsible
  for water management and giving them authority to manage
  surface water and groundwater on an integrated basis;

- increasing investment in water infrastructure;

- providing incentives for more efficient use of water in all sectors, particularly by improving pricing systems;

- creating market mechanisms for the transfer of water rights; and

- setting aside sufficient water to preserve critical ecosystems.

Positive developments over the last 30 years give grounds for hope that the three North American countries will be able to make significant progress along these lines by 2025. In the United States, total and per capita water use has actually declined since 1980 as a result of improved efficiency and structural changes in the economy. All three countries have strengthened their laws and regulations governing the quality of water, but inadequate enforcement of those laws and regulations remains a problem. State and local governments—particularly in the United States—have conducted a number of successful experiments in creating market mechanisms for the transfer of water rights.

There are important differences in the regulatory regimes, patterns of historical development, and overall availability of water resources among the three countries. In Mexico, water resources are enshrined in the country's constitution as part of the national patrimony and are therefore formally under state control; whereas in the United States and Canada, private citizens and corporations can acquire legal title to specific water resources under the prior appropriation doctrine of "first in use, first in right." The United States has led the world in building dams and massive water diversion projects, using federal dollars as a means to create farms and cities in the desert. Of all the countries that are members of the Organization for Economic Coordination and Development (OECD), Canada has the largest amount of water resources per capita, although more than half of these resources are in northward flowing rivers in northern Canada and therefore are not accessible to population centers in the southern part of the country. The separation of population centers from tropical southern states that have a disproportionate share of the country's water is also a problem in Mexico.

Despite these and other differences, water management in the three countries has three common characteristics. In all three countries, water management is very fragmented and highly political, with most key decisions made at the local level. Federal decisions with respect to water allocation and investment in infrastructure are typically made in reaction to specific demands and pressures from local interests that have the ear of their political representatives. None of the three countries has established adequate processes to make long-term decisions about allocating scarce water resources between and across regions or even across water basins. Finally, despite some successful experiments, none of the countries has put in place comprehensive market-based policies and mechanisms that will enable water to be priced at levels that encourage conservation while protecting the interests of poorer citizens and protecting ecosystems.

Nevertheless, North America has developed a set of bilateral and trilateral institutions that have untapped potential to help overcome these weaknesses. The two most important bilateral institutions are (1) the International Boundary and Water Commission (IBWC), which is responsible for implementing the 1944 treaty and other agreements between the United States and Mexico related to allocating the waters of the Rio Grande/Rio Bravo River and its major tributaries between the two countries, and (2) the International Joint Commission (IJC), which was established 100 years ago by Canada and the United States under the Boundary Waters Treaty of 1907 and is responsible for implementing the treaty and carrying out research and joint planning efforts between the two countries with respect to issues involving their shared waters. In addition, under the Great Lakes Water Quality Agreement of 1972, the United States and Canada cooperate in cleaning up pollution in the Great Lakes.

Three other institutions—one trilateral and two bilateral—were established in the early 1990s to help mitigate the perceived negative social and environmental impacts of the North American Free Trade Agreement (NAFTA). The North American Commission for Environmental Cooperation (NACEC) was created by the environmental side agreement to NAFTA among Canada, Mexico, and the United States in 1993. At the same time, in response to pressure for greater investment in environmental infrastructure in the border region and concerns that increased trade between the two countries under NAFTA would lead to further degradation of the border environment, the United States and Mexico created the Border Environment Cooperation Commission (BECC) and the North American Development Bank (NADBANK).

All these institutions have provided valuable services and, to differing degrees, are regarded as models for similar regimes elsewhere in the world. The IBWC has successfully maintained and operated the Elephant Butte, Amistad, and Falcon reservoirs and has enabled the United States and Mexico to meet their obligations under the 1944 treaty and subsequent additions, with the partial exception of the dispute about Mexico's water debt that arose as a result of the drought in that country between 1992 and 2002. The IJC has enhanced cooperation and prevented disputes between the United States and Canada on a number of contentious issues and has successfully sponsored an innovative planning process for water basins. NACEC has provided a forum in which citizens' groups in all three countries can present claims of improper enforcement of environmental laws of their respective countries, and the commission has carried out valuable capacity building, particularly in Mexico. The BECC has certified hundreds of projects related to wastewater treatment, drinking water, and solid waste that would not otherwise have been built; NADBANK (with the help of grants awarded by the of U.S. Environmental Protection Agency) has arranged the financing for these projects.

These institutions have the potential to accomplish far more, however, if the three governments would commit the political will and resources required. For example, the IBWC, BECC, and NADBANK could cooperate on programs designed to create and support a watershed-based binational planning process carried out by local stakeholders within parameters established by the two federal governments. The IJC and the Great Lakes Secretariat could be the catalysts for a similar process along the U.S.-Canadian border. NACEC could be given the autonomy and financial resources required to identify issues related to enforcement of environmental laws in all three countries and to propose innovative solutions for any problems that are found. With additional political and financial support, the institutions could help water management authorities in all three countries overcome resistance to taking the steps needed to meet the challenges identified above.

Strengthening these institutions would benefit the broader global community as well. Many other countries face water management problems that are far more severe than those in North America. Perhaps the greatest environmental disaster of the last 100 years is the drying out of Central Asia's Aral Sea, which has occurred because of the diversion of the lake's two principal feeders—the Amu Darya and Syr Darya Rivers—in order to cultivate vast quantities of cotton and rice. Salt and chemical residues blown from the exposed lake bed have poisoned millions of acres of land and affected the health of millions of people downwind of the Aral Sea. A similar disaster looms in Africa, because Lake Chad has shrunk to 10 percent of its original size as a result of massive irrigation projects and huge withdrawals of water to offset drought conditions.

An even greater disaster could result from the depletion of aquifers in China, India, and Pakistan. Fred Pearce, an author who specializes in water management issues, estimates that several hundred million people in those three countries are subsisting on crops grown with fossil water that cannot be quickly replenished with rainwater and that the resulting overdraft ranges between 120 and 160 million acre-feet per year.[28] When the farmers growing those crops can no longer extract the necessary groundwater, millions of people could starve. North American institutions responsible for water management have the opportunity—and some would say the obligation—to work with other countries to help them avert these disasters and get on the path toward more sustainable water management.

Before examining these themes in a North American context, it is necessary to look at the situation in each of the three countries individually.

CANADA

Water is more central to Canadians' image of their country than it is to the population of either the United States or Mexico. Yet it has been argued that the gap between this self-image—the "myth of water abundance"—and the reality of the actual availability of water in Canada as well as current uses and management practices is greater than it is in any other country in the world. Many Canadians believe that Canada has roughly one-quarter of the world's supply of freshwater, whereas the reality is that Canada has approximately 6.5 percent of the world's renewable water supply, as do the United States, China, and Indonesia.

Canada has a relatively large supply of water per capita, but each region does not necessarily have a large supply of water. Most Canadians live in the southern part of the country—far from some of the larger sources of water. Certain regions are already experiencing water shortages, and climate change is likely to make this situation worse. The myth of water abundance, moreover, has led Canadians to tolerate substandard water management practices, ranging from failure to en-force pollution control regulations, to underinvestment in water infra-structure, to dysfunctional water pricing structures that are at variance with their expressed commitment to environmental values. According to John Sprague, "there must be a continued campaign to get Canadi-ans to abandon the myth of water abundance and to adopt a realistic view of their water supply. Otherwise, we will make policy decisions based on misinformation, and this cannot help but have serious eco-nomic, political, and ecological consequences."[29]

In addition to the need for a more realistic understanding of its wa-ter resources, Canada needs to take a number of specific steps to man-age these resources in a more sustainable manner. First, Canada needs to obtain better data on both the quantity and the quality of the coun-try's water supply. Because provinces and territories carry out all basic water management functions, including issuing permits to withdraw water, they are the main source of data related to water quantity; the federal government lacks detailed nationwide data on additions to and withdrawals from the water supply. This problem is particularly severe when it comes to groundwater, because good nationwide information on withdrawals simply does not exist.

Canada does not operate a national program to monitor the quality of water, and provincial or sectoral monitoring programs do not use the same standards to measure water quality. Therefore, it has been difficult to assess water quality across the whole country. The first na-tional assessment, based on methodology developed by the Canadian Council of Ministers of the Environment, was published in 2003 and was based on data from 319 monitoring stations concentrated in urban areas.[30] One would hope that future assessments will be based on more data points and will use improved methodology.

A related, but broader, need is to strengthen the role of the federal government in Canada's water management. Few federal laws directly address water use, because Canada's Constitution Act of 1867 gave provinces jurisdiction over this area, with three key exceptions: the federal government has jurisdiction in the fields of fisheries, naviga-tion, and boundary waters. Under the Fisheries Act, the federal gov-ernment has the power—but not the duty—to require dam owners to ensure that there is adequate water downriver to protect the fish. The federal government also has the authority to require projects affecting fisheries or navigation to go through an environmental assessment process. In practice, however, Ottawa has been reluctant to use these powers because of a desire to avoid confrontations with provinces over issues related to the country's natural resources. Canada has had greater success with managing boundary waters; together with the United States, the Canadian government has made considerable progress in achieving the goal of the Great Lakes Water Quality Agreement: to restore and maintain the chemical, physical, and biological integrity of the ecosystem of the Great Lakes basin.

The weakness of the federal government is most apparent in Canada's approach to controlling water pollution. The Canadian Environmental Protection Act of 1999, which regulates toxic substances and ocean dumping, as well as other federal and provincial laws dealing with water pollution all take the same basic approach. The regulations start with a broad prohibition on all pollution but then lay out broad exceptions to these blanket prohibitions; the laws almost always allow pollution as long as it is in accordance with a permit. To the extent that polluters are not covered by other exceptions, they will apply for a permit, which will usually be granted with a limitation based on maximum concentrations of a pollutant per unit of effluent or maximum quantities of a pollutant per unit of production.

This approach to controlling water pollution has three major deficiencies:

- It enables polluters to manipulate the limitations by either diluting the pollutant in question or redefining "production."

- It does not cover many nonpoint sources of pollution.

- It does not control actual environmental outcomes through binding standards related to water quality.

In contrast to the binding water quality standards established by the U.S. Environmental Protection Agency (EPA) under the U.S. Clean Water Act and Safe Drinking Water Act, Canada's federal and provincial water quality standards have been promulgated in the form of voluntary guidelines that are frequently followed in the breach. Since the 1970s, there have been many calls to introduce binding regulations related to water quality, but thus far, these calls have not been answered.

The result of these deficiencies is unacceptable water quality in many places, particularly outside of major urban areas. The assessment conducted by the Council of Ministers of the Environment in 2003 found that 51 percent of the stations showed good to excellent performance in achieving local water quality objectives for protection of aquatic life, 28 percent showed fair performance, and 21 percent showed marginal or poor performance.[31] No countrywide review of the quality of groundwater is currently available, but the limited data available raise serious issues about the quality of drinking water. Two recent episodes of serious dysfunction in municipal water supply in Walkerton, Ontario, and in North Battleford, Saskatchewan, have led to severe consequences on residents' health. Contamination of rural household wells is also a concern. Depending on the region, 20–40 percent of rural wells surveyed have occurrences of coliform bacteria in excess of the guidelines set for drinking water, and about 15 percent of rural wells exceed guidelines set for nitrates.

Canada's federal and provincial governments have reacted to increased public concern over water quality by developing comprehensive strategies, such as the 2002 Quebec Water Strategy, and also by promulgating new legislation or regulations, such as the Council of Ministers of the Environment's Sustainable Water and Sewage Systems Act for Ontario as well as water regulations for Saskatchewan in 2002 under the Environmental Management and Protection Act. Municipal water treatment systems have been upgraded and operational standards have been improved. There has also been a slight increase in the percentage of people connected to sewers to approximately 75 percent connected.

Canada will not see fundamental improvement, however, until the country addresses nonpoint source pollution from agricultural, municipal, and industrial sources and makes a significant investment in water infrastructure. The OECD's Environmental Performance Review of Canada conducted in 2004 estimates that, at the present rate, it may well take another 20 years of effort (and more than US$100 billion of expenditures) before Canada fully equips itself with the municipal wastewater infrastructure it needs, even without taking into account the significant investment required to upgrade drinking water systems.[32]

The issue of infrastructure brings up another basic water management need that Canada must address: incentives for conservation. Partly because of the myth of water abundance, Canadians have not paid much attention to conserving water until very recently. Canada's per capita water use is approximately 1.5 million cubic meters per year— second only to the level in the United States. Production of thermal power is the primary reason for withdrawing water, followed by withdrawals used for manufacturing, municipal services, agriculture, and mining. Even if one looks at domestic water use alone, however, Canada's daily use of domestic water averages 343 liters per day—second only to the U.S. average of 382 liters per day and roughly 50 percent higher than the European average. In addition to the myth of water abundance, this high level of domestic consumption is encouraged by the lowest municipal water prices among Western industrialized countries, including the United States. In many Canadian municipalities, water revenues are not even sufficient to cover the cost of water service and do not reflect the true value of the resource.

The solution to the problem of consumption is not just higher prices, but pricing mechanisms that encourage conservation while enabling users with low incomes to meet their essential water needs at a reasonable cost. A recent report from Environment Canada shows both great diversity in water pricing schemes across the country and a pattern of perverse incentives from a conservation standpoint. The most striking finding in the report is that 37 percent of Canadians pay a flat rate for their water regardless of the quantity that they consume. The significance of this finding is highlighted by the fact that water consumption was 70 percent higher when users faced these types of rates than when they faced volume-based rates. Among the remaining 63 percent of users facing volume-based rates, 39 percent paid the same amount per liter no matter how much water they consumed, 13 percent paid rates that declined as the volume consumed increased, and only 10 percent paid rates that increased with the volume of water consumed.[33]

In the short term, Canada's municipalities need to raise their rates to levels that cover the full costs of service in a manner that encourages conservation and protects low-income users. The best way to accomplish these goals is to have a relatively low rate for a minimum monthly quantity of water used per household and to increase rates for amounts consumed that exceed the minimum. To maximize conservation, municipal water utilities should couple this block pricing approach with conservation education programs and financial incentives for users to install appliances that save water, such as low-flush toilets and low-flow showerheads.

In the longer term, utilities must improve the efficiency of water use in their own operations, particularly by reducing leakage from their own pipes. In addition, provinces must phase out the practice of granting long-term water permits to agricultural, industrial, and thermoelectric customers at no cost or at a very low cost. Seven of thirteen provinces levy some sort of one-time or recurring fee for these permits; the remaining provinces (including Quebec and Alberta) levy no fee at all. Only when larger-scale users pay something close to the real value of the water they use will they have an incentive to exploit their tremendous potential for water savings through process improvements and water recycling. At the same time, provincial and local governments will gain the resources to make the investments in water infrastructure that the country needs.

The current practice of granting long-term permits to agricultural and industrial users has also inhibited the development of market-based mechanisms in areas where water is scarce. Canadians tend to look at water markets with a very skeptical eye through the lens of the "commons or commodity" debate. As will be argued at greater length later in this chapter, experiments in the United States and other countries have shown that it is possible to obtain many of the efficiency benefits of market-based transfers while protecting the special status of water as an essential and place-based resource. Substantively, Canada must restrict water transfers to a particular basin and set aside sufficient quantities of water for ecosystems, native peoples, and other claimants whose rights might not be protected by the market alone. Procedurally, Canadians need to reach agreement on the rules for market process through a bottom-up process that involves all the stakeholders in the basin in question.

A number of Canadian commentators have expressed concerns about the possibility of exporting bulk water to the United States. Two of the grounds for these concerns are (1) the failure explicitly to exclude water from the scope of NAFTA, particularly the procedures to resolve investment disputes spelled out in Article 11, and (2) comments made by politicians, business leaders, and other advocates of greater economic integration in North America suggesting that bulk water exports from Canada to the United States could play a positive role in such integration and should not be ruled out. Good faith application of the principles proposed in the preceding paragraph would rule out interbasin transfers within and between Canada and the United States and thereby put these concerns to rest.

Addressing all these needs would go a long way toward putting Canada on a path leading to sustainable water management. But resolving these problems will not be enough to deal with a fundamental shift in Canada's future water supply. Canada, Russia, and, to a lesser extent, Alaska will be presented with significant new opportunities and challenges as climate change opens up their northern regions to resource extraction and economic development. Russia and Canada are already making competing claims of rights to exploit the Arctic Ocean. Canadian government officials and entrepreneurs are already thinking about the implications of an ice-free Northwest Passage. If easier access to the resources found in northern Canada sets off a gold rush similar to what has been seen elsewhere in the world, the national and global impacts on the environment could be far greater than what was experienced at Prudhoe Bay and Fort McMurray. These impacts would be particularly great for the great river basins of the north, which are currently relatively pristine.

As a democracy whose self-image is deeply connected to the grandeur and beauty of its natural environment, Canada will face some of the most difficult choices in its history when it deals with opening up its northern territories because of the impact of climate change. It would be a tragedy if Canadians allowed one of the most beautiful and least-degraded areas on the planet to be irreparably damaged because the country was unable to make some very hard choices in time to protect its natural resources.

UNITED STATES

The United States faces many of the same challenges and opportunities with respect to water management as Canada does. The United States has roughly the same total annual renewable water supply as Canada has, although the per capita supply of water is much lower in the United States because of its larger population (for example, the lower 48 states have a total supply that is about 40 percent larger than southern Canada's is, but they have much less water per capita than southern Canada has). Like Canada, the United States is a heavy consumer of water, leading the world with an annual abstraction of 1,730 cubic meters per capita, as compared with Canada's second-place abstraction of 1,430 cubic meters per capita.

The United States also faces many of the same challenges as Canada does when it comes to water management. Responsibility for managing the water supply is fragmented among many agencies at different levels of government and, at least until recently, little attempt has been made to coordinate water policy across basins or even within basins. There are serious shortcomings in enforcing regulations related to water quality, particularly outside of major cities and with respect to nonpoint source pollution. The United States has a huge backlog of unmet needs for maintenance, repair, and extension of water treatment and drinking water infrastructure. Much more needs to be done to encourage water conservation in all sectors, including developing public education programs and offering targeted subsidies for appliances and systems that use water more efficiently.

Although the price of water has increased and pricing structures have been modified to encourage conservation in different parts of the country over the last 15 years, the price of water in most parts of the country still does not reflect the true economic value of the resource. This is particularly the case for groundwater, which is being withdrawn from aquifers at unsustainable rates, resulting in increasing subsidence. There has been some experimentation with market-based water transfers in California and other states, but much more needs to be done. Finally, the United States will face many of the same hard choices in dealing with the impact of climate change in Alaska that Canada faces with respect to its northern territories.

Despite these similarities, the United States differs from Canada in two important respects. The first is both geographical and cultural and can be summed up by using the term "Cadillac Desert" to define it. As the United States expanded westward and particularly after it acquired vast territories in California and the Southwest from Mexico in the Treaty of Guadalupe Hidalgo in 1848, settlers in the U.S. desert sought to ensure their future by making the desert bloom. To achieve their goal, they needed huge amounts of water—from the Colorado and Rio Grande Rivers as well as from the great aquifers under the desert surface—and transferring this water from where it was to where they wanted it required huge amounts of money for the construction of dams, reservoirs, canals, and other water infrastructure. The only source of these funds was the federal government in Washington, D.C.

Therefore, starting in the early 1870s, following the end of the Civil War, 100 years of the Cadillac Desert began. Voters in the Western states and their elected representatives used their political clout in Washington to obtain billions of dollars in federal appropriations to fund the dams, reservoirs, and other infrastructure necessary to supply water for millions of acres of irrigated fields and for the towns and cities that grew up with these areas. With the creation of the Bureau of Reclamation in 1902, this process accelerated and reached its apogee with the construction of the Hoover Dam and other great dams in the West during the New Deal era in the 1930s. By then, the focus of the Cadillac Desert had broadened to include not only huge diversion projects built to bring water to rapidly growing desert cities such as Los Angeles but also the production of cheap hydroelectric power in the Pacific Northwest. It can be argued that, without this cheap hydropower provided by the great dams, the United States could not have produced the aluminum needed to make the fighter planes that helped the Allies win World War II.

A huge political and cultural irony accompanies this unparalleled act of economic and ecological hubris. From the country's beginnings in the seventeenth-century settlements in Virginia and Massachusetts, the United States has prided itself on its culture of rugged individualism and freedom from government control. Yet, when it comes to economic development, the people have consistently relied on the federal government to provide them with the tools needed to succeed. From canals and railroads to land grant colleges, to the federal highway system, to the military-industrial complex, the federal government has been central to U.S. economic development. Even today, the federal government controls more than 40 percent of the land in the United States and more than 60 percent of the land in certain Western states.

Nowhere has the federal role been more important than in water management. The economies of the most rapidly growing parts of the United States would simply not exist if the federal government had not subsidized the water infrastructure necessary to sustain them. In theory, the recipients of this federal largesse were supposed to pay back the federal government's investment over time, but, in practice, they have been required to pay back only a tiny fraction of that investment. It is ironic that—at least with respect to water management—the most successful U.S. export has been a strategy of state-driven economic development based on heavily subsidized water infrastructure. The legacy of the Hoover Dam lives on not only in Canada and Mexico—which have copied the U.S. model to a significant extent—but also in the great dams in Itaipu, Bratsk, Narmada, and Three Gorges.

Domestically, the results of the experience of the Cadillac Desert have been mixed. On the positive side of the ledger, the federal government's financial support has made the dynamic and expanding economy of the American Southwest possible. On the negative side, the provision of low-cost water from subsidized diversions has led to an artificially large agricultural sector that cultivates such crops as cotton and alfalfa on irrigated land that would not be economically sustainable if water were priced closer to its true marginal cost. The availability of water at a small fraction of its true value has also encouraged wasteful practices in all sectors of the economy and has discouraged conservation. Overallocation of Colorado River stream flows for irrigation and municipal uses has deprived ecosystems, such as the marshes in the Bay of California, of the water that they need to survive. Today, powerful agricultural and other interests feel entitled to cheap federal water, and they are well positioned to oppose reduced allocations or price increases. Institutionally, however, the history of the Cadillac Desert has given the federal government a level of involvement and control that could be used to promote better water management practices.

On the water supply side, the U.S. Department of the Interior controls the water rights associated with federal lands through the Bureau of Land Management and the National Park Service. The U.S. Department of Agriculture has similar authority with respect to national forests through the U.S. Forest Service. The Department of the Interior's Bureau of Reclamation has jurisdiction over the construction and maintenance of dams, reservoirs, and other infrastructure involving federally controlled waters. Not only do these agencies have direct influence over domestic users of federal water through water contracts and control over critical infrastructure, but they also have indirect influence through their power to grant or withhold federal funding and other types of support to state and local water management agencies and their customers. Although this influence has not been used to any great extent recently because of the user-friendly attitudes of the current administration, the power remains available to a future administration with a more reform-minded agenda.

With respect to water quality, the Clean Water Act and the Safe Drinking Water Act, both administered by the U.S. Environmental Protection Agency, give the federal government the authority to set binding nationwide standards for pollution discharge and water quality standards. The EPA has exercised this authority extensively in the 35 years since its creation and has achieved substantial improvements in water quality across the country. One of the keys to the EPA's success in this regard has been its delegation of responsibility for implementation and enforcement of its standards to the agency's 10 regional offices, which, in turn, delegate authority to the appropriate agencies in the states within their respective regions. Each state—or, in some cases, a group of states sharing a particular watershed—is required to develop a plan for complying with a particular standard or set of standards over a specific period of time. This delegation process creates partnerships among different levels of government and enables the federal government to obtain a broad consensus on ways to improve the quality of the country's water.

It is helpful to examine specific trends in meeting standards set for water quality over the past decade. The share of the U.S. population served by community water systems (273 million residents in 2003) that received water that met all health-based drinking water standards increased from 79 percent in 1993 to 90 percent in 2003—below the EPA's strategic objective of reaching 95 percent by 2008.[34] The number of individual violations of water quality standards has remained high, and episodes such as the discovery of high levels of lead in the tap water of Washington. D.C., in 2004 have raised concerns about various water companies' failure to comply with reporting requirements related to the quality of drinking water elsewhere in the country. Many water systems have installed treatment systems to control corrosion, and some cities and states have made large investments for the removal of lead pipes. The EPA tightened standards for arsenic in 2001; it has taken steps to improve the technical, financial, and managerial capacity of water systems; and it has required states to assess the susceptibility to contamination of all sources of drinking water. There are also serious problems with the quality of the water in rivers, lakes, estuaries, and coastal waters, including eutrophication (oxygen depletion caused by algae growth) resulting from agricultural runoff, mercury and acid deposits that come from power plant emissions, and beach closures attributable to sewage spills and urban runoff.

The United States has made significant progress in controlling point source water pollution. In 1996, the latest year for which data are available, about 71 percent of the U.S. population—more than the average for OECD member countries—was connected to public wastewater treatment plants. The EPA projects that share to rise to 88 percent in 2016—a level that will require an expenditure of US$120 billion in 1996 dollars between 1996 and 2016. In 1996, more than 90 percent of wastewater from the population served by sewerage received at least secondary treatment. Much of the progress in expanding wastewater treatment infrastructure can be attributed to the Clean Water State Revolving Fund program that was launched by the EPA in 1987 and provides funds to individual states for their wastewater treatment needs.

As part of this program, each state operates its own fund, thereby allowing the state to establish its own priorities. The states provide funding equal to 20 percent of the federal contribution, although the states have been increasing their contribution by issuing bonds for specific projects. Even though Congress has reduced the federal contribution to the EPA's funding program substantially in recent years, from 1989 to 2004 the fund received a total of US$50 billion, including US$22 billion from the federal government.[35] This investment has led to major improvements in the water quality in rivers, lakes, and estuaries across the country, notably in Lake Erie and the Potomac River, where people can now fish and swim.

The United States has had less success in controlling nonpoint source pollution. The Clean Water Act requires each state to identify waters that cannot meet water quality standards without control of nonpoint source pollution, to inventory the nonpoint sources responsible for this failure, and to strengthen existing programs designed to control those sources. In 2000, the EPA used this authority to enter into a partnership with the states to reduce nonpoint source pollution, according to which each state is required to assess its nonpoint sources and to develop a program for addressing them. Once the EPA approves a state's program, the state is eligible for federal funding of up to 60 percent of the implementation costs. The Coastal Zone Management Act and the 1990 reauthorization amendments to this act also foster cooperation between the state and federal governments in measures taken to reduce nonpoint sources of pollution in coastal waters.

These collaborative efforts between the federal government and the states have led to significant reductions in nitrogen and phosphorus loadings in critical estuaries such as the Chesapeake Bay as well as improvements in pesticide control, storm water management, and erosion control. But these improvements have been overtaken by continuing increases in nonpoint source water pollution from urban runoff and from agricultural discharges. The growing concentration of beef, hog, and poultry operations has led to increasing discharges of nutrient surpluses and animal wastes into U.S. waters. Although the Clean Water Act gives the EPA the authority to require large animal feedlots to obtain pollution permits as point sources and to implement nutrient management plans, the agency is not authorized to limit the overall volume of agricultural discharges from all sources into U.S. waters. Efforts to obtain this authority indirectly by establishing limits on total discharges into specific bodies of water have met strong resistance from agricultural and other interests and their political patrons. The agro-environmental programs implemented by the U.S. Department of Agriculture, particularly the Conservation Reserve Program, have led to a modest reduction in agricultural runoff by giving farmers an economic incentive to take vulnerable acreage near streams out of cultivation.

An emerging problem with nonpoint source pollution that is of great concern to the United States and its North American neighbors is the discharge of small quantities of "emerging contaminants," including those from pharmaceuticals, cosmetics, and antibacterial soaps. A study conducted by the U.S. Geological Survey in 2002 detected such compounds in 80 percent of the 139 streams examined, many of which were downstream of urban areas.[36] Of particular concern are the "endocrine disrupters"—chemicals in the environment that mimic hormones when they get into the human body. This category includes a broad array of chemicals—ranging from natural and synthetic hormones to chemicals in certain cosmetics, shampoos, shaving lotions, skin creams, dishwashing liquids, pesticides, flame retardants, plastics, and antibacterial soaps—which have effects at exceedingly low concentrations. Because so many of these chemicals bind to the same receptors as natural hormones do, their effects add up. Scientists are not concerned about the impact on human health of tiny quantities of any one of these chemicals in isolation, but the cumulative effect could become significant over time. The harmful impacts on fish and other marine species—including the feminization of males and increased numbers of individuals with both male and female characteristics—are already in evidence.

With respect to water pricing, the United States faces many of the same challenges as Canada does. The U.S. water industry is highly diversified and fragmented, with more than 161,000 public water supply utilities: 53,400 municipal water systems serving 273 million people and 107,800 nonmunicipal systems serving 30 million people. This fragmentation has produced a wide diversity of water pricing structures, with water prices generally lower for businesses than they are for households. The marginal costs of meeting increased water demand have spurred efforts to strengthen the need for conservation when setting prices for water. Almost all water networks now meter water consumption and charge for it according to the volume consumed. The spread of metering has been accompanied by a decline in the average amount of water consumed, particularly in large urban areas like New York City. Over the last several decades, approximately 25 percent of U.S. water utilities have switched from decreasing-block to increasing-block tariff structures in order to encourage conservation. Each of these tariff types now accounts for nearly one-third of household water tariff structures, with uniform volumetric pricing accounting for almost another third.

Despite these improvements, however, water services remain underpriced and water consumption is at a high level. Aside from consumers' general resistance to higher prices, three major factors contribute to this unsatisfactory situation. The first is the availability of continuing federal subsidies for water supply and water treatment infrastructure, particularly in the interest of extending service to smaller communities and assuring that they have an acceptable quality of drinking water. Although the total amount of these subsidies (primarily from the EPA Drinking Water State Revolving Fund) has been declining in recent years, the subsidies still make it possible for local agencies responsible for water management to refrain from applying the "user pays" principle. These subsidies are particularly important in the agricultural sector, where they take the form of below-market pricing of federal water and failure to recapture the cost of federal investments for water diversion. The second factor contributing to the low price of water is the continuing culture of the Cadillac Desert, which has led irrigators and other water users to expect the federal government to support unsustainable patterns of water use and to bail them out when they encounter a problem. (For example, irrigators in the Klamath Basin of Oregon have recently been successful in getting the federal government to release the water they wanted, in direct contravention of the Endangered Species Act.) The third factor is the resistance of large industrial users in the Midwest and other areas with plentiful water supplies to increasing-block pricing structures.

An important tool for overcoming these obstacles to increasing prices as a way to encourage conservation is the use of market-based mechanisms for the transfer of water rights. A drought from 1987 to 1992 in northern California and decreasing availability of surface water from the Colorado River, for example, have forced Los Angeles and San Diego to accept a reduction in total long-distance water transfers from 6.5 billion cubic meters per year to 4 billion cubic meters by 2010 (currently about 4.5 billion cubic meters are transferred annually). Both cities have responded by adopting more progressive price structures (although their average price for drinking water is still low by OECD standards) and by providing financial incentives for the installation of low-flush toilets and water-efficient washing machines. By 2020, the volume of water saved as a result of these measures is projected to meet the needs of one-third of Los Angeles' added population and one-quarter of San Diego's. Closing the remaining gap through price increases and conservation alone would require the two cities to lower their per capita water demand from the current 600 liters to 300 liters and, in drought years, to something approaching the average demand in Europe and Japan—180 liters—a goal that may be impossible to achieve. Water markets, however, could help bridge the gap. Under rules established pursuant to the California Water Transfer Act of 1996, agencies responsible for water management in the two California cities may buy water from irrigation districts via annual contracts and pay the Los Angeles Metropolitan Water District to transport the water. Although prices have doubled since trading began in 1991 and issues with respect to salinity remain, transfer of water rights from irrigators in California and elsewhere will play an increasingly important role in meeting southern California's water needs.

Market-based transfers of water rights from irrigation districts to municipalities has also played an important role in managing the effects of the scarcity of water and in avoiding conflict along the U.S. border with Mexico. The Rio Grande Water Master system established in the Texas Lower Valley after extended litigation, for example, has established a clear hierarchy of historical water rights and enabled municipalities to acquire rights to agricultural water on a temporary or permanent basis. Under Texas Senate Bill 1, the state has been divided into regional planning districts for purposes of identifying improvements in the efficiency of water use and water allocation procedures. The Paseo del Norte Task Force has initiated a bilateral planning process involving key stakeholders in El Paso and Juarez; the goal of the effort is to encourage conservation and better management processes in the water basin the two countries share.

These efforts highlight the need to create planning processes for transferring rights within water basins that involve all relevant stakeholders throughout the United States as well as in Canada and Mexico. Only if local stakeholders are able to participate in setting the rules for allocating water when the resource is scarce will they be comfortable in permitting market-based transfers in accordance with those rules. An example of such basin-based planning is the New York City Watershed Memorandum of Agreement, which was signed in 1997 by New York City, the state of New York, the EPA, the cities and towns of the Catskills-Delaware watershed from which New York City gets 90 percent of its water, watershed residents, and nongovernmental organizations (NGOs). The agreement supplemented New York City's existing watershed protection program by providing $300 million for land acquisition and $400 million for partnership programs designed to protect water quality in the region. New York City supplied most of the funds but also received federal support. The city's total expenditures in complying with the federal Surface Water Treatment Rule since applying for a filtration waiver in 1991 amount to less than US$2 billion, compared with estimated filtration costs of US$6 billion that the city has avoided.

The above example demonstrates that the United States has the tools—notably, strong federal legislation and the capacity to enforce that legislation—to do a far better job of managing its water resources than it has done in the past. Unfortunately, when it comes to water management, as it does in so many other areas, the United States tends to do the right thing only after exploring all other alternatives. It is to be hoped that, over the next few decades, the United States will be able to short-circuit this process by learning from past experience. At stake is not only the welfare of U.S. citizens but also the ability of North America as a whole to manage its water resources in a more sustainable manner and thereby to serve as an example to the rest of the world.

MEXICO

Mexico faces many of the same water management challenges as Canada and the United States face but starts from a lower base in terms of water availability, water infrastructure, and enforcement capability. Mexico's extraction of water is approximately 800 cubic meters per capita per year, as compared to 1,730 cubic meters in the United States and 1,430 cubic meters in Canada. Mexico has made substantial progress in meeting the targets set in its National Water Plan for providing access to the water supply, sanitation services, and wastewater treatment, although performance in rural areas has lagged that in urban areas. The country's greatest success has been the increase in the proportion of drinking water that is disinfected to more than 95 percent, which has dramatically decreased the number of cases of gastro-intestinal diseases and has caused cholera to be eradicated.

Mexico has also made considerable progress in decentralizing water management by delegating the administration of the National Water Commission's programs to the state level, encouraging passage of state water laws and creation of state water commissions, and creating 25 councils responsible for managing water basins. The National Water Commission has also transferred the administration of water districts to user associations, which now have management and financial responsibility for operating and maintaining their irrigation systems. Finally, Mexico has increased the transparency of its water management not only by recording water abstraction rights and permits for wastewater discharge in a public register that is accessible on the Internet but also by greatly improving its systems that maintain information about its water. The country has also promoted the participation of stakeholders in the decisionmaking process related to water management.

Despite this progress, Mexico's use of its water resources remains unsustainable. According to the OECD's most recent Environmental Performance Review of Mexico (issued in 2003), investment in water infrastructure, already low by OECD standards, fell in real terms during the 1990s.[37] In order to achieve a sustainable pattern of water use by 2025, the current level of investment in infrastructure would have to be doubled. A little more than 25 percent of urban wastewater is treated. Few wastewater utilities have met the 2000 deadline for limiting effluents, and industrial discharges are largely untreated. Many water utilities are caught in a perverse cycle in which they cannot make their customers pay their water bills, causing the utilities to be unable to provide good service, which, in turn, makes customers even more reluctant to pay their bills. Laws and regulations are not adequately enforced because of resource constraints. Water losses from irrigation and drinking water systems remain high. Aquifers are being depleted at unsustainable rates (according to a recent National Ecology Institute study, 100 of Mexico's 180 most important aquifers are now "overexploited"),[38] and ecosystems are being deprived of the water necessary for their survival.

In addition, because Mexico's population and industrial centers are concentrated in the arid regions of central and northern Mexico—areas that are most vulnerable to the likely reduction of surface water flows resulting from climate change—the country remains particularly vulnerable to climate change. This vulnerability is not just a concern for Mexico; it is also a concern for the United States. Illegal emigration from Mexico into the United States is already a contentious political issue in the United States and a major challenge to good relations between the two countries. The problem will become far worse if millions of Mexicans lose their ability to make a living in Mexico because of inadequate water supplies. This prospect makes it even more critical for the United States and Mexico to increase collaborative efforts to improve water management and to handle the problem of water scarcity.

Before discussing several of Mexico's water management challenges in greater depth, it is important to mention several aspects of the country's legal and political systems that distinguish Mexico from the United States and Canada. Mexico inherited from Spain a natural law tradition under which the state owned all the resources of the nation on behalf of the people as part of the national patrimony. Thus the state's ownership of water resources has been enshrined in the Mexican Constitution. Even though the state may grant private parties the right to use a portion of those resources for a specific period of time, the government retains underlying ownership and control of those resources. In theory, this ownership should give the state the ability to impose a rational scheme of water management on its citizens. In practice, however, ownership has led the Mexican government to use water abstraction rights as a political tool to win and reward supporters at the local level.

Mexico faces two fundamental and related challenges to achieving sustainable water management by 2025: shortage of state capacity and shortage of fiscal resources. It is ironic that Mexico, which has a culture of deference to vice-regal authority, has a federal government that cannot impose its authority at the state and local level or provide its poorer citizens with basic social services; whereas the United States, with its "don't tread on me" distrust of government power, has created a veritable Leviathan that has been the underlying force behind the country's social and economic development. Mexico's political leadership, most notably President Felipe Calderón and his predecessor, Vicente Fox, is fully aware of these problems and has been making efforts to strengthen the rule of law and to achieve fiscal reform (the recent increase in business taxes passed by the national legislature is a step forward). In the meantime, however, the country will need to rely on help from state and local governments, the private sector, and its northern neighbors to effect a transition to more sustainable water management.

The government of Mexico has created a legal framework that can accommodate the cooperation that is needed. In addition to delegating authority for water management to states, municipalities, and the private sector as well as improving the quality and transparency of information related to the environment, Mexico has laid the foundation not only for planning at the water basin level by creating 25 councils to deal with water basins but also for adopting a more market-based approach to water management. In 1982, Mexico established a system of water abstraction charges, the level of which is set in the annual Federal Law on Water Taxes. In 1991, the government introduced pollution taxes, with annual rates established in the same law. The National Water Law permits banking and trading in water, and trading or swapping water used for irrigation is a common practice. Abstraction and pollution charges need to be systematized, increased over time, and enforced, but the basic framework is in place.

Nevertheless, Mexico could take at least three additional steps to improve its water management without placing undue stress on the power or resources of the federal government. The first step is to provide financial and technical assistance to municipal water authorities and irrigation districts to improve capacity and efficiency. There are significant gaps between the best performing and worst performing water utilities Mexico in terms of both financial efficiency (the ratio of water that consumers actually pay for and the amount of water delivered to them) and physical efficiency (the ratio of the amount of water actually delivered to customers and the amount of water produced). As of 2001, financial efficiency ranged from approximately 95 percent in Monterrey to less than 50 percent in Heroica Nogales and other poorer communities. Physical efficiency ranged from higher than 80 percent in Matamoros to lower than 40 percent in Acapulco. Both urban and rural communities exhibit similar efficiency gradients for electricity used in water pumping and distribution.

It is no accident that most of the utilities that are the most efficient both financially and physically are located within the U.S.-Mexican border region. As part of an overall effort to upgrade water treatment and supply infrastructure in the border region, the BECC and NAD-BANK, supported by grant funds from the EPA, have provided technical and financial assistance to help many utility companies extend and upgrade their drinking water systems and to improve their training and management practices. The EPA has also funded the Watergy Program being implemented by the Alliance to Save Energy and its Mexican partners and is helping water utilities design and implement plans to improve their water management and energy efficiency simultaneously. Several Mexican cities, including Vera Cruz, have already made significant improvements in the financial and physical efficiency of their water utilities by participating in this program.

A related step that Mexico could take to improve its water management is to reform water pricing so that both urban and rural inhabitants would cover the cost of system upgrades and conservation could be encouraged. Increasing prices for water services, particularly those provided to poorer Mexicans, is only politically possible if it is done gradually and accompanied by improvements in the quality of the services. Experience in getting water treatment and drinking water projects certified by the BECC and financed by the NADBANK has shown that border communities will agree to increasing prices over time in order to pay for projects that they themselves have identified as critical to improving their quality of life. An important complementary step is to require Mexico's industrial sector to pre-treat and recycle its wastewater to the maximum extent possible, and higher cost of water can provide an incentive. Finally, the price of water delivered to irrigation districts must be gradually increased in order to encourage conservation and a shift to higher-value crops. Implementing these price increases will be much easier if irrigation districts receive technical and financial assistance for improving their water distribution and in-field irrigation infrastructure. Here again the BECC and NADBANK have shown the way by using their retained earnings to fund system upgrades in Delicias and other irrigation districts on both sides of the border.

The third critical step that would improve Mexico's water management is to make it possible for the National Water Commission and state and local agencies that are responsible for water management to do a better job of planning for the future in light of the likely effects of climate change. No matter what measures are implemented, reductions in surface water supplies and an increased demand for drinking water will lead to fundamental changes in water consumption in the arid regions of northern and central Mexico. The more that can be done to anticipate those changes, the less disruptive they will be. The following measures can help Mexico minimize inevitable disruptions and buy time for an orderly transition to an economy that will surely be affected by the scarcity of water:

- providing incentives and assistance to promote water conservation in all sectors;

- helping irrigation districts phase out cultivation of thirsty, low-value crops such as cotton and alfalfa; and

- strengthening mechanisms used to transfer water rights to municipalities and to allocate water in times of extreme scarcity.

In light of the high level of Mexican migration, the United States has a strong motivation to assist Mexico in this effort.

SUMMARY AND POLICY RECOMMENDATIONS

Despite their geographic, historical, cultural, and economic differences, the three North American countries face similar challenges in improving water management. All three must improve the amount and quality of their data on water supply, particularly with respect to groundwater. All three must strengthen the legal framework governing water management at all levels of government and must devote more resources to enforcement of laws and regulations. All countries must adopt water pricing structures that encourage conservation and phase out subsidies that contravene the principles of user pays and polluter pays. All three must also substantially increase their investment in upgrading and expanding their water supply and pollution control infrastructure.

All three nations, particularly Mexico and Canada, need to offset structural weaknesses in their federal government's capacity by empowering and helping local governments and private stakeholders to establish councils responsible for planning for water basins that will incorporate all sources and uses into a water plan for the basins. These councils could then develop pricing and allocation structures that would simultaneously encourage conservation, enable water rights to be transferred from lower-value uses to higher-value uses, set aside water for critical ecosystems, and prepare contingency plans for periods when water is extremely scarce. Federal governments in all three countries, bilateral institutions (such as the International Joint Commission, the Boundary and Water Commission, the Border Environment Co-operation Commission, and the North American Development Bank) and multilateral institutions (such as the North American Commission for Environmental Cooperation) should all support this process by developing appropriate legal frameworks and providing analytical and financial support for water management plans prepared by basin councils within those frameworks.

Underlying these changes must be a transformation of the water management culture in North America from a culture of never-ending abundance to a culture of long-term sustainability. In the past, all three North American countries have treated water as an unlimited resource that could be drawn down at will to support the march of progress and the god-given right of North Americans to enjoy an ever improving standard of living. Particularly in the United States and Canada, huge sums of public money have been poured into major diversions of water to support economic development in places that did not have the water necessary to support that development in the first place. Experience demonstrates that these interbasin diversion projects—particularly long-distance transfers of bulk water—pose several problems: (1) they cannot be economically justified on a cost-recovery basis; (2) they cause large, and often unanticipated, damage to the basins from which the water is transferred; and (3) they encourage wasteful practices. Such projects have been possible only because the broader public in North America has not been adequately informed of their long-term consequences or given the opportunity to participate in making the decisions to approve the projects.

One theme of this section of this chapter has been the need to increase the sharing of experiences, joint decisionmaking, and overall cooperation among Canada, the United States, and Mexico in moving North America toward more sustainable management of its water resources. Another theme has been the need to incorporate more realistic pricing structures and market-transfer mechanisms into an overall strategy for achieving this goal. But these themes should not be misconstrued as support for an overall strategy of North American integration that is designed to remove political and regulatory obstacles to the more systematic exploitation of the continent's water resources in order to generate higher economic returns for specific industrial and financial interests. There is a risk that the Security and Prosperity Partnership and other current projects to promote North American integration might be hijacked for this purpose. Concerned Americans and Mexicans should join concerned Canadians in making sure that this does not happen.

This issue goes beyond legitimate Canadian concerns about exporting bulk water from Canada to the United States. Climate change is already opening up the Artic territories of Canada and Alaska to commerce and resource extraction. In theory, it may be possible to conduct those activities in a manner that is socially and environmentally sustainable. Experience would suggest, however, that, absent strong intervention by federal, state, and provincial governments based on transparent decisionmaking processes involving all stakeholders, these activities will cause widespread environmental damage to sensitive ecosystems and will lead to the displacement of native peoples. One need only look at the Athabasca tailing ponds to get a preview of what may lie ahead. The manner in which decisions about development of the Artic region are made in Canada and the United States will be a test of the strength of their democratic institutions.

It is important to look at all the challenges to water management the three countries face through the prism of climate change—a phenomenon that intensifies all of them:

- Climate change decreases the supply of water and increases the demand for water in arid regions.

- It disrupts current patterns of water supply and use and puts additional pressure on already stressed water infrastructure.

- It invites unsustainable exploitation of water and other resources in the Arctic.

- It enhances the probability of conflict within and between North American countries over scarce water resources.

- It adds a layer of complexity and uncertainty to democratic decisionmaking.

- Finally, climate change poses a significant threat to North American biodiversity in large part because of the ramifications on the availability of water.

Even if the improvements to sustainable water management discussed in this section are made, North America will find it difficult to meet these intensified challenges. Despite the difficulties, however, North America cannot afford to fail to ensure the sustainability of its natural resources.

BIODIVERSITY

OVERVIEW

At no time in history has the rate, scale, and number of drivers of environmental change been so great or the consequences so threatening to the human enterprise. Humans are the dominant change agents on earth, and numerous ongoing processes driven by human activity are drastically altering ecosystems, their functioning, and their services. According to a report issued by the Commission for Environmental Cooperation in 2001, "In North America, as in much of the world, humans are reshaping the environment and using up many parts of it faster than nature can renew itself. The three countries have ecological footprints that exceed their biocapacity and their average per capita footprint is above the world's average."[39] One can readily surmise that the state of North American biodiversity in 2025 will differ from present conditions in many ways.

Stellar's sea cow, Allen's 13-lined ground squirrel, Bachman's warbler, the Labrador duck, the passenger pigeon, the Sulcate blind snake, the Vegas Valley leopard frog, the Tecopa pupfish, the American chestnut moth, the acorn pearly mussel, and the bigleaf scurfpea—these are just some of the species that have been permanently lost from North America's landscape in recent years. They were exterminated on the heels of habitat loss and fragmentation, pollution, and overhunting, vacating wetlands, grasslands, deserts, forests, oceans, and rivers. The implications for these ecosystems have been many, complex, cascading, and difficult to measure in quantitative terms. But there is no doubt: humanity has not been enriched by their absence.

Moreover, North America hosts unwelcome guests—the Asian long-horned beetle, emerald ash borer, kudzu, cheat grass, European starling, brown rat, red imported fire ant, Formosan termite, chestnut blight, black carp, zebra mussel, green crab, West Nile virus, and so many more. They have arrived via international trade, tourism, and transport. Not only do they fail to replace what the continent has lost, they threaten what remains. Ultimately, these invasive species (harmful non-native species) contribute to social instability and economic hardship, thereby placing constraints on the conservation of biodiversity, sustainable development, and economic growth.

In 2025, North American ecosystems will be a composite of stalwart natives and eager transplants. The drivers of change they have faced previously will remain, if not become exaggerated, and new ones (for example, global climate change and emerging biotechnologies) with direct and synergistic consequences will have emerged in readily apparent ways. Species composition, abundance, and behavior will determine the structure and function of the ecosystem and thus have substantial implications for water supplies, agricultural and energy productivity, disease transmission and treatment—ultimately, the well-being of human beings.

The decisions made by North American policymakers and consumers, past and present, will determine the state of biodiversity in 2025 as well as the quality of life for every person in North America and beyond. Fundamentally, well-informed policy decisions are based on sound science resulting from biodiversity inventories, monitoring, and research. The motivation and ability to make such decisions is a reflection of society's values—the inherent value of biodiversity as well as the valuation of the services that biodiversity provides for human use. There is no statistically precise way of placing a value on biodiversity. However, estimates suggest that the global market value of products derived from biodiversity (referred to as "genetic resources") is on the order of US$500–US$800 billion annually,[40] whereas the estimated economic value of ecosystem services is US$33.3 trillion per year.[41] Despite the uncertainties associated with this calculation, it is clear that biodiversity represents an irreplaceable support of immense value to the world's societies, yet it is largely unaccounted for in the markets and policies of the world's nations. (See table 2.5 and box 2.1 for further information of the valuation of biodiversity and North America's economic dependence on it.)

Many policymakers are surprised to learn that North American biodiversity and its conservation are poorly understood. Although it is a region that has two of the most economically wealthy and competitive OECD nations and immense biological wealth, North America lacks much of the basic information needed to conserve biodiversity today, let alone project the challenges and solutions to its sustainability

Table 2.5. Examples of Biodiversity's Importance

Inherent Values	Market Value Products	Ecosystem Services
Aesthetics (beauty)	Biofuel	Carbon storage
Cultural identity	Food (agricultural products)	Climate regulation
Stress relief	Industrial materials	Pollination
Sense of connectedness	Pharmaceuticals	Erosion control
Inspiration and wonder	Pesticides	Nutrient cycling
Romantic context	Botanical medicines	Soil creation
Spiritual practice and solace	Cosmetics	Water cycling
Security	Ornamental plants	Seed production
	Nontraditional pets	Disease and pest resistance
	Arts and crafts	Storm resilience

in 2025. When it comes to protection of the habitats on which species depend, there is a complex but basically distressing situation in all three countries. The biological wealth of North America has been squandered in the past, and the lack of political and financial support for biological studies now hampers the ability to know where, when, and how to act in North America's own future best interest. Biodiversity—even though *Homo sapiens'* security is fully dependent upon it—has not been sufficiently valued by North America's policymakers or its citizenry. The state of the environment in 2025 rests fully on two interdependent questions:

- How much do the three countries care about the state of biodiversity?

- How much do they care about the quality of human life?

This section will provide a general overview of the current state of North American marine, aquatic, and terrestrial systems and explore the fundamental drivers of environmental change in North America that will shape the ecosystems and their services in 2025. The discussion will also outline potential government responses (national, binational, and trilateral) that could serve to minimize the threats to the security of North American biodiversity and will also highlight some of the proactive policy and institutional measures that are currently under way in Canada, Mexico, and United States. North America is already a global leader in many ways. It now has the potential to be-

Box 2.1. The Value of Biodiversity

Domestic and international trade patterns create an ecological footprint on major ecosystems, especially western forests, the Great Plains, the Mississippi River, the Great Lakes, and ocean areas such as the Gulf of Maine. These patterns are dynamic; they are affected by new approaches to agriculture and biotechnology, by the changing demands of both domestic and international consumers, and through side effects such as the introduction of exotic species via transportation of people and goods.

North America is home to great wealth—both biological and financial—the former is indeed the cause of the latter. All three countries of North America rank within the high human development group on the human development index developed by the United Nations Development Program. From heavy industry to tourism, subsistence agriculture, and fishing, North Americans depend on natural resources for their survival and well-being. Yet, in general, the population seems to be unaware of the extent of people's dependence on these resources, the connectivity of their condition, and the precariousness of their situation.

The environment is critical for social and economic development as well as for the well-being of humans. For example, compared with financial, material, and human assets, natural assets account for 26 percent of the wealth of low-income countries and, on average, somewhat less in higher-income countries.[1] Changes in environmental services, such as climate regulation, can affect all assets and, in turn, humans' well-being—the ability of people to live the kind of lives they value in terms of security, health, social relations, and material needs.

North American society is complex, and its use of biodiversity is simultaneously crude and sophisticated, harmful and productive, consumptive and sustainable. These contrasts are not new. The destruction of forests in the eastern United States peaked more than 100 years ago,[2*] and now many areas have been restored to wooded status, with many ecological benefits. Yet unsustainable use of forests continues in all three countries today. The social and economic sectors—such as agriculture, forestry, fisheries, and industrial production—play a dual role in shaping the interaction between the environment and society. They are instrumental in utilizing ecosystem services and natural resources, yet they also affect ecosystem services and are affected by changes in the ecosystem.

Biodiversity valuation at the macro level is a difficult and controversial the task.[3] Fortunately, through the work of resource and environmental economists, it is possible to provide some measure of "existence values" and to define in some detail the economic benefits derived from the use of natural areas and even complex resource bases. Typically, however, it is only when ecologically rich regions or individual stocks of plants and animals are degraded or otherwise depleted that the true measure of their worth becomes apparent.

Following are highlights of some of the unique issues associated with the economic dependence on biodiversity in North America:

- Canada derives a very significant portion of its wealth and export revenues from the use of natural resources. Of these sources, none is more significant than forests, which account for the largest single line in Canada's export earnings. The plains of both Canada and the United States have become the most important breadbasket for the world, and the International Food Policy Research Institute believes this role will continue for decades to come. The massive ecological footprint arising from this agricultural base is now being gradually altered to accommodate important ecological values better.

- Mexico is the center of origin of many cultivars and other well-known plants. The indigenous peoples of Mexico have succeeded in domesticating roughly 100 species of plants and use more than 5,000 plant species to fulfill their diverse subsistence needs.[4] The positive contribution of Mexican indigenous communities to the preservation of the world's genetic heritage of plants is well recognized.[5] Mexico's rich biodiversity is exploited for an extensive variety of productive ends, including food, clothing, construction materials, and firewood, among others, and for aesthetic and artistic values (such as handicrafts, ornamental use, and literature) as well as for religious and mystical reasons (sites for worship, amulets, myths, and legends).

- The United States is generating many of the new developments in agricultural biotechnology that are likely to be applied in the coming years. Genetically engineered crops may have the capacities to produce pesticides and vaccines as well as food, and faster-growing trees and shrubs may be able to increase biomass production in support of biofuels. The promises of these advances are becoming the source of much controversy and divisiveness within and among the countries of North America, however. People are concerned about the potential effects biotechnology on human and animal health as well as on biodiversity. The issues associated with biotechnology will emerge as some of the most economically important decisions to be taken in the course of the next decade.

Sustainable development inherently acknowledges the value of all the various forms of natural capital, of which biodiversity is a key element. Biodiversity is a source of wealth and welfare, and its value to society will increase over time—if it is well tended. It therefore makes sense, even from an economic point of view, to both utilize and protect biodiversity. A comprehensive approach to biosecurity—one that integrates intergenerational equity with current needs—is called for.

1. World Bank, "Where Is the Wealth of Nations?" Washington, D.C., 2006.
2. United Nations Environment Programme, "North America's Environment," Washington, D.C., 2002.
3. For a useful guide, see *Handbook of Biodiversity Valuation: A Guide for Policy Makers*, http://earthmind.net/rivers/docs/oecd-handbook-biodiversity-valuation.pdf.
4. CONABIO, "La Diversidad Biológica de México: Estudio País," Mexico City, 1998.
5. Carpentier and Herrmann, "Maize and Biodiversity: The Effects of Transgenic Maize in Mexico," Issues Summary, Council for Environmental Cooperation, Montreal, Quebec, 2002.

come a leader in biosecurity, demonstrating to the world that Canada, Mexico, and the United States have the foresight and capacity to conserve biodiversity and protect all that depend upon it.

CURRENT STATE OF NORTH AMERICAN ECOSYSTEMS

Human actions have already had a profound effect on the extent, distribution, and condition of all of the major ecosystems in North America. There are many indications that the capacity of ecosystems to provide the goods and services (listed in table 2.1) on which the population depends is rapidly declining. Although data are generally available for mapping the extent of North American ecosystems,[42] they are typically either lacking or incomplete when it comes to analyses of the condition of the ecosystem. Some scientists have attempted to develop "indicators" of the structure and function of ecosystems,[43] but this approach is fraught with technical difficulties and often unsubstantiated assumptions. Moreover, the condition of the ecosystem tends to be highly focused on the species in a particular site, reflecting the particular biogeographic context, past history of environmental impacts, and the current matrices and intensity of human influences. From a policymaking perspective, this means that the issues facing pine forests in British Columbia are likely to be quite different from those affecting Mississippi or Oaxaca. Thus, effective policymaking needs to consider regional priorities and still be meaningful at the local level. Only through greater investments in biodiversity inventories, monitoring, and data synthesis will policymakers be able to build the scientific understanding of biological change and decisionmaking capacity in North America.

It is helpful to have a general overview of the state of marine, aquatic, and terrestrial systems in North America to serve as a benchmark for the later discussions of major drivers of ecological change and recommendations for mitigating the changes. Related sample statistics are given in box 2.2. Box 2.3 describes the current ecological footprints that exist in North America.

Coastal and Marine Ecosystems

The shared marine regions of Canada, the United States, and Mexico are affected by human activity both directly and indirectly. These regions are influenced by atmospheric chemistry and temperature, are the ultimate recipients of the soil erosion and pollutants resulting from poor land use practices, and are under increasing pressure to supply natural resources (such as fisheries) and space to accommodate human demands. Multiple and cumulative threats have already undermined the functioning of many North American marine systems.

The public is slowly coming to realize that marine biodiversity is being lost at alarming rates, as genetically unique populations of marine organisms are extirpated through overharvesting. Commercially driven extinction is a recurring problem in all three countries and is brought on by what appears to be serial mismanagement of profitable fisheries. The Atlantic finfish catch off the eastern coast of North America has declined from 2.5 million tons in 1971 to less than 500,000 tons in 1994.[44]

Box 2.2. North America's Biodiversity: Facts and Figures

Coastal and Marine Systems

- Fisheries have declined precipitously since the mid-1980s; 21 of 43 groundfish stocks in Canada's North Atlantic are in decline, 16 others are at the point of maximum sustainable yield.

- Nearly one-third of the United States' federally managed fishery species are overfished.

- A total of 26 distinct groups of salmon are listed under the United States' Endangered Species Act.

Freshwater Systems

- North America holds about 13 percent of the world's renewable freshwater (excluding glaciers and ice caps).

- Canada alone hosts 24 percent of the world's wetland area.

- In the United States (excluding Alaska), 50 percent of original wetland areas has been lost, in Mexico 35 percent has been lost, and in Canada almost 15 percent has been lost.

- About one-third of the region's threatened and endangered species depends on wetlands.

- Since 1900, 123 freshwater animal species have been recorded as extinct; work by Canadian scientists suggests a further extinction rate of 4 percent per decade.

- Water extraction from many of the region's aquifers (underground sources)— for example the Ogalla Aquifer underlying major agricultural areas in the Midwestern Plains states—exceeds the rate of renewal.

Terrestrial Systems

- Overall, the variety of terrestrial zones of North America translates into a continent that is rich in diversity. Mexico alone houses 10 percent of the planet's terrestrial biodiversity and much of its endemism.

- Forests cover about 26 percent of North America's land area, representing 12 percent of the world's forests.

- Canada has about 30 percent of the world's boreal forests—the largest forest ecosystem in North America.

- Forest cover has been reduced by almost 40 percent in the past two centuries, and, in general, forests and other terrestrial ecosystems are becoming increasingly fragmented, biologically impoverished, and weakened.

- The continent has at least 235 threatened species of mammals, birds, reptiles. and amphibians, of which 14 are shared by all three countries, 35 by Mexico and the United States, 15 by Canada and the United States, and 7 by Canada and Mexico.

- North America contains approximately 11 percent of world's agricultural lands.

Source: United Nations Environment Programme, "North America's Environment: A Thirty-Year State of the Environment and Policy Retrospective," Washington, D.C., 2002.

Box 2.3. Some Facts About Current Ecological Footprints in North America

The ecological footprint refers to the land and water area required to produce and sustain natural resources as well as to absorb the waste generated by a person using the prevailing technology.[1] This number can then be compared with the available resources at the country, regional, or global level (known as biocapacity). Biocapacity is affected by degradation processes, such as deforestation and land erosion; the footprint is driven by population growth, consumption patterns, and technology.

In all three countries, biocapacity has been decreasing, whereas the footprint has been increasing. In 2003, North Americans required 7.7 hectares on average to sustain their consumption patterns, but the region's biocapacity was only 4.7 hectares. Thus, the region exceeded its biological capacity by more than 60 percent. At current trends, this ecological deficit could increase substantially by 2025.[2]

Furthermore, it is important to note that North America's global impact is disproportionately large. The continent's inability to meet the needs of the population within the region will place greater demands on the resources of other countries.[3]

- North Americans use more water per person per year than any other people.

- North America leads the world in the manufacture and use of pesticides.

- In 2004, despite hosting only 5 percent of the world's population, North America accounted for 26.15 percent of global carbon dioxide emissions.[4]

- In 1998, per capita annual consumption of gasoline for motor vehicles in North America was nine times the world's average.

- In 1997, the U.S. transportation sector accounted for more than one-third of the world's total energy used for transportation.

- In 2006, North America's overall ecological footprint was four times the world's average.[5]

More sustainable consumption and production patterns, as well as more investments in conservation and restoration of the natural habitats, are urgently needed.

---

1. Global Footprint Network, http://www.footprintnetwork.com.
2. Estimations based on ibid., http://www.footprintnetwork.org/download.php?id=305.
3. Statistic from United Nations Environment Programme, "North America's Environment: A Thirty-Year State of the Environment and Policy Retrospective," Washington, D.C., 2002.
4. Carbon Dioxide Information Analysis Center, List of Sovereign States by Man-made Carbon Dioxide Emissions, United Nations, New York, 2004
5. Global Footprint Network, "Ecological Footprint and Biocapacity," 2006, http://www.footprintnetwork.com.

Whether large-scale or small-scale, habitat alteration is dramatically undermining the functioning of marine systems, especially because much of this development is taking place in areas that are the most important ecologically: estuaries and wetlands that serve as feeding areas, nurseries, and crucial places for maintaining hydrological balances. Estuaries, in particular, are a key issue in North America, because the bulk of the coastal population lives in estuarine areas, and these areas support many of the continent's commercial and recreational fisheries.

The increasing density of human population in the coastal plains has ramifications for biodiversity, because coastal development clearly parallels population growth. Approximately half the North American population lives within 130 kilometers of the coast, and population growth rates are higher in the coastal margin than they are in any other part of the continent. In fact, U.S. population growth in the coastal zone is four times the national average; by 2025, three-quarters of the U.S. population will live in coastal areas. North American coral reefs are especially vulnerable to pressures brought about by increasing density of humans along the coast.

Land-based sources of pollution enter watersheds and eventually find their way to coastal waters. Such pollutants include nutrients, pesticides, heavy metals, hydrocarbons, and debris. Nutrient pollution, in the form of nitrogen from agricultural wastes and fertilizers that enter coastal systems through runoff and sewage, causes imbalances in coastal systems through eutrophication (excessive plant decay, oxygen depletion, and so forth).

Invasive species also constitute a form of pollution. Species that are not indigenous to an area are often released inadvertently through ship ballast discharges and hull fouling. Invasive species are also deliberately introduced into marine systems for aquaculture and other purposes, causing a restructuring of the biotic community as the foreigners outcompete locals for food and space, and the result is usually greatly reduced biodiversity.

Aquatic Ecosystems

It is still possible to locate remarkable bodies of water in all three countries of North America. These bodies of water support diverse aquatic fauna, with all trophic levels intact, including mature top predators. Many of these habitats are in the broad belt of the boreal forest stretching across northern Canada and Alaska. These lands are now under considerable pressure from forest operations, power dams, and mining; thus, even some of the most isolated areas experience pressures that include mercury contamination of fish as a consequence of mining and disturbance of sediments when dams are constructed, loss of spawning habitat as a consequence of road construction, and the opening of lakes to more intensive exploitation.

Even though some North American aquatic ecosystems are being maintained in quite impeccable condition, they are the exception. Human population and development pressures in North America are among the most intense in any part of the world. Throughout North America, wetlands are among the most precious of all aquatic habitats and among the most threatened. The wetland areas of Canada are by far the largest—127 million hectares; the United States has 43 million hectares, and Mexico has 2 million hectares.[45]

Water basins or watersheds are the fundamental units of management when it comes to aquatic organisms. The habitat within these basins is being drastically changed as water tables are lowered, run-off patterns changed, contaminants added, impoundments created, and channelization carried out. Throughout North America, as sewage processing and industrial wastewater treatment are improved, the stress on aquatic ecosystems is reduced. However, some of the most troubling problems today arise from the nonpoint source contaminants, such as those from agricultural land use and golf courses; from recombinant forms of pollution, such as those found in alpine lakes; and from the fast pace and scale of development activities.

Freshwater ecosystems are likely to be the most biologically invaded systems in North America. Unintentional introduction of foreign organisms occurs through recreational activities, escape of fish and wildlife, and water garden plantings. Intentional introductions result from fish stocking (both for recreation and management purposes), aquaculture, release of unwanted pets, and other sources. Furthermore, the connectivity created between previously isolated rivers permits intensive competition among once isolated species and allows invasive species to move freely. The consequence to the rich aquatic fauna is catastrophic. Despite tremendous economic significance and intensive use of the region's aquatic systems, a proper understanding of these systems is, without a doubt, less than is needed for adequate protection of North America's biodiversity.

Terrestrial Ecosystems

Terrestrial ecosystems have no political boundaries, and species (other than those native to the region) know no national borders. The migration of species, the ranging of animals, the distribution of flora, and the definition of ecological and even geographical features transcend state, provincial, territorial, and even national borders. A number of species migrate within North America, including bats, birds, butterflies, whales, and other marine mammals and fish. A significant proportion of the plant and animal species in North America is threatened.

The significance of transboundary animal migrations for North American ecosystems is twofold. First, if a refuge, staging, nesting, or wintering habitat is lost in any one of the three North American countries visited by a particular species, the survival of this species can be threatened as a result. Second, local and national measures alone may be inadequate to protect the many forms of biodiversity that cross political borders, which are delineated by humans. An estimated 2 billion to 5 billion birds pass from northern regions of the continent into the tropics each year.

The primary threat to North American biodiversity is related to human activities and the loss and degradation of habitats that these activities cause. Unsustainable land use is driving land degradation—in the form of soil erosion, nutrient depletion, water scarcity and salinity—and this has cumulative adverse impacts on food security, biodiversity, and carbon storage. It has been estimated that about half of the continent's most diverse terrestrial ecosystems are now severely degraded.

Invasive species are also an important national and transboundary issue for the conservation of terrestrial biodiversity, especially in forest ecosystems. Invasive species pose serious threats to wildlife, plants, and ecosystem integrity—largely as a consequence of competition, predation, disease, parasitism, and hybridization. In combination with climate change and land use change, invasive species are already causing rippling effects throughout terrestrial ecosystems.

FUNDAMENTAL DRIVERS OF CHANGE

Humanity as a whole relies on the earth's natural capital through a complex web of interactions. All human activities either augment or undermine these interactions, but some have far greater consequences than others do. Generally speaking, the spatial and temporal scale of the activity's footprint on natural systems determines its effects. Biodiversity has adequate resilience to recover from small-scale, acute assaults. However, large-scale, chronic, and novel perturbations often have devastating consequences, leading to population declines and possibly species extinctions.

To envision the challenges to and requirements for conserving biodiversity in 2025, policymakers need to understand the human-driven processes shaping biodiversity as well as their effect on supporting physical systems (water, land, climate, and air). Fundamentally, decisionmakers need to ask the following questions:

- What are the main factors driving declines in biodiversity and degradation of the physical environment?

- What is the specific effect and current trends of these drivers on biodiversity and how are they likely to change in the future?

- What are the implications of these changes for biological systems and the well-being of human beings?

- How can the negative impacts of these drivers be minimized and the opportunities for increasing the quality of human life be maximized?

On the basis of the answers to such questions, the most pressing challenges to conserving biodiversity can be identified and alternative futures can be developed for 2025 and beyond.

Although the scientific literature and popular press reports tend to give the impression that the human activities (for example, habitat destruction and pollution) leading to the loss of biodiversity are straightforward and readily arrested, in actuality, these activities are intertwined across landscapes and geopolitical boundaries through both biophysical and socioeconomic processes. No driver and no recipient ecosystem is independent, although for the purposes of this report, they are presented individually. Furthermore, given the paucity of baseline data on North American biodiversity and ecosystem dynamics in particular, caution is required when projecting both the degree of change attributed to specific drivers and the resultant future condition. Nonetheless, it is possible to identify driver trajectories that point to likely biodiversity scenarios at the ecosystem level.

A group of scientists constructed scenarios of global changes in biodiversity for the year 2100; these are largely informed by global climate, vegetation, and land use models, as well as by expert knowledge of current levels of biodiversity and biotic interactions in terrestrial and aquatic ecosystems.[46] The North American overview presented in this report is informed by the work of this group as well as by more recent assessments conducted for North America in particular, such as the report by the Commission for Environmental Cooperation (CEC) on critical and emerging environmental trends for North America,[47] as well as by the United Nations Environment Programme's 30-year retrospective on the North American environment.[48] Ultimately, all these projections are encapsulated in uncertainties, and some of the unknowns are literally beyond human imagination. For example, 20 years before they were invented, it was impossible to predict the degree to which televisions and computers would dominate cultural norms. Similarly, it is impossible to anticipate the specific location and scale of human conflicts and disease epidemics or the emergence and consequences of the advanced technologies that will influence North American landscapes and people by 2025.

Nonetheless, this section provides an overview of the most likely key ecological drivers of environmental change that will influence the state of North American biodiversity and the well-being of its population in 2025 and beyond. All these ecological drivers are in actuality "secondary" drivers of ecological change; the primary drivers are the human activities that have generated and will continue to generate these disturbances. Human behaviors, in turn, are the result of human capacities and values, individual and cultural identities, and a sense of for what or for whom (such as family, community, a guiding spirit) human actions are ultimately undertaken. (Boxes 2.4 and 2.5 provide further information on the socioeconomic drivers of ecological change, including the anticipated trajectories of their influence on biodiversity in 2025.)

CHANGES IN LAND USE

Land use change typically translates into habitat destruction, degradation, and fragmentation. Forests are replaced by shopping malls, wetlands by condominiums, deserts by golf courses, prairies by intensive agriculture, and so on. Both globally and throughout North America, changes in land use have been, are now, and are likely to remain the single greatest driver of biodiversity loss. This change has resulted in the decline of populations and the extinction of various species across most, if not all, groups of plants and animals (taxonomic groups). Fur-

---

Box 2.4. The Impact of Socioeconomic Drivers of Ecological Change

---

All the factors listed below fundamentally result from the perception that humans are apart from, rather than a part of, ecological systems. The plus and minus signs in brackets indicate the direction of the influence on North America's native biodiversity over the next 20 years: if a factor is more likely to contribute to its decline, this is indicated by [−]; if it is more likely to contribute to recovery, this is indicated by [+].

- **Human population:** The number of people inhabiting North America in 2025, both through births and immigration, is estimated to increase from 70 million to just over half a billion people.[1] Urbanization will increase, altering cultures and lifestyles, further reducing the bond between humans and nature (discussed in box 2.5) and undermining the countries' capacity to manage ecosystems that cannot recover by themselves. [−]

- **Consumption of natural resources:** The demand for natural resources is likely to increase in association with the growth of the human population (although human population growth and consumption are not always directly correlated) and with the desire to reduce North America's dependence on foreign countries, especially in the energy sector. [−]

- **Political conflict:** Although North America is generally considered a cooperative region in the world, conflicts over land and natural resources (especially water) are likely to exacerbate in the coming decades, as human population increases and rapidly changing environmental conditions place human beings in ever greater positions of uncertainty and resource limitation. History indicates that political conflict can take a considerable toll on biodiversity, as individuals and groups focus on fulfilling their immediate needs in times of conflict. [−]

---

1. Estimation based on data from Instituto Nacional de Estadística, Geografía e Informática (INEGI), Statistics Canada, and the U.S. Census Bureau.

---

thermore, changes in land use compound the impacts of other environmental stressors, especially global climate change and biological invasion (to be discussed below).

Change in the use of land is directly driven by human needs and human wants. Natural resources are extracted from various ecosystems for shelter, fuel, fiber, food, and recreation. Land is cleared to support agriculture, dwellings, transportation routes, places of business, and grounds for sports. And although land use change has enabled humans to garner an ever increasing proportion of the earth's resources, the changes have also limited the capacity of ecosystems to maintain the services they provide, such as food production; infectious disease resistance; and the regulation of climate, air, and water quality.

Rarely is any effort made to return human-modified land to its natural state, although small-scale attempts are being made (in the prairie pothole region, for example). More typically, one type of change in

---

Box 2.5. The Bond Between Humans and Nature

The single greatest driver of environmental degradation is the human perception that people are apart from, rather than a part of, ecological systems. Contributing factors to this perception include declines in environmental education; the popularity of television, video games, and other forms of technology for recreation; economic models that are incongruent with ecological principles; and religious perspectives that promote human domination of the environment. The increasing lack of interest in natural environments translates into a decline in the value placed on the environment as well as a decrease in knowledge of environmental issues. This decline in values and knowledge is conveyed and reinforced over generations through academic curriculums and standards, parenting choices, institutions, and socioeconomic practices.

Recently, scientists and spiritual leaders concerned about the state of the environment have been voicing the same opinion: if biodiversity and the well-being of humans are to be protected, people need to be reconnected to their natural environment (that is, the bond between humans and nature needs to be rebuilt). World-renowned scientist E.O. Wilson recently intertwined spirituality and the conservation of biodiversity in his book, *The Creation: An Appeal to Save Life on Earth.*[1] Various religious leaders are coming together to address environmental issues and are calling for actions that foster the conservation of biodiversity. For example, the Evangelical church has produced a program, entitled "On the Care of Creation: An Evangelical Declaration on the Care of Creation."[2] Many of the "earth-honoring" principles being put forth by spiritual leaders and conservation biologists have found their way into policymaking through the United Nations Earth Charter Initiative—a declaration signed by thousands of organizations that "seeks to inspire in all peoples a sense of global interdependence and shared responsibility for the well-being of the human family and the larger living world."[3] (More information on the bond between humans and nature, as it relates to the conservation of biodiversity, is provided in the discussion of the No Child Left Inside Initiative below.)

---

1. E.O. Wilson, *The Creation: An Appeal to Save Life on Earth* (New York: W.W. Norton, 2006).
2. See http://www.creationcare.org/resources/declaration.php.
3. See http://www.earthcharter.org/.

---

land use facilitates another change. Road building often literally paves the way for people to gain access to formerly remote areas and convert them to other uses. Increasingly, agricultural land is developed for suburban home sites. However, this trend is expected to change, perhaps dramatically; by 2025, the growing demand for biofuels may drive the dynamics of land use change in North America to such a degree that currently developed lands and those set aside for conservation purposes will be placed into intensive agricultural production.

Although the impact of the increasing rate and scale of land use change in North America over the coming decade is likely to be far lower than the effect in other regions of the world (such as South America), the changes will, nonetheless, have escalating consequences for biodiversity. These alterations will vary greatly among ecosystems, reflecting their unique composition and ecological dynamics, the spatial and temporal scale and intensity of land use, and the dynamics of other drivers influencing the system.

Decisions related to land use have generally been considered an issue for local decisionmakers. However, as the footprint of land use grows, it is clear that local management can have wide-ranging consequences. More comprehensive national and regional policy decisions regarding the use and protection of land may become warranted. In 2025, policymakers will be faced with the challenge of meeting immediate human resource needs while securing the capacity of the ecosystems to support the human enterprise over the long term. The trade-offs will be many and the consequences—to both biodiversity and humanity—great.

GLOBAL CLIMATE CHANGE

Living organisms must track the climate regimes appropriate for their survival, adapt to the new conditions, or become extinct. Over the past 150,000 years, atmospheric carbon dioxide (CO_2) and temperature have been closely correlated, strongly suggesting that the two are coupled. In the 1970s, climatologists began to warn that steadily increasing CO_2 levels would cause the earth to experience rapid rises in temperature, induced in part by emissions of greenhouse gases resulting from the burning of fossil fuels, intensified land use, and reduction in forest cover. Climatologists projected that global temperatures would rise significantly in the coming decades. Biologists projected that species would respond to climate change in dramatic ways: ranges would shift, natural communities would be disrupted, and mass extinctions of some species would occur.

Carbon dioxide emissions from fossil fuel burning and industrial processes have been accelerating at a global scale, with their growth rate increasing from 1.1 percent y^{-1} for 1990–1999 to less than 3 percent y^{-1} for 2000–2004. The emissions growth rate since 2000 was greater than the rate for the most fossil fuel intensive emissions projected in scenarios developed by the Intergovernmental Panel on Climate Change in the late 1990s.[49] Data collected in 2004 show that the three NAFTA countries contributed 7,126,860 thousands of metric tons of carbon dioxide emissions per year—a figure equivalent to 26.15 percent of the world's annual emissions.[50] Even if this trend declines, climate change is expected to exacerbate the biodiversity crisis. Species most at risk as a result of climate change are those that (1) are already at the upper limits of their physiological tolerance to temperature and/or dryness; (2) have highly specific habitat and/or feeding requirements; and/or (3) are bound by barriers to dispersal. Although there will undoubtedly be variation in the type, rate, and degree of response that species make to global warming, observations of population declines, species extinctions, and range and phonological shifts attributed to climate change are already being reported for a diversity of taxonomic groups in a number of ecosystems. For example, the range of Edith's checkerspot butterfly in North America has changed in accordance with a western regional climate shift. Recent events in the marine environment, where just a slight increase in the sea's surface temperature has led to extensive coral bleaching and mortality (up to 90 percent) in most tropical oceans, are believed to be largely a consequence of a steadily rising baseline of marine temperatures. In the Yellowstone area of the Rocky Mountains, grizzly bears are dependent on white bark pine forests for forage and cover. Evidence suggests that regional climate change is enabling the mountain pine beetle, a pest of white bark pine, to extend its range into altitudes that were previously too cold for its survival. As a result, white bark pine populations are experiencing significant loss—a loss believed to threaten the grizzly bear's survival.

At the regional level, changes will vary, and some are anticipated to be quite dramatic (as illustrated in figure 2.9). In drought-stricken regions, where water tables are already drawn down by excessive use, climate change may result in permanent damage to vegetation and the ecosystem. In the Far North, the extended ice-free and snow-free periods will prevent coastal carnivores from maintaining their ice flow-based hunting regimes, and the destruction of permafrost will have major repercussions for both plant and animal communities. In the South, both mangrove systems and coral reefs are unlikely to keep up with rates of sea level rise and to cope with the stresses (including disease) caused by warming waters. Coastal estuaries and barrier islands, already highly stressed and weakened by overuse and degradation, are highly vulnerable to ecological collapse in the face of severe storm events and the rise of sea levels.

Throughout North America, policymakers and natural resource biologists are going to be challenged to deal with wildlife and ecosystem management issues like never before. Hard decisions will need to be made about where and how to allocate resources as species ranges

Figure 2.9. How North America Will Feel the Heat

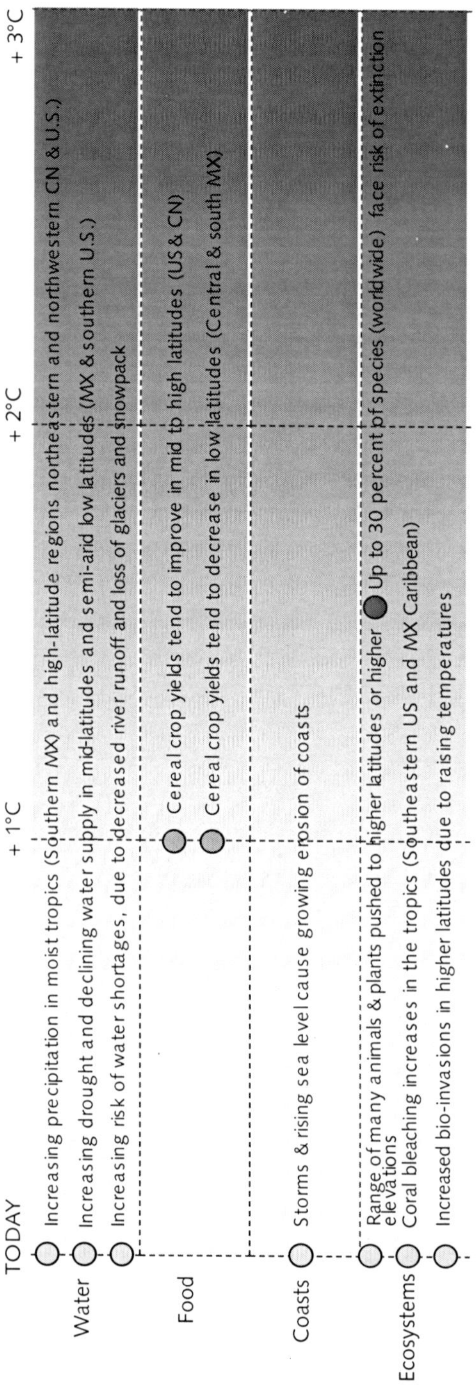

Source: Adapted from "Changing Climate," Supplement to National Geographic, October 2007.

shift, populations become increasingly isolated, and ecological relationships are uncoupled and become newly initiated.

To minimize the repercussions of climate change, North America is likely to move away from its dependence on fossil fuels. The Intergovernmental Panel on Climate Change (IPCC) projects that biomass will provide a significantly increasing proportion of global energy needs over the next century. The potential implications for biodiversity are profound: areas now set aside to conserve biodiversity and ecological processes, as well as to support agricultural production, will be sought after for the production of energy. Upcoming meetings sponsored by the IPCC and the associated Kyoto Protocol will greatly influence what and how the governments of North America will address the implications of climate change for biodiversity and the well-being of human beings and how successfully they will do so.

INVASIVE SPECIES

Invasive species are non-native species whose introduction and/or spread harms or threatens to harm biodiversity, economies, or human health. Invasive species are among the three top drivers of environmental change globally (along with habitat destruction and climate change) but may be the primary driver in certain regions and ecosystems, especially islands and aquatic environments. Invasive species are already causing severe ecological damage in North America and have been implicated in the endangerment of specific species, the degradation of aquatic and terrestrial environments, and the alteration of bio-geochemical cycles. These species have, for example, caused harm to approximately half of the species listed under the United States' Endangered Species Act,[51] and they are a contributing factor in 68 percent of the region's fish extinctions over the past century.[52] Furthermore, it is clear that the impacts of invasive species on biodiversity and ecosystem services can impede environmental conservation (even in supposed protected areas), sustainable development, and economic growth. David Pimentel and his colleagues estimate that invasive species already costs the United States more than US$100 billion annually; thus, economic damage and control costs for the whole of North America are clearly much higher.[53]

The globalization of trade, travel, and transport is greatly increasing the rate at which organisms are transported around the world as well as the number and diversity of species being moved. Intentional introductions of invasive species occur when non-native organisms are introduced into the natural environment for specific reasons (for example, aquaculture production, erosion control, development assistance, or "freeing" of pets and research subjects) and later cause harm to the environment. Unintentional introductions of invasive species take place when harmful non-native species are imported as "hitchhikers" on people and products and dispersed into the environment or when they escape from captivity. The diversity and degree of the introductions of invasive species will follow the patterns and trends of globalization. Land use change and climate change are likely to facilitate biological invasion by making habitats more challenging for native species and more hospitable to invasive species. Because disturbed habitats often favor rapid colonizers, these habitats are particularly vulnerable to the invasion of non-native species.

In 2025, a much greater percentage of North America's biodiversity will undoubtedly consist of non-native species. However, this increase in diversity may very well be more detrimental than beneficial. A certain amount of human adaptation and innovation will be necessary to address the challenge. For example, the countries of North America currently lack sufficient and safe technologies for the mechanical and chemical control of invasive species on the scale that will be required. Furthermore, how ecosystems and their services will change is very difficult to predict, especially because the biology of many of these newcomers is not well documented within their native range, there is no inventory of the non-native species that have already been introduced into North America, and it is impossible to determine which species will be the next to arrive.

North American governments' response to the problem of invasive species has thus far been inadequate to counter their increasing toll on the environment and society, and there is little evidence that this situation will soon change. Although both the United States and Canada have developed national plans for the management of invasive species, the countries have yet to fully find the political will and to commit the financial resources and staff to implement the plans adequately. In Mexico, the issue of invasive species is still largely the concern of academic and research institutions and has received little government attention aside from projects associated with the Commission for Environmental Cooperation. Although all taxonomic groups of organisms (mammals, birds, and so forth) include species that are invasive in North America, policymakers need to be particularly concerned about pathogenic microbes and fungi as well as insects. Because they can produce many generations in a relatively short time period, they are better able to adapt to changing environmental conditions than other groups of organisms are and may thus become increasingly dominant forces in the shaping of ecosystems and the quality of the human condition.

NITROGEN DEPOSITION

In terrestrial systems, nitrogen deposition places a key constraint on the net primary productivity (total plant growth) by disrupting ecological processes such as plant/soil nutrient relations and increasing soil acidification and aluminum mobility. Plants, of course, play key roles in water, nutrient, and energy cycling, and they also provide food, cover, and reproductive sites for various animals. Not all plants are equally affected by nitrogen deposition. Recent studies in New England and Europe indicate that some forests receiving chronic nitrogen inputs may decline in productivity and experience greater mortality and that slow nitrogen-cycling coniferous forests (pines, spruce, hemlock, and so forth) may be replaced by fast-growing and fast nitrogen-cycling deciduous forests (those that are largely composed of trees that shed their leaves, such as oaks, hickories, maples, and so forth).[54] Many invasive trees (*Ailanthus altissima,* the tree of heaven, for example) are likely to take advantage of conifer loss. Clearly, excess nitrogen can cause cascading impacts throughout terrestrial ecosystems.

Nitrogen deposition also has an impact on the atmosphere as well as on aquatic and marine systems. It can contribute to global warming by increasing emissions of nitrogenous greenhouse gases from soil and by reducing methane soil uptake. Nitrogen excess can decrease water quality, have toxic effects on freshwater plants and animals, and cause eutrophication in coastal marine waters.

Nitrogen deposition is greatest in the urban fringes of the northern temperate zone and lowest in areas that are far removed from sources of pollution—the Arctic region and southern temperate forests, for example. Human population growth and consequent increases in fossil fuel use during the twentieth century have caused large increases in nitrogen deposition in North America and elsewhere. Although some ecosystems may have benefited from nitrogen's fertilizing effect and have slightly increased their capacity to sequester carbon (an important aspect of climate change mitigation), most terrestrial ecosystems are negatively affected by increasing nitrogen levels.

Nitrogen emissions (in the form of nitrogen oxide or nitrogen dioxide) from human-created sources are expected to increase dramatically in the coming years. Even though it is clear that nitrogen deposition will also increase, the degree of change, interaction with the climate system, and ultimate impact on biodiversity are not readily apparent. In theory, the ecosystems that are the most nitrogen-limited (such as most forests in North America) will see the largest impact of increased nitrogen deposition on biodiversity; plant species with high growth rates (many of which are likely to be invasive species) are likely to out-compete slower-growing species and steadily influence other changes in the system. If this proves to be the case, temperate and boreal forests, as well as Arctic and alpine systems, are likely to suffer the greatest consequences of nitrogen deposition, whereas deserts and tropic forests will be least affected.

Part of the problem in projecting the consequences of nitrogen deposition in 2025 lies in the current lack of understanding of the role of nitrogen cycling in various ecosystems and how this is affected by other drivers of environmental change (such as climate change or certain types of invasive plants). The paucity of existing data on current levels of nitrogen in various terrestrial ecosystems, deposition rates, and biological responses also makes projections difficult. Although elaborate computational models have been developed to assist in finding answers to these questions, all models are only as good as the conceptual framework and data on which they are based.

BIODIVERSITY RESPONSES

Species will respond to the various environmental drivers in diverse ways. Although the lack of scientific baseline information for most species in North America makes it impossible to project to what degree species will respond,[55] two fundamental generalizations can be made:

- Some species—those that are habitat or dietary specialists or have small range sizes—will have the least ability to adapt to the changing conditions. By 2025, an unforeseeable number of these species will be extinct. Each one lost represents a biological legacy that spans back some 3 billion years. What they had to offer to the future well-being of the world's population will never be known.

■ Conversely, other groups of organisms–such as microbes, insects, and invasive plants that reproduce rapidly and in large numbers are likely to be able to capitalize on the changes and become serious threats to native biodiversity, agricultural systems, and even human health. Only time will tell what impact these groups will have on the world's ecosystems.

From the perspective of biodiversity management, it is important to recognize that the species in North America that are generally considered to be the most charismatic and deserving of conservation dollars–wolves, bears, and birds of prey, for example–are not necessarily those that will be the most directly threatened by rapidly changing environmental conditions. In many cases, such as that of the grizzly bear mentioned above, the impact on the charismatic large vertebrates will be indirect, coming via the effects on their food supply or habitat, for example. Thus, in order to protect the icons of conservation in North America, investments need to be made for the protection of all the elements of biodiversity, regardless of whether the public considers a certain species "charming" or "icky." Basically, this effort calls for the wildlife management agencies in North America to adopt an ecosystem approach to the conservation of biodiversity, as called for in the Convention on Biological Diversity.[56]

Thus far, the governments of North America have a relatively poor track record of undertaking efforts to conserve ecosystems as a whole. In fact, North America has done very little to address the declines of some of the most threatened groups of organisms critical to the health of ecosystems when those species have not engendered much interest in the public psyche. For example, amphibians (frogs, toads, and salamanders) are the most threatened taxonomic group of organisms in the world. Over the two decades, the amphibian population of North America and elsewhere has suffered a severe decline, and some species have even become extinct, primarily as a result of habitat loss and an invasive microscopic fungus (*Batrachochytrium dendrobatidis*) that infects the skin and causes severe die-offs.[57] Despite all the scientific evidence of the decline and the potential consequences for species that prey upon or are controlled by amphibians (such as many insect pests, including mosquitoes), the governments of North America as well as many nongovernmental organizations have done very little to address the problem.

Box 2.6. Recommended Steps for Protecting North America's Biodiversity

---

- Support education and outreach efforts that aim to raise awareness of ecological principles, promote biodiversity conservation measures, and foster the bond between humans and nature.

- Whenever possible, base policy decisions on sound science.

- View healthy ecological systems as the support structure for economic growth.

- When adequate scientific information is not available, invest in efforts to obtain such information and adopt a precautionary decisionmaking approach in the interim.

- Implement an ecosystem approach to natural resource management that is based on ecological units of organizations (such as watersheds) rather than on jurisdictional boundaries.

- Seek active collaboration among governments and nongovernmental organizations at all levels in order to implement "best practices" in conservation measures. When necessary, provide capacity-building programs to agencies to ensure that the bar of implementation is set as high as possible.

- Adopt policy measures that recognize the complexity of natural systems (biocomplexity) and take a long-term perspective of ecological systems and services (that is, consider the needs of multiple human generations) yet are flexible enough to address the rapid and uncertain changes facing biodiversity. To do this, policymakers must recognize that focusing public attention and resources on the threat of relatively small-scale dramatic events (such as terrorist attacks) undermines the human and financial resources needed to address the subtle, gradual socioeconomic and environmental changes that are causing so many substantial negative impacts in North America.

- Base policy decisions on economic models that are congruent with ecological principles.

- When considering new technologies (such as genetic modification), energy programs (such as biofuel production), and trade agreements, evaluate their potential impacts on biodiversity and implement measures to minimize these impacts. Whenever possible, use these tools proactively to foster the protection of biodiversity.

- Fully engage in regional and international instruments intended to address the drivers of environmental change and designed to secure the services provided by biodiversity and ecosystems. (Some of these instruments are listed in box 2.7.)

RECOMMENDATIONS

Policy Principles

Although humans have the capacity for rationalization, their actions often suggest otherwise. When governments create policies that undermine the integrity of ecological systems, they fail to behave rationally.

Box 2.7. Sample Frameworks that Address the Drivers of Environmental Change and Biodiversity in North America

---

Regional Frameworks

- Commission for Environmental Cooperation (http://www.cec.org/)

- North American Plant Protection Convention (http://www.nappo.org/)

- Trilateral Committee for Wildlife and Ecosystem Conservation and Management (http://www.trilat.org/table_cites/cites_vi_mtg/vi_mtg_cites_report_eng.htm)

- North American Forest Commission (http://www.fs.fed.us/global/nafc/)

Global Frameworks

- Convention on Biological Diversity (http://www.cbd.int/default.shtml) and the associated Cartagena Protocol on Biosafety (http://www.cbd.int/biosafety/default.shtml)

- Intergovernmental Panel on Climate Change (http://www.ipcc.ch/) and the associated Kyoto Protocol (http://unfccc.int/kyoto_protocol/items/2830.php)

- International Plant Protection Convention (http://www.ippc.int/IPP/En/default.jsp)

- Ramsar Convention on Wetlands (http://www.ramsar.org)

- United Nations Convention to Combat Desertification (http://www.unccd.int/)

- United Nations Framework Convention on Climate Change (http://unfccc.int/2860.php)

In order to minimize the impact of the major drivers of environmental change by 2025, policymakers need to shift their paradigm of decisionmaking—in terms of impetus, tools and approaches, spatial and temporal scale, and direction. At a minimum, policymakers in North America need to adopt and institutionalize the principles listed in box 2.6. Many of these principles have already been called for at national and international levels, but governments have thus far shown little commitment to ensuring biosecurity by putting them into practice.

There is reason to be optimistic, however. Policymakers have shown that, when they have the will to protect North American biodiversity, successes are possible. For example, sound and effectively implemented policies have had a number of positive results:

- the reduction of ozone-depleting chlorinated fluorocarbons to almost zero,

- protection of approximately 13 percent of the region's land area,

- stabilized desertification (drying) and recovery of dry lands,

- a slowdown in the loss of wetlands, and

- reduction in point source pollution.

The following specific recommendations are provided as a starting point for Canada, the United States, and Mexico in their efforts to strengthen their regionwide approach to conserving biodiversity. (Examples of initiatives already in line with these recommendations are described in box 2.8.) By no means is the list of recommendations meant to be exhaustive; rather, it is provided as a way to demonstrate the feasibility of implementing the recommendations and to point out projects that could serve as the basis for initiating national or regional efforts. Policymakers are encouraged to build on current successes and to avoid creating new projects that will further deplete resources that are already limited.

Educational Programs

Far greater investments in environmental education are needed in order to foster sustainable living practices by North Americans as well as to build public support for government policies aimed at addressing the major drivers of environmental change. These educational programs can serve a range of purposes and address different audiences. Specific recommendations include the following:

- Foster and support legislation (including grant programs) that promotes and supports teaching and learning about the environment at all levels of education, especially elementary and secondary schools. For example, the United States' No Child Left Inside Act of 2007 aims to provide incentives for state educational agencies in the United States to create a State Environmental Literacy Plan for integrating environmental education into the curriculum for kindergarten through grade 12 in order to ensure that graduates are environmentally literate.[58] (Boxes 2.5 and 2.8 provide more information about this initiative.)

- Through the North American Association for Environmental Education (NAAEE) and relevant partners (such as the CEC), develop/assemble curriculum materials for use in environmental education programs that focus on the interdependence and connectivity of North American ecosystems (for example, wildlife migration, influence of climate, and trade patterns). The NAAEE

Box 2.8. Current Initiatives That Address Key Recommendations

---

- **No Child Left Inside Initiative:** Richard Louv's recent book, *Last Child in the Woods,* points out that children are increasingly alienated from nature because of their attraction to video games, television, shopping malls, and so forth, and the implications of this trend are significant for children's health and creativity as well as for the value they place on the environment and their understanding of environmental issues. Largely inspired by this work, state and provinces in the United States and Canada have joined with environmental education organizations to foster No Child Left Inside Initiatives aimed at rebuilding the connection between human beings and nature. For example, Ontario's minister of education, Kathleen Wynne, recently decided to integrate environmental education across the curriculum from kindergarten through grade 12. The intent of this measure is to ensure that high school graduates will have an understanding of the relationship between humans and their environment as well as knowledge of practices that will ensure sustainable living. Connecticut's governor, M. Jodi Rell, has implemented a project coordinated by the Connecticut Department of Environmental Protection to encourage the state's families and visitors to enjoy all the recreational resources and outdoor activities available in Connecticut's state parks, forests, and waterways.

- **Habitattitude™ and Stop Aquatic Hitchhikers™:** Both of these campaigns are designed to prevent the introduction and spread of invasive species. The former initiative aims to achieve this goal by educating pet owners about choice of appropriate pets, pet care, and alternatives to the release of unwanted pets. (More information can be found at http://www.pijac.org and at http://www .habitattitude.ca/en/aboutus/.) Stop Aquatic Hitchhikers focuses on educating boaters and other water recreationists to remove mud, plants, and animals from their equipment before moving it from one location to another. (More information on this program can be found at http://www.protectyourwaters. net/.) A number of stakeholders are involved in both campaigns, which unite federal agencies with the private sector and are based on social marketing principles. Although the campaigns originated in the United States, they have been adopted in Canada; Mexico has also expressed an interest in implementing a Spanish-language version of both programs.

- **AAAS Science and Technology Policy Fellowships:** The American Association for the Advancement of Science (AAAS) implements a variety of science- and technology-oriented fellowships for recent postdoctoral scientists and those in the middle of their careers. The fellowships are designed (1) to educate scientists and engineers on the intricacies of federal policymaking, (2) to provide scientific expertise and analysis to support decisionmakers confronting increasingly complex scientific and technical issues, (3) to foster positive exchanges between scientists and policymakers, (4) to empower scientists and engineers to conduct policy-relevant research that addresses the environmental challenges facing society, and (5) to increase the involvement and visibility of scientists and engineers in the public policy realm. After their fellowships end, many recipients establish careers within U.S. federal government agencies or as policy advisers under the auspices of NGOs, think tanks, and private corporations. (More information about the AAAS fellowships can be found at http://fellowships.aaas.org.)

- **Mexico's Program of Payments for Environmental Services:** This program is aimed at providing cash incentives to landowners to enable them to maintain the

(continued next page)

Box 2.8 (*continued*)

natural land cover in their plots. The initiative effectively attempts to internalize the wider value of the services the ecosystem provides. Currently, the range of services includes carbon, water, and biodiversity. Future challenges include consolidation of support areas and improvement in monitoring, but the principle is extremely valuable. Under this program, landowners can voluntarily commit to conserve their forests in exchange for receiving an annual per hectare payment for up to five years. In 2006, more than US$20 million was allocated, providing payments for conservation of more than 200,000 hectares of land.

■ **CONABIO´s Program for Mexican Collective Biological Resources:** Most of the remaining natural areas in Mexico lie in the indigenous community's land or in ejidos—areas where land is collectively owned. This program is aimed at strengthening the community's capacity to appropriate the land's biological resources and develop them into marketable products. Among the mechanisms being developed to reach the marketplace are geographical indications and collective trademarks. The products being developed include traditional distillates from agave, natural fibers, aromatic oils, and spring water, among others. This program adds to a growing range of initiatives aimed at opening market alternatives for sustainable products that are produced by the region's biodiversity. These initiatives are key to promoting alternatives to maintaining inhabitants' traditional livelihoods and conserving biodiversity.

■ **Mitigation and Conservation Banks in the United States:** Conservation and mitigation banks are ecosystem or resource areas that have been restored, established, enhanced, or preserved for the purpose of providing compensation for the unavoidable impacts of environmental change on resources or endangered species. In an effort to create a mechanism to offset the impact of development on biodiversity, conservation banks are being used to provide incentives for landowners in areas with a high level of biodiversity to manage the areas for conservation, providing a basis for zero-net-impact development and ensuring a funding mechanism for conservation activities. Thus far, conservation banks for both habitats and endangered species have been created. These initiatives are key to ensuring meaningful in-kind compensation, rather than monetary compensation. There are a number of mitigation and conservation banks across the United States.

---

has created guidelines for achieving excellence in materials used for environmental education.[59]

■ Implement regionwide multistakeholder outreach campaigns based on social marketing principles and aimed at reducing the impact of the major drivers of environmental change.[60] Whenever possible, build on existing programs. (Box 2.8 provides two examples of campaigns that address invasive species.)

■ Through the CEC and relevant partners, create a North American-based environmental education course for decisionmakers modeled on the Organization for Tropical Studies' course for

U.S. decisionmakers, entitled "Conservation and Development in Tropical Countries: Insights and Implications."[61]

Scientific Programs

The paucity of scientific information on North American biodiversity is the most significant factor limiting the capacity of the region's policymakers to make well-informed, timely, and strategic decisions in this area. Implementing the following recommendations would help fill the gap by creating or reinforcing existing inventory and monitoring programs; supporting field research on the causes of environmental change; and providing timely, scientifically accurate, and comprehensible information to the policymaking community and federal agencies:

- At the national level, establish or strengthen biological inventory and monitoring programs that are designed to measure the degree, direction, and consequences of ecological change. Build on existing agency and NGO capacities as well as citizen-based monitoring programs (such as Christmas bird counts). In general, data are available for marketed goods and services, but they need to be greatly strengthened for the biological factors that support them.

- Substantially increase funds to support academics', NGOs', and agency scientists' research on the drivers of environmental change. Develop a mechanism for enacting trinational research initiatives by creating a network of the appropriate scientific agencies in the United States, Canada, and Mexico.

- Through the CEC and relevant partners, create a biodiversity clearinghouse mechanism for North American decisionmakers in order to provide them with scientific information that they need that is timely and packaged for their understanding and application. This portal should be organized by environmental drivers and ecosystems and should provide links to relevant databases and reports that can be readily used by decisionmakers. Policymakers should also subscribe to scientific journals specifically designed to communicate advances in science to readers involved in decisionmaking in the field of ecology. Examples of such publications include *BioScience* (http://www.aibs.org/bioscience), *Conservation Magazine* (http://www.conbio.org/Publications/

ConservationMagazine), and *Frontiers in Ecology and the Environment* (http://www.frontiersinecology.org/instructions.php).

- Create a North America-wide fellowship program for placing exceptional environmental scientists as advisers in government agencies for two years. This capacity-building program will help educate decisionmakers about pressing environmental issues and will also train scientists to communicate their findings to policymakers in a timely and effective manner. (Box 2-8 describes a program that can serve as a potential model.)

Economic Incentives

Various economic tools can be applied at international, national, and local levels in order minimize the negative impact of human activities on the region's biodiversity. These tools include tax policy, fines and levies, royalties, user fees, property rights, licenses, eases, bonds, and deposits as well as institutional mechanisms. The following economic incentives can help attract private investment in conserving North America's biodiversity:

- On a national level, evaluate subsidies provided to the agricultural and energy sectors to determine their potential to affect and/or protect biodiversity. Biodiversity is a public good necessitating public investment. In 2001, economists estimated that, of the US$1.9 trillion in government subsidies going to support agriculture and fossil fuel production, transportation, and other human activities globally, approximately US$1.4 trillion were "perverse" subsidies   subsidies for activities that work against the conservation of biodiversity.[62] It should be noted that some legislation (such as the U.S. Farm Bill) may contain provisions that foster biodiversity conservation and others that facilitate drivers of environmental change. Where possible, governments should redirect ecologically harmful subsidies immediately and seek ways to create an eco-centric approach to subsidy programs over time.

- At the regional and national level, develop economic incentive programs that encourage civil society to invest in the conservation of North America's biodiversity by fostering measures that protect the land and practices that lead to sustainable living practices. The fate of much of North America's biodiversity is controlled by private landowners and private companies. The World Business Council for Sustainable Development and the International Union for the Conservation of Nature (ICUN) have published a useful reference on this topic for policymakers and the private sector.[63]

- Through relevant federal agencies, provide grants and fellow-ships that foster collaboration between ecologists and economists in the development of ecologically congruent economic models. Although the terms "economics" and "ecology" stem from the same Greek word, ecos (meaning home), economic models are often incongruent with ecological principles. For example, economic models are often based on the assumption that resources are unlimited and that systems are closed (self-contained). In reality, all resources have finite limits and ecological systems are interconnected and interdependent. The discrepancy between ecological processes and economic models has greatly contributed to policy decisions that facilitate—and even promote—the major drivers of environmental change.

Governance Programs

The state of biodiversity in North America is influenced by decisions made by the governments of Canada, Mexico, and the United States, as well as by every other country in the world. In order to make well-informed decisions in the midst of rapid changes in North America's biodiversity, policymakers need to have access to technical experts and also to one another so that they can identify and address problems in current policies, implement effective policies designed to protect the continent's biodiversity as well as the world's, and ensure that each country's policies are consistent with those of its neighbors. The following recommendations suggest specific ways to achieve this goal:

- Sponsor a biannual, two-day meeting of high-level North American decisionmakers from each country's ministries that have responsibility for biodiversity, agriculture, and trade (at a minimum). Ideally, the meeting should be a joint venture of the CEC, North American Plant Protection Convention, and Trilateral Committee for Wildlife and Ecosystem Conservation and Management (some of the regional frameworks listed in box 2.7). The first day of the meeting would be dedicated to briefings on key

biodiversity issues presented by technical experts who have ample experience working with policymakers. On the second day, a
working format could be provided to participants to enable decisionmakers and their key staff to seek decisionmaking advice
from these technical experts. At the end of the meeting, representatives of each country's agencies should be asked to offer a
pledge to seek new or expanded initiatives, state their goals along
these lines, and provide a mechanism for reporting progress.

- At the national level, establish interagency task forces to focus
  on key drivers of environmental change from a multisector perspective. At a minimum, these task forces should be used for the
  following purposes: (1) to evaluate gaps and inconsistencies in
  relevant policies across the federal agencies (for example, one
  agency promoting trade and another trying to prevent biological
  invasion); (2) to develop new policies aimed at protecting biodiversity that are congruently supported across all federal agencies; and (3) to develop across-the-board budgets, arrangements
  for staff to share facilities, and other mechanisms that will help
  promote resource sharing, information exchange, and capacity
  building. It is critical that the federal agencies carefully consider
  which staff members to assign to these task forces, because the
  effectiveness of the task forces depends on participants who are
  technically savvy in both science and policymaking and are also
  proactive and visionary.

- Fully engage the governments of North America in international
  frameworks that deal with environmental issues. Because the
  scale of influence and impact of the most pressing environmental issues is global, international cooperation and consultation
  are necessary aspects of problem resolution. The governments
  of North America need to work within existing international
  frameworks (as listed in box 2.7) to promote and implement
  policies that protect the region's biodiversity and population.

CONCLUSION

The North American environment will face unprecedented pressures
between now and 2025. Even if all the recommendations proposed in
this chapter were adopted, natural systems in all three North American

countries would still experience disruption caused by climate change that is already built into the climate system because of existing concentrations of greenhouse gases in the atmosphere and unavoidable short- to medium-term increases in those concentrations. The more arid midcontinental regions of the United States, northern Mexico, and southern Canada are likely to experience reduced flows of surface water and changes in precipitation, including longer periods of drought. Coastal areas, particularly along the Atlantic seaboard and the Gulf of Mexico, will probably have to contend with at least a modest rise in sea levels and stronger storm surges. Ecosystems will change in response to shifting climate patterns, and many of the species that depend on those ecosystems will be endangered or lost.

As indicated by the discussion in this chapter, however, the impacts of these changes can be managed in a way that makes it possible to avoid harmful disruption to most North Americans' quality of life if action is taken now. Starting right away is particularly important with respect to climate change, because there is no hope of keeping atmospheric concentrations of greenhouse gases below 450 parts per million (the level at which average temperature increases can probably be held to 2°C) unless North America, and particularly the United States, leads by example and persuades China, India, and other developing countries to follow. As the discussion of climate change demonstrated, such leadership will require commitment to concrete steps to cut North American greenhouse gas emissions by 60 percent or more by 2050. Achieving reductions of this magnitude will require far-reaching changes in policy and incentive structures as well as accelerated deployment of more climate-friendly technologies across North America.

Climate change not only reduces water availability in areas of North America that are already stressed and threatens North American biodiversity but also opens up large areas of northern Canada and Alaska that were previously inaccessible to development. Even today there are signs of a potentially vicious cycle in which growing demand for fossil energy in the United States, China, and other countries raises both greenhouse gas emissions and energy prices, thereby putting irresistible pressure on those controlling energy resources in northern Canada and Alaska to develop those resources. Development of those resources then, in turn, puts pressure on scarce water supplies and biodiversity and in this way adds to the negative effects of climate change. This cycle is already at work in the Athabasca tar sands and could rapidly spread to other areas. Keeping this cycle in check will require a strong political commitment by concerned North Americans and their political representatives.

The changes in behavior needed to keep the impacts of climate change, reductions in water availability, and loss of biodiversity within acceptable limits between now and 2025 will only take place on the scale required if there is a transformation in public attitudes throughout North America. North Americans need to appreciate the value of the ecological services provided by their natural systems; understand the pressures that their increasing environmental footprint is putting on nature's ability to provide those services; and be willing to make short-term sacrifices, such as paying higher prices for energy and water in order to ensure that those services will be provided in the future. Instead of perceiving their environment as a resource to be exploited, North Americans will have to perceive it as something of great value that must be protected. This transformation in public attitudes will take place only if there is an informed public discussion based on better data and analysis about current trends and what can be done to reverse them. This is the reason this chapter has emphasized monitoring, improved data and analysis, public education, and greater public participation in decisionmaking processes.

The good news for the continent is that Canada, the United States, and Mexico have already taken initial steps to reduce greenhouse gas emissions through energy efficiency and deployment of more climate-friendly technologies, to improve management of scarce water resources by encouraging conservation and recycling and reducing pollution, and to protect ecosystems and control invasive species. The three countries now need to accelerate those trends by implementing the user pays and polluter pays principles; by using market mechanisms to encourage resource conservation and more environmentally friendly behavior; and by strengthening existing mechanisms for cooperation at the local, national, and regional levels.

What North Americans do or do not do between now and 2025 will have consequences that will not be experienced until many years thereafter. The next few decades are arguably the most important decades in history in terms of the future of the North American environment. One can only hope that North Americans will find the wisdom and the strength to act accordingly.

NOTES

1. Matthew Bramley, *The Case for Deep Reductions: Canada's Role in Preventing Dangerous Climate Change* (Vancouver: David Suzuki Foundation, 2005), p. 11.

2. About half of the uncertainty in projecting temperature increases is attributable to differences in emissions trend scenarios; the remaining half is because of differences between climate models.

3. The Royal Society, "Joint Science Academies' Statement: Global Response to Climate Change," http://www.royalsoc.ac.uk/document.asp?id=3222.

4. Bramley, *The Case for Deep Reductions*, p. 17.

5. Council of the European Union, "22 and 23 March Presidency Conclusions," 7619/1/05 REV, Brussels, 2005, pp. 15–16.

6. International Climate Change Taskforce, "Meeting the Climate Challenge: Recommendations of the International Climate Change Taskforce," p. ix, http://www.americanprogress.org/site/pp.asp?c=biJRJ8OVF&b=306503.

7. German Advisory Council on Global Change, "Climate Protection Strategies for the 21st Century: Kyoto and Beyond," pp. 9–21, http://www.wbgu.de/wbgu_sn2003_engl.html.

8. National Roundtable on the Environment and the Economy, "A Canadian Perspective on Dangerous Anthropogenic Interference with the Climate System," Draft Report, Ottawa, August 2005, pp. 3–4.

9. Each of the six primary greenhouse gases—CO_2, N_2O, CH_4, SF_6, PFCs, and HFCs—generates a different level of radiative forcing in the atmosphere. CO_2e provides a standardized measure of the radiative forcing expected from a mixture of GHGs in terms of the concentration of CO_2 that would have the some forcing effect.

10. Bramley, *The Case for Deep Reductions*, p. 20.

11. C. Keeling et al., "Atmospheric CO_2 Concentrations (ppmv) Derived from In Situ Air Samples Collected at Mauna Loa Observatory, Hawaii," http://cdiac.esd.ornl.gov/ftp/trends/co2/maunaloa.co2.

12. Bramley, *The Case for Deep Reductions*, p. 27

13. United Nations Framework Convention on Climate Change, Preamble, http://unfccc.int/essential_background/convention/background/items/1349.php.

14. *Climate Analysis Indicators Tool (CAIT)*, Version 3.0, World Resources Institute, Washington, D.C., http://cait.wri.org.

15. United Nations Framework Convention on Climate Change, Article 3.1, http://unfccc.int/essential_background/convention/background/items/1349.php.

16. Bramley, *The Case for Deep Reductions*, p. 28.

17. Ibid., p. 31.

18. M. Den Elzen and M. Meinhausen, "Meeting the EU 2°C Climate Tar-

get: Global and Regional Emission Implications," pp. 27–29. Netherlands Environmental Assessment Agency, 2005, www.rivm.nl/bibliotheek/rapporten/728001031.pdf.

19. Derived from B. Hare and M. Meinhausen, "How Much Warming Are We Committed to and How Much Can Be Avoided?" PIK Report No. 93, 2004, p. 26, http://www.pik-potsdam.de/pik_web/publications/pik_reports/reports/pr.93/pr93.pdf.

20. UNFCCC, "GHG Emission Profiles for Annex I Parties," http://unfccc.int/ghg_emissions_data/items/3954.php.

21. "Mexico: Third National Communication to the UNFCCC," Powerpoint presentation, http://regserver.unfccc.int/seors/file_storage/pluakyjv66tzwr5.pdf.

22. Bramley, *The Case for Deep Reductions*, p. 31.

23. D. Woynillowicz et al., *Oil Sands Fever: The Environmental Implications of Canada's Oil Sands Rush* (Drayton Valley, Alberta: Pembina Institute, 2005), p. 22.

24. A. Footitt, *Climate Change Policy and Canada's Oil Sand Resources: An Update and Appraisal of Canada's New Regulatory Framework for Air Emissions* (Norwich: Tyndall Centre for Climate Research, 2007), p. 20.

25. Woynillowicz et al., *Oil Sands Fever*, p. 20.

26. M. McCulloch et al., *Carbon Neutral 2020: A Leadership Opportunity in Canada's Oil Sands* (Drayton Valley: Pembina Institute, 2006), p. 3.

27. Woynillowicz et al., *Oil Sands Fever*, p. 9.

28. F. Pearce, *When the Rivers Run Dry: Water—The Defining Crisis of the Twenty-First Century* (Boston: Beacon Press, 2006), as referred to in F. Mitchell, "The Coming Water Crisis," *Environment Yale* (Spring 2007), p. 9.

29. J.B. Sprague, "Great Wet North? Canada's Myth of Water Abundance," chapter 2 in *Eau Canada: The Future of Canada's Water* (Vancouver: UBC Press, 2007), p. 32.

30. Organization for Economic Cooperation and Development (OECD), *OECD Environmental Performance Reviews: Canada* (Paris: OECD, 2004), p. 58.

31. Ibid.

32. Ibid., 64.

33. S. Renzetti, "Are the Prices Right? Balancing Efficiency, Equity and Sustainability in Water Pricing," chapter 13 in *Eau Canada: The Future of Canada's Water*, pp. 264–265.

34. Organization for Economic Cooperation and Development (OECD), *OECD Environmental Performance Reviews: United States* (Paris: OECD, 2005), p. 67.

35. Ibid. p. 73.

36. U.S. Geological Survey, "Water Quality Data for Pharmaceuticals, Hormones, and Other Organic Wastewater Contaminants in U.S. Streams, 1999–2000," USGS Open-File Report 02-94, Iowa City, Iowa, Abstract.

37. Organization for Economic Cooperation and Development (OECD), *OECD Environmental Performance Reviews: Mexico City* (Paris: OECD, 2003), p. 57.

38. A. Guevara-Sangines, section entitled "A clearly unsustainable pattern of groundwater use," in "Water Subsidies and Aquifer depletion in Mexico's Arid Regions," Human Development Report 2006, Human Development Report Office Occasional Paper, UNDP, 2006/23.

39. Commission for Environmental Cooperation, "The North American Mosaic: A State of the Environment Report," Montreal, 2001.

40. Ten Kate and Laird, *The Commercial Use of Biodiversity: Access to Genetic Resources and Benefit Sharing* (London: Earthscan Publications, 2002).

41. Costanza et al., *Nature,* no. 387 (1997), pp. 253–260.

42. For example, see http://www.worldwildlife.org/science/ecoregions/assessments.cfm.

43. For example, see http://www.heinzctr.org/ecosystems/report.html.

44. Hanson et al., *Securing the Continent's Biological Wealth: Toward Effective Biodiversity Conservation in North America* (Montreal: Commission for Environmental Cooperation, 2000).

45. Ibid.

46. Sala et al., *Science,* no. 287 (2000), pp. 1770–1774.

47. Commission for Environmental Cooperation, *Understanding and Anticipating Environmental Change in North America: Building Blocks for Better Public Policy* (Montreal: Commission for Environmental Cooperation, 2003).

48. "Retrospective," Washington, D.C., 2002.

49. Raupach et al., "Global and Regional Drivers of Accelerating CO_2 Emissions," Harvard University, Cambridge, 2007.

50. Carbon Dioxide Information Analysis Center, List of Sovereign States by Man-Made Carbon Dioxide Emissions, United Nations, New York, 2004.

51. Wilcove et al., *BioScience* 48 (1999): 607–615.

52. Miller et al., *Fisheries* (14): 22–38.

53. David Pimentel, ed., *Biological Invasions: Economic and Environmental Costs of Alien Plant, Animal, and Microbe Species* (Washington, D.C.: CRC Press, 2002).

54. See the discussion in Fenn et al., "Nitrogen Excess in North American

Ecosystems: Predisposing Factors, Ecosystem Responses, and Management Strategies," *Ecological Applications* 8 (1998): 706–733.

55. Baseline information consists of data on population status and trends that are generated through inventories and monitoring programs and on biological research on the direction and degree of various drivers on specific species in specific ecosystems.

56. See http://www.cbd.int/programmes/cross-cutting/ecosystem/default.shtml.

57. See http://www.issg.org/database/species/ecology.asp?si=123&fr=1&sts.

58. See http://www.cbf.org/site/DocServer/No_Child_Left_Inside_Act.pdf ?docID=9503.

59. See http://www.naaee.org/npeee/materials.php.

60. Bartels and Nelissen, eds., *Marketing for Sustainability: Towards Transactional Policy-Making* (Amsterdam: IOS Press, 2002).

61. See http://www.ots.ac.cr/%7Epcambientales/es/ots-8.shtml.

62. Myers and Kent, *Perverse Subsidies: How Tax Dollars Can Undercut the Environment* (Washington, D.C.: Island Press, 2001).

63. Stone et al., *Business and Biodiversity: A Guide for the Private Sector* (Gland, Switzerland: IUCN-World Conservation Union, 1999).

OUTLOOK FOR LABOR MOBILITY

B. LINDSAY LOWELL

International mobility is of critical importance to the future of the economy of the North American nations of Canada, Mexico, and the United States. It can be argued that the greatest determining factor for the future of labor flows is the economic growth rate of the three countries, particularly Mexico, and this rate might determine future labor flows. At the same time, population trends in postindustrial Canada and the United States will generate a latent demand for more workers than might be supplied domestically, while population trends in developing nations, particularly Mexico, make it likely that they will take up the slack.

Much of the contemporary literature on globalization focuses principally on the liberalization of trade and investment as well as, to a lesser extent, on labor mobility and its direct or indirect implications for a nation's economy. Nevertheless, the international migration of labor is embedded in the current trend of economic globalization. Economic linkages serve as bridges for the international movement not only of goods and capital but also of people. Such changes in the global economy have led to the creation of a new international division of labor—the shifting labor markets that arise from changing the geographic specialization of global production patterns.

The flow of people across national borders will undoubtedly continue in North America, as will the social, political, and economic challenges that accompany this trend. In 2000, the United Nations estimated that, of a global population of 6 billion people, about 175 million—or 3 percent of the world's population—were international migrants. The level of Mexican migration into the United States was greater, with 9 percent of Mexican-born individuals living in the United States. Canada has fewer Mexican migrants—roughly 30,000, compared with 9 million in the United States. But thousands of Mexicans are admitted to Canada to work in the agricultural sector, and Mexican exports to Canada are ranked third—only China and the United States get more exports from Mexico.

This chapter will first describe the population projections and the general conclusion that population growth is slowing in all three North American nations, albeit with more immediate impacts in Canada and the United States because of the aging of the populations in those two countries. The report will then discuss the possible implications of these population trends for the labor force, the economy, and the generation of demand for international migration to these nations. Mexican emigration will be treated separately because of its unique characteristics—specifically its size, substantial illegal subpopulation, and developmental status in the North American context and under the North American Free Trade Agreement (NAFTA). Finally, the conclusion will offer some general comments on policy related to the role of population projections, the part migration plays in offsetting a country's slow-growing and aging populations, and appropriate policy responses to Mexican migration.

POPULATION PROJECTIONS AND THEIR IMPLICATIONS

The broad-brush strokes of describing the history of population growth and predicting its future are well recognized. The booming growth of the initial stages of demographic transition—declines in mortality rates preceding declines in fertility rates—gives way to ever slower growth. In the late stages of the demographic transition, this trend sets into play a dynamic whereby a country's population consists of ever fewer young people relative to older people who are living longer. While *all* migrants are not necessarily workers, and labor mobility is the topic covered in this chapter, any discussion of future labor mobility necessarily includes the role that all migrants play in tomorrow's population picture. International migration affects the economy by supplying workers, but the total number of immigrants also affects the dynamics of tomorrow's population, and this, in turn, has implications for the economy.

The rate of population growth in the United States and Canada has been slowing since early in the last century; in Mexico the rate has been slowing since the 1970s. Most observers and statistical agencies fully expect that, absent rather unlikely rebounds in fertility rates, the long-running trends in slowing population growth will continue. As figure 3.1 clearly demonstrates, projections show continued steep declines in the rate of growth through 2050 in the United States, Canada, and Mexico, as well as in most of the world. Today, the U.S. and Canadian populations are growing at a rate of about 1 percent annually, whereas Mexico's population is growing at an annual rate of a little under 1.5 percent. By 2025, the population of all three nations is projected to grow at roughly 0.75 percent annually, with further declines projected through the middle of the century.

Figure 3.1. Population Growth in Canada, Mexico, and the United States, 1995–2050 (estimated)

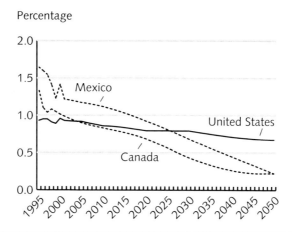

Source: U.S. Census Bureau, International Database.

Nevertheless, declining rates of growth do not mean negative growth of the population—that is, the total number of people living in North America is not projected to decline. Given projected fertility and mortality rates—and, perhaps more important, projected rates of immigration—the total population of North America will continue to grow, albeit more slowly than if either fertility levels were, say, at historic levels or immigration were to increase to unprecedented levels—several times higher than has been the case in recent years.

According to the U.S. Census Bureau's projections of North American populations from 2000 to 2025, the U.S. population is projected to grow from 285 million to 350 million, Canada's from 31 million to 38 million, and Mexico's from 100 million to 130 million. In each case, international mobility plays a key role in the projection. The fertility rate in the three countries has declined to such an extent that immigrants and their children will make up at least two-thirds of the increase in the population of the United States. In Canada, net immigration will contribute from 70 percent today to more than 90 percent of the net growth of its population by 2030.[1] At the same time, emigrants from Mexico will reduce Mexico's potential population growth by nearly an equivalent amount.

However, all population projections rely on assumptions about rates of migration that are not as stable as future rates of mortality or fertility. Indeed, the United Nations' projections of emigration from Mexico and immigration into the United States and Canada simply assume fixed numbers from about 2010 through the middle of the century—that is, they assume no change in the rate of migration at all. But the U.S. Census Bureau's latest round of projections assumes that total immigration will dip in the next decade, only to increase thereafter into the United States and Canada, as the impact of aging increases the demand for immigrant labor. In parallel fashion, the projections assume declining rates of emigration from Mexico through the middle of the century, as Mexico's economy strengthens and absorbs the continually smaller cohorts of persons of working age.

The UN's projections seem too static, but what if the U.S. Census Bureau's projections are based on too strong a set of assumptions about the future pattern of migration? In fact, recent trends in migration into the United States in particular, but also into Canada, suggest that the number of migrants has increased in recent years. One Canadian forecast expects international immigration to rise from the 265,000 range targeted in 2007 to a peak of 360,000 by 2024.[2] And the number of emigrants from Mexico—even in light of the slight decline during the recent, post-2001 economic cycle—is likely to rebound somewhat and could easily remain at levels that are higher than the Census Bureau's calculations based on levels of just a half-decade ago. A comparison of projections modeled on the U.S. Census Bureau's assumptions about migration with those assuming migration levels more characteristic of what has actually been the case in recent years demonstrates that the population growth that has been projected could be much higher.[3] All these caveats simply demonstrate that the empirical basis for projections, as is well known, is rather weak over time frames that are longer than one to two decades.

PRIMARY IMPACT ON THE LABOR FORCE

Nevertheless, existing projections permit analysts to readily infer that, absent seismic changes in the levels of international migration, population growth will slow down and the number of elderly will increase. These trends will affect the supply of tomorrow's labor force in two primary and reinforcing ways.

First, the working-age population will either decline or grow more slowly than it did in the past. Because smaller populations have fewer workers and fewer consumers, a slowdown in the rate of growth could translate into reductions in the level of the country's potential economic output. Particular industries or certain localities may be more affected than others will be, and labor shortages could even result. The degree to which this is true partly depends on changes in capital investments, changes in the technology of production, and the demand abroad for goods and services.

Second, reductions in the fertility rate mean that there are fewer young people today relative to the number born several decades ago. The baby boom generation is aging, and the momentum of longer life expectancies and declining fertility rates will translate into elderly persons making up a larger share of the total population. This trend places a strain on "pay-as-you-go" retirement systems and shifts the balance of the labor force toward more elderly workers—a development that could lead to lower labor productivity. The first effect means that younger workers might be expected to take on more of the burden for paying for elderly, retired workers, and more immigrants may help to keep the system solvent. The second effect means that there may be an increased demand for younger workers, who are more productive than older workers are. Therefore, the demand for immigrants is increased, in part, because they are typically young and may boost overall productivity. The effect of these scenarios also depends on changes in investment and technology as well as changes in labor force participation by women and the elderly.

In the short to medium term, slowing population growth and an aging population will have a stronger impact on the United States and Canada than on Mexico. Mexico's population will increasingly follow the same trend, however. The fertility rate in Mexico is approaching 10 to 15 births per thousand persons—the range the United States and Canada are experiencing today. Indeed, Mexico has only two to three decades before its aging population begins to be as large, relatively speaking, as those of the United States and Canada, countries that started their demographic transitions decades earlier.

What these trends suggest is that there will be shortages of domestic supplies of labor, particularly in the United States and Canada, and a latent demand for immigrant labor. Figure 3.2 shows that the U.S. labor force will actually decline if immigration were to stop, whereas immigration at about today's levels would generate growth to 170 million workers by 2025; there will be a difference of 20 million assuming lower or higher levels of immigration. It is hard to imagine a decline in the number of workers; therefore, there is likely to be a robust demand for immigrants. Most observers agree with such a conclusion, but there are offsetting possibilities. One includes the rarely mentioned—but rather obvious—option of simply accepting the possibly lower rates of economic growth that could be associated with slower growth of both the population and the labor force. But if one accepts the inevitability of a demand for immigrants as a result of a country's aging population, how effectively can alternatives offset that demand and how many immigrants will be needed? At the same time, even though emigration could benefit Mexico through migrant remittances, for example, Mexico could potentially benefit from retaining workers for its domestic needs, especially as the country's population growth begins to slow. However, unless this trend generates demand that retains potential emigrants, how likely is it that Mexico's mass emigration will slow down in the near future?

In 2000, the United Nations Population Division issued a controversial report entitled *Replacement Migration: Is It a Solution to Declining and Aging Populations*?[4] Given the extremely low fertility rate and increased longevity of the population of many developed countries, replacement migration is defined as "the international migration that would be needed to offset declines in the size of population [and] the declines in the population of working age, as well as to offset the overall ageing of a population." In fact, without significant new num-

Figure 3.2. Size of U.S. Labor Force, Depending on Rates of Immigration, 2000–2025 (estimated)

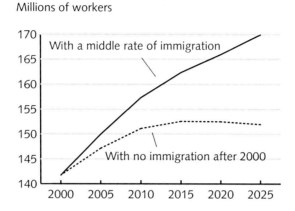

Source: Jeffrey S. Passel, "U.S. Population and Labor Force, 2025: Two Projections of the Future of the North American Labour Mobility, 2025" (presentation at Center for Strategic and International Studies, Washington, D.C., March 23, 2007).

bers of migrants, many European countries will experience declining populations.

Yet, because of the generous immigration policies adopted by the United States and Canada, the prospect for growth is more positive, but these nations will also experience an increasingly large population of elderly dependents. At the same time, most scholars believe that simply increasing the number of immigrants—even several times more than today's already high levels—cannot effectively offset the trends driving the aging of the country's population. Therefore, it is important to come to a better understanding of how the demographic and skill characteristics of immigrants—independently and in combination with other policies related to aging and immigration—can play a significant part in addressing the demands of an aging population.

To answer the question posed in the title of its report, the United Nations calculated the number of immigrants required in the coming century to maintain the peak projected size of the total population, the size of the working-age population, and the ratio of workers to the elderly. The report concluded that maintaining total population size would require about the same current flow of migrants for the United States and most countries of the European Union. For Italy, Japan, the Republic of Korea, and Europe as a whole, however, offsetting population decline would require a level of immigration much higher than these countries have experienced in recent years. Most countries would need a significantly larger number of migrants to offset declines in their working-age population. According to the report, "the levels of migration needed to offset population ageing (i.e., maintain potential support ratios) are extremely large, and [for all countries] entail vastly more immigration than occurred in the past."[5]

For example, figure 3.3 shows the ratio of all workers to the elderly population aged 65 and over that would result from current levels of immigration to the United States. The number of immigrants being admitted to the United States is at a historic high. Yet, even assuming such "medium levels" of immigration, the ratio of workers to the elderly population would reach 2.8 by 2025, which is not substantively greater than the ratio of 2.5 that would be reached in the absence of any migration. In both scenarios, the ratio drops quite significantly from today's ratio of about 4 workers relative to the elderly population.

Indeed, the number of immigrants required to maintain the size of today's working-age population, much less to maintain the ratio of workers to the elderly, would be much greater than most policymakers would be willing to accept. For example, the United Nations estimates that about 47 million migrants would be needed to maintain the overall size of the U.S. population until 2050 and that about 79 million migrants would be needed to maintain a constant size of the 15–64 year-old age group. But about 674 million migrants would be needed to maintain a constant old-age dependency ratio. Nevertheless, even though the UN report recognized that immigration is not the only solution, its authors reinforced for many observers that international migration must be an important part of any strategy to combat population decline and aging.

MIGRATION'S ROLE IN TOMORROW'S LABOR FORCE
Just what role immigration will play in addressing demographic changes is still debatable. Opposition to immigration remains strong in many countries. Negative public opinion may well restrict any options that require substantial increases in the number of immigrants admitted. During the past decade, however, even countries with little

Figure 3.3. Number of Workers per Elderly Person in the United States, Assuming Immigration Is Cut Off after 2005 (estimated)

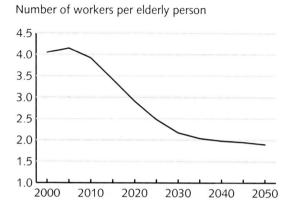

Number of workers per elderly person

Source: Jeffrey S. Passel, "U.S. Population and Labor Force, 2025: Two Projections of the Future of the North American Labour Mobility, 2025" (presentation at Center for Strategic and International Studies, Washington, D.C., March 23, 2007).

Note: Elderly is defined as older than 65 years of age.

tradition of immigration have acknowledged that they have sizable immigrant populations and are likely to continue to admit immigrants. The option that is discussed most often is a temporary worker program that would admit immigrants to contribute to the labor force but not as permanent residents likely to take advantage of the government's benefit programs.

What is also open to debate, however, are the kinds of immigrants that will be admitted. When governments select immigrants, they often base their admission criteria on level of skills, pre-existing connections to the host country (such as colonial ties or trade agreements), family ties, humanitarian interests, and other factors. Governments often cite a preference for highly skilled migrants, who, officials believe, will contribute most to the economy and will be the easiest to integrate. However, businesses often seek laborers with lower-level skills. It is highly likely that international migration will play an important role in addressing the demographic trends already unfolding in most developed countries. But there is a lack of detailed information about what type of role immigrants will play, particularly if policymakers alter the profile or characteristics of immigrants.

Nevertheless, it is fairly easy to understand why researchers find that immigration in and of itself will not radically alter the demographic future. For example, immigrants make up 12 percent of the U.S. population, and current rates of immigration add just over 1 million immigrants yearly to an existing base of about 37 million. Thus, it would take a great deal of new immigrants over a substantial period of time to change the demographic structure of a population of 300 million. That basic insight plays itself out in many ways in the research literature but should not detract from the fact that immigration does have an impact on population outcomes, as evidenced by the fact that the high levels of immigration in Canada and the United States over the past two decades place the two countries at an advantage over Europe in terms of demographic growth. Yet the demographic models indicate that immigration alone has minimal impacts on the age structure of a population.[6] Immigrants—particularly those of working age—add to the population at different steps of the age pyramid, but even radically admitting only the youngest immigrants has little immediate impact. Any demographic structure has its own momentum and takes a long time to develop and stabilize.

The population age distribution depends primarily on the fertility and the age pattern of mortality rather than on migration. Population projections have been run testing several scenarios with different assumptions about fertility rates, mortality rates, and immigration levels.[7] The findings indicate that different assumptions about fertility rates have the largest impact on the projected size of the population aged 0–14, whereas assumptions about mortality rates have the greatest impact on the size of the population aged 65 and over. Changing the number of assumed immigrants has the greatest impact on the working-age population (ages 15–64). Regardless, the built-in momentum of a population's historical age structure means that, absent extreme shocks, it takes time to change the average age of a country's population—it is not easy to reverse the aging process.

Therefore, it is not surprising that many observers argue that there should be an emphasis on increasing the fertility rate by adopting pronatalist policies.[8] This is especially the case in Europe, where fertility rates have declined well below the levels needed to maintain a stable population size. Scholars' opinions on the applicability of this option, however, are divided. For example, general fertility trends mask substantial differences across countries, and high fertility rates are sometimes associated with unequal socioeconomic opportunities for women. As a strategy, increasing a country's fertility rate also has the significant disadvantage of requiring a substantial period of time before it generates population growth, especially that of working-age persons.[9] Stated more prosaically, inducing women to have more children is difficult, requiring, at a minimum, affordable child care options that permit women to work. If women were to drop out of the labor force to have more children, this would exacerbate the problem of having too few young workers.[10]

One of the most effective ways of bolstering the number of workers is for a country to have more persons who choose to participate in its labor force. Almost everywhere, rates of female participation, despite historic gains in the past three decades, are lower than those of males. Bringing more women into the labor force, therefore, is one of the most viable ways of maintaining the number of available workers.[11] Of course, there are other options—for example, decreasing the unemployment rate of the youngest workers; increasing labor participation by the elderly; or increasing the retirement age of the elderly, who are living longer, healthier lives, an option that is mentioned most often. Alternatively, the number of full-time workhours could be increased, capital investment and new technologies could improve workers' productivity, or everyone could simply accept a lower standard of living.[12] A combination of the above factors can expand the size of the current labor force significantly or offset demand. In many European countries, even modest increases in the number of immigrants could play a significant role in offsetting the effects of an aging population if the labor force were first expanded by increasing the low participation rates and encouraging early retirement.[13] Indeed, as figure 3.4 shows, greater proportions of elderly Canadians already appear to be remaining in the labor force; this trend could continue.

All the approaches discussed thus far focus on numbers only—for example, more immigrants or more births, or more women or more elderly in the labor force, and so forth. But immigrants can spur economic growth in several ways, and a bigger economy can itself offset many of the productivity and financial problems created by the aging of a country's population. Other economic analyses focus on maintaining a certain level of growth of the per capita gross domestic product (GDP) rather than maintaining a certain population size or ratio. At the same time, a declining workforce may not be a problem if the fewer

Figure 3.4. Age of Retirement in Canada, 1976–2004

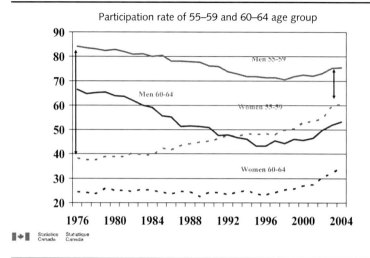

Source: Pamela White, director of demography, Statistics Canada, "Aging: Canada's Demographic
Challenge in the Twenty-first Century," roundtable presentation, North American Future, 2025,
Project, Center for Strategic and International Studies, Washington, D.C., March 23, 2007.

people who are working are more productive, increase overall earnings and taxes, and generate more government revenue that will fund
retirement systems. In addition, nondemographic factors have to be
examined, such as demand differences across sectors, the mobility and
flexibility of the domestic and foreign labor force, the impact of new
technological advances, and the globalization of markets (including
international labor markets). In other words, analysts need to take into
account the impact that immigrants may have on a country's economy;
even though highly skilled immigrants are generally seen as having a
positive economic impact, there is some disagreement on this issue.

A study group of eminent social scientists assembled by the U.S. National Academy of Sciences in 1997 came to the following conclusions:

- Immigrants pay more in taxes at the federal level than they receive in federal benefits.

- Immigrants, especially unauthorized residents, cost more to
  states and localities than they pay in taxes.

- Immigrants with low-level skills depress the wages of low-skilled
  domestic workers.

But these experts also found that immigrants generate a small but positive boost to the country's gross national product by generating increased returns on capital that are greater than their adverse impact on wages.[14] However, a recent trade-based model finds that immigrants reduce the gross national product by a small amount.[15] And even the fairly standard consensus that immigrants with low-level skills reduce the wages of low-skilled native workers has recently been looked at from another angle. It may also be that, by taking low-paying jobs, immigrants place native workers in the position of weighing their opportunity costs and pursuing more education, which, in turn, could generate more human capital and productivity growth.[16] Most economists agree that the economic contribution of immigrants depends on their skill levels; thus, low-skilled immigrants may reduce the wages of low-skilled native workers, even while boosting the wage of "complementary" highly skilled native workers.[17] At the same time, well-educated individuals are thought to boost productivity and highly skilled immigrants are often seen as a particular boon to the economy.

Another position is evident in the economic geography literature, which suggests that innovation thrives when human capital is agglomerated in areas with many specialists and skilled migrants. One can point to the fact that the booming "new economy" of the late 1990s in the United States was fueled by historic productivity gains, one-third of which came from the field of information technology and, in turn, foreign workers fueled one-quarter of the growth in the labor force engaged in this field.[18] It should also be noted that immigrants started about one-third of Silicon Valley's high-tech startup businesses.[19]

At least one study attempts to capture some of the complexity involved in the economic attributes of immigrants and their impact on the fiscal burden and capital shortages of aging societies.[20] The study begins with a global model that includes the United States, Europe, and Japan and assumes twice the level of just low-skilled and just high-skilled immigrants. Because immigrants bring and accumulate capital, they contribute to productivity growth in the model and, to play out this insight, the researchers estimate the impact of doubling the number of elderly well-to-do immigrants. The major projected impact comes through a doubling of the number of high-skilled immigrants into the United States with favorable spillovers to other industrial nations. Indeed, the transfer of public goods and social costs that comes with low-skilled immigrants can even have adverse effects. Only the migration of highly skilled workers has a meaningful and favorable impact in this model, although the authors question whether or not the doubling that they build into the model would be politically palatable.

Nevertheless, given the right circumstances, it is not difficult to imagine that the number of skilled workers admitted into the country could increase significantly. Furthermore, a significant portion of skilled immigrants comes through family-based admissions, and there are policies that might increase the number of highly skilled immigrants entering this way.[21] Furthermore, the skill level of immigrants coming to the United States has been increasing over the past couple of decades, and that trend is likely to continue. What is more, the number of temporary highly skilled immigrants who are working in the United States has grown remarkably in the past decade. Temporary workers have the additional advantage of not needing to draw on financial assistance from the government, primarily because most of these workers are single and young and they leave the country after working for a few years.[22] In light of these circumstances, doubling the number of skilled immigrants might not be as difficult to achieve as it might otherwise be assumed.

In short, population trends in Canada and the United States will probably generate a demand for workers that cannot be met domestically. International migrants are likely to make up the slack. Nevertheless, it is equally clear that the number of migrants required to make up for the loss of young workers relative to older persons is far beyond what most observers would consider reasonable. What is more, domestic responses in the form of labor force participation rates and new technologies, for example, could themselves reduce the apparent need for growing numbers of foreign workers. Therefore, it is difficult to predict how many international workers will be *needed,* because the strength of domestic adjustments is not yet known and may be susceptible to changes in policy. It is certain, however, that there *will be* a large supply of international migrants because of the vacuum in the labor market in the future as well as past trends that suggest that powerful forces are driving international migration.

CHALLENGES FOR IMMIGRATION POLICY

If immigration numbers are unlikely to be high enough to offset the aging of the population and the future decline in the growth of the labor force, immigration could make a more effective contribution to offsetting these trends if it contributes to productivity growth. Here the skill composition of immigrants will make a difference, and admission policies may play an important role in supplying labor markets with workers who have the right mix of skills in the right geographic settings. A shared challenge for both nations will be to design an admission system that efficiently selects immigrants to supply the evolving needs of the labor force.

On the surface, Canada and the United States have very different policies for admitting immigrants, and the two countries certainly face different challenges. The centerpiece of Canada's immigration policy is its points-based selection process, which is designed to admit immigrants with the right skill sets, particularly highly skilled immigrants. In contrast, U.S. immigration policy is heavily based on family ties, and the country also has a large unauthorized workforce; therefore, a large proportion of the migrant population in the United States has little education. In 2000, about 40 percent of the immigrants arriving in Canada and 20 percent of those arriving in the United States had college degrees. It is often presumed that, as a result, Canadian immigrants are a better fit for the economy than U.S. immigrants are.

However, research in both nations finds that immigrants do not perform optimally in the job market. And the presumption that the Canadian and U.S. legal admission systems lead to markedly different outcomes for skilled workers may overstate the case. Canadians are very concerned that their skilled immigrants often fail to find jobs that are commensurate with their skills—that is, they are underemployed—this despite the fact that Canadians have expended considerable effort to award points for language ability, education, and so forth, and to make sure that newcomers receive proper accreditation for their skills in the Canadian labor market. [23] A small body of U.S. research also finds evidence of underemployment even among highly skilled immigrants. At the same time, researchers have found that the only significant difference between the two nations in how much immigrants earn is attributable to the United States' large population of Latino immigrants who draw down average earnings—in other words, differences in labor market outcomes appear not to be strongly correlated with legal admission policies.[24] This finding underscores the fact that the United States has particular problems with unauthorized migration, especially from Mexico and Central America.

Getting admission policies right will remain a difficult challenge, because workers coming from developing nations may not readily integrate into postindustrial economies. Given greater competition among nations that receive a large number of immigrants, it may also be increasingly difficult for North America to attract the best and brightest immigrants. Moreover, if one presumes that developing nations will increasingly offer good jobs, such that potential emigrants may choose to stay at home, it will become even more difficult to tweak existing policies in a way that will attract "ideal" immigrants to North America. Perhaps part of the solution lies in capitalizing on the compatibility and growing integration of the economies in the North American nations and to explore a more efficiently managed system of labor mobility between them.

MEXICAN EMIGRATION: CUMULATING AND DIVERSIFYING
The number of migrants moving between the North American nations has been increasing, but the volume remains relatively small. Mexico is the North American partner that has the largest single source of migrants in the United States. Today, Mexicans make up about 27 percent of the U.S. foreign-born population and Canadians account for another 2.5 percent. A growing number of Mexicans are migrating farther north to Canada, partly in response to being actively sought out,[25] albeit the number of Mexicans in Canada remains rather small. Mexicans make up less than 1 percent of Canada's foreign-born population, whereas U.S. natives make up about another 5 percent.

Thus, Mexican emigration to the United States deserves special consideration because of its magnitude and because the forces driving it are well researched and hold insights to potential migration to Canada. At the end of World War II, only 500,000 Mexicans were living in the United States. However, the mid-1960s marked the passage of more liberal legal immigration policies as well as the end of the *Bracero* temporary agricultural work program—both of which set in motion a growing volume of legal and illegal migration. By 2006, a total of 12 million Mexican-born persons were living in the United States. Thus, between 1970 and 2006, the Mexican- born population of the United States grew an amazing 15-fold—doubling every 8–9 years.

As North America enters the early years of the twenty-first century, there is little doubt that the flow of migrants will continue, but there are questions about the magnitude of the future migration flow, its demographic composition, its "circularity" or transnational ties, immigrants' legal status, and their choice of where to settle. A "residual" estimate of the size of the unauthorized population residing in the United States is made by subtracting the legal immigrant population from the total immigrant population. That method suggests that, as of March 2006, there was a total of 11.5 million unauthorized residents in the United States, 6.5 million of whom were Mexicans, who make up 57 percent of the total immigrant population. Unauthorized residents from elsewhere in Latin America, particularly from Central America, make up another 24 percent of the unauthorized population living in the United States.

The number of Mexican-born residents residing in the United States has been growing as a result of the in-migration of new migrants. During the 1980s, net Mexican migration—combining both legal and illegal immigrants—averaged approximately 250,000 each year. By the early 1990s, estimates suggested a larger flow of 370,000 a year;[26] by the late 1990s, net Mexican migration exceeded an average of 500,000 per year. Indeed, it is estimated that, between the late 1990s and the present, at least 80 percent of all Mexican migrants were unauthorized.[27]

Many factors are responsible for the rapid increase in Mexican migration into the United States during the late 1990s. One major reason, generally agreed upon by all observers, is the legalization of some 2 million Mexicans in 1987–1988. The new legal status of these formerly unauthorized persons enabled them, in turn, to spur further migration by sponsoring family members and hosting others. Another reason for the increase is the lack of any meaningful worksite enforcement of hiring limitations and new methods of border enforcement that simply routed migrants to new entry routes.

Figure 3.5 shows that the most obvious reason for the migration surge, however, was the booming U.S. economy. Both Mexican migration and the "new economy" really took off in the latter part of the 1990s, as records for economic growth were surpassed through the first year of the twenty-first century. All Mexican employment indicators took off as well, causing U.S. unemployment rates to plummet, employment ratios to increase, and wage gains to reach historic highs. The age-old story of supply and demand worked exceedingly well during this time. In fact, as the data in the figure clearly show, trends in the flow of incoming Mexican migrants correlate very well with the growth in the U.S. economy and the U.S. national rate of employment.

Figure 3.5. Annual Average Migration of Mexicans to the United States and the Rate of Employment in the United States, 1991–2005

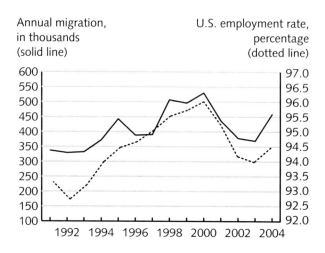

Source: B. Lindsay Lowell, Carla Perderzini, and Jeffrey Passel, "The Demography of Mexico/U.S. Migration," in *Mexico-U.S. Migration Management: A Binational Approach,* ed. Agustin Escobar and Susan Martin (Mexico City: CIESAS-Occidente, forthcoming).

The future trend of Mexican migration is of great interest to all stakeholders in Mexico and the United States. Will Mexican migration continue at high levels over the coming years, or will forces come into play that will moderate future migration? Some social scientists believe that Mexican migration is driven by powerful social forces that have cumulated over time and will not readily dissipate, and that, in the medium to long term, it is likely that levels of migration will continue to be high.[28] However, as the United States experienced in the late 1990s, Mexican migration is responsive to economic forces, and most observers hold to the belief that, like all other historical instances of mass migration, future Mexican migration will ultimately slow down. According to this scenario, the growth of the Mexican population will continue to slow in the wake of dropping fertility rates, and, at some point, Mexico's economic development will generate enough jobs to keep job seekers at home.[29] Indeed, Mexico's total fertility rate is less than one-third of what it was in 1960, dropping from about 7 children born per woman to about 2.4—or just above the replacement level.[30] At the same time, Mexico's economy in the immediate years following the implementation of NAFTA in 1994 grew strongly and appears to be poised to do so again.

In fact, official projections of net migration from Mexico all agree that the trend will be declining; these include forecasts made by the U.S. Census Bureau, Mexico's premier statistical agency, and the United Nations. The Mexican projections are model-based, that is, they predict future emigration rates based on known associations with forecasted demographic and economic variables. The projections made by both the United States and the United Nations are based simply on an assumption that the number of emigrants will decline; this last round of projections explicitly assumes a declining rate of Mexican emigration, with the greatest reduction in rates expected to occur in the second decade of the century. However, it is quite likely that these assumptions will be revised in the next round of projections, because recent trends suggest ongoing high levels of immigration. Increasingly, observers are less sanguine about the possibility that international labor mobility will temporize and are more likely to believe that several factors will reinforce current levels of Mexican emigration.

Factors Driving Future Emigration

The new strategy for enforcing U.S. borders, which began in 1994, has had marked effects on cross-border movement, even though the strategy does not seem to have deterred migrants. In addition, as shown in figure 3.6, in the past, Mexicans have tended to emigrate to the United States for temporary stays. However, because increased enforcement has made crossing the border more difficult and dangerous, many migrants who previously may have moved back to Mexico now choose to stay in the United States for longer periods after making it across the border. Hence, the increase in the immigrant population in the late 1990s partly reflects not new migration but, rather, more emigrants remaining in the United States on a permanent basis. Nevertheless, decreases in return migration are primarily attributable to increases in urban employment of migrants in year-round and permanent jobs as well as to the growth of Mexican communities in the United States. (For example, in 2000, Los Angeles alone had 1.5 million Mexican-born residents—double the number living there at the start of the decade.[31])

For the past century, most Mexican migration has originated in a few rural communities in central Mexico and has gone to well-known locations in Texas, California, or Chicago. Both the origins and the

Figure 3.6. Annual Flow of Mexicans to the United States and Average Length of Stay, 1993–2005

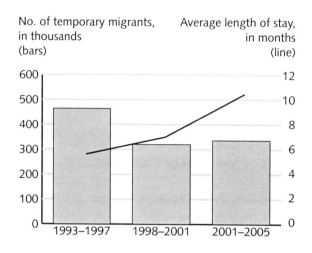

Source: Elena Zúñiga Herrera, "Demographic And Labor Force Projections:The Case of Mexico" (presentation to the Center for Strategic and International Studies, Washington, D.C., March 23, 2007.

Note: Data are for Mexicans who are not U.S. persons or legal immigrants.

destinations of Mexican migrants have become more varied over the past one or two decades, however. The greatest shift in settlement of Mexican immigrants has been away from the traditional location in which they were concentrated—California—where, in 1990, 58 percent of Mexican migrants could be found. In spite of growing numbers of Mexican immigrants living in California, only 38 percent of all Mexican residents in the United States were living there in 2006. Moreover, there has been extraordinarily large growth of the population residing in all states other than the four traditional states in which Mexicans settled, with the share of Mexican immigrants in these newly settled areas increasing from 12 percent in 1990 to 31 percent in 2006. This new settlement pattern has a self-perpetuating aspect: the greater dispersion of Mexican migration means that there are more locations where employers can hire Mexican labor, more contacts for Mexican migration networks, and more places where Mexican families can put down roots.

Coupled with the emergence of new settlement areas in the United States has been a dispersal of the origins of migration from new states within Mexico. However, the trend toward new origins in Mexico has not been as dramatic as the one seen in new destinations in the United States. Although the share of Mexican migrants coming from states in southern and southeastern Mexico has remained relatively small, the number of migrants from these areas has increased—from 9 percent to 13 percent—over the past 15 years. Many observers believe that there is an emerging trend of Mexicans migrating from new origins—they are coming from new, often southern states—and other evidence suggests a growing number of migrants from urban centers as compared with those from rural areas.[32] This trend bears watching and suggests that a widening of the potential pool could supply more migrants either in conjunction with or in addition to existing traditional sources.

NAFTA and Future Migration Scenarios

The North American Free Trade Agreement, which the three nations signed in 1993 and went into effect the following year, primarily covers the movement of goods across borders and cooperation at the borders. Even though the passage of NAFTA by the U.S. Congress was motivated primarily by the promise that the agreement would reduce northward migration from Mexico, NAFTA includes few mechanisms to manage or to reduce migration. The "NAFTA visa" facilitates temporary movement of highly skilled persons between the three nations, and about 60,000 Canadians and 5,000 Mexicans avail themselves of this visa. A substantial number of Canadians have taken advantage of this visa, whereas the opportunity has barely made a dent in the large inflow of Mexican migrants. At the same time, those who successfully advocated NAFTA as a curb on migration relied solely on free trade to boost Mexico's economic development, but they ultimately provided no investments or other mechanisms to foster such development.

Indeed, it is evident that NAFTA has not curbed migration substantially and may have even increased it somewhat. The empirical data clearly show that post-NAFTA emigration has increased to high levels that were not anticipated in the early 1990s, even if NAFTA had not been enacted. Most all analysts concur that any curbing impact of NAFTA will only occur if its job-generating impacts coincide with a reduction in the size of the coming-of-age labor force and other factors. In fact, NAFTA certainly stimulated some additional emigration because, for example, the price of corn imported by the United States plummeted, undermining Mexico's market and subsistence corn farmers.

In addition, NAFTA introduced the notion of a "migration hump," which refers to a period during which rapid economic growth destabilizes traditional economic activities and therefore releases labor, adding to the pool of potential emigrants. Over the longer run, it is likely that marketplaces will adjust, generating new industries and jobs that absorb labor, but when that will occur is uncertain. There is even a theoretical possibility that freer NAFTA-related trade boosts freer migration.

Even though NAFTA has not had a substantial impact on either lowering or increasing migration thus far, the impact of trade policies and other national policies can affect future migration. A team of researchers led by social scientists from the University of California at Los Angeles has conducted a number of exercises that give an idea of how national policies might affect future migration.[33] Their model notes that immigration and trade interact in several important ways:

- The presence or absence of immigrants in a country has an impact on the relative price of goods and thus trade flows.

- Openness to trade affects wage levels and thus incentives to immigrate.

- Immigrant workers' financial remittances have an impact on a country's balance of payments and thus trade flows.

- Remittances further fuel investment and growth in regions from which migrants come, thus affecting wages, prices, trade, and migration.

These researchers' model includes three types of policy scenarios: (1) a change in migration policy, with a direct impact on migration and indirect impacts on trade; (2) a change in trade policy, with a direct impact on trade and indirect impacts on migration; and (3) a change in both policies. The model's projections include changes in migration or trade policies, which can be more restrictive or open, and also includes both the U.S. and Canadian policies in the mix of impacts on Mexican emigration. An assumption about restrictive migration policy is one that would cause up to 6 million Mexicans to be deported; an open policy would result in either maintenance of the status quo or the legalization of the status of up to 6 million workers who are currently unauthorized. An assumption about trade policy is that it will either shift toward an expansion of preferences within NAFTA for all products or shift toward multilateral trade liberalization of manufactured goods.

Generally speaking and somewhat surprisingly, the results of the model based on policy changes indicate that changes in migration policies have impacts that are an order of magnitude greater than those in scenarios involving changes in trade policies. Therefore, NAFTA studies that ignore labor markets miss the primary driver of integration and the primary source of both gains and conflict. But scenarios that take into account the effect of migration on trade show that this impact can also be large, confirming that a model incorporating both changes is important to understanding either phenomenon.

The model's findings on migration are wide-ranging. At one extreme, the model projects that massive deportations of 4 million workers of Mexican origin would lead to a sharp drop in the GDP of the United States—about 1.2 percent (US$130 billion)—whereas the initial gains Mexico would realize in its GDP from more labor would be balanced against losses in foreign exchange and economic development because of reduced remittances sent from Mexican workers in the United States. At the other extreme, as table 3.1 shows, the legalization of unauthorized migrants might create gains of 0.6 percent in U.S. GDP, with only modest declines in Mexico's GDP of 0.3 percent. In this scenario, migrants themselves are the big winners; wages for other workers in the United States would show modest declines as a result of assumed legislation that would lead to an increase in the immigration of about 350,000 low-skilled workers. This scenario has potential consequences for the country's labor supply, income, and productivity level—all of which generate a total of US$14 billion in the production of capital goods. These outcomes offset one another, but the distribution of the effects among industries is varied; for example industries projected to gain more than US$3 billion are leather, wood, and paper; chemicals, rubber, and plastics; motor vehicles and automobile parts; nonelectric machinery; and construction.

In short, any extreme in policies related to the mobility of Mexican labor can have marked impacts on the economies of both the United States and Mexico; and those impacts are likely to be uneven, with low-skilled workers benefiting or losing more than, say, owners of capital who would also be affected. It is important to note that these modeled assumptions envision changes in the flow of migrants as largely

Table 3.1. Impact of Regularization/Legalization of Migrants' Status on U.S. GDP

	Mexico	Rest of Latin America	U.S.	Canada
Increase in unskilled labor migration to: (in thousands of people)	−100	185		
Change in GDP, in: (percent change from base)	−0.29	−0.09	0.63	0.2
Real Wages for unskilled workers in: (change in dollars)	2	0.5		
Real Wages for skilled workers in: (change in dollars)	79	5		
Remittances from immigrants in U.S. to: (percent change from base)	6.5	7		
Change in trade balance (millions)	−343	−674	−7466	−40

	U.S (native)	U.S. (Mexican migrant)	U.S. (Latin American migrant)
Real Wages for unskilled workers in: (change in dollars)	50	3104	3076
Real wages for skilled workers in: (change in dollars)	84		

Source: Raul Hinojosa Ojeda, Robert McCleery, Fernando De Paolis and Terrie Walmsley, "North American Competitiveness and Labor Market Interdependence," presentation to the Center for Strategic and International Studies, Washington, D.C., March 23, 2007.

determined by active (or inactive) choices of policies related to migration. Trade policies, as already noted, apparently have a much less significant impact on both the flow of future migrants and the future economic growth of Mexico and the United States. Other scenarios that take into account policies combining bilateral policies that have an impact on both trade *and* migration—as well as unilateral policies that independently affect economic growth in either nation—might generate different outcomes that can be more favorable or less favorable.

CONCLUSIONS AND POLICY RECOMMENDATIONS

Even though the literature recognizes that a combination of responses will be needed, social scientists tend to discuss the role of immigration in isolation, rather than as part of a set of solutions to tomorrow's population trends. Immigration offers possible solutions to two problems created by the aging of the Canadian and U.S. populations. In the first place, a dynamic economy demands workers in their most productive ages; as the labor force ages, that demand will be harder to meet. These demands are for highly skilled and knowledgeable workers in the technologically driven sectors of the economy as well as for low-skilled workers in the less glamorous jobs that must be done, particularly those that address the provision of services and the needs of the aging population. Second, with ever fewer young workers paying money into the system and ever more dependents drawing money out, the decades-old pay-as-you-go retirement system will be increasingly unable to make ends meet. As part of a set of policy changes, immigration can help meet the demand for young workers as well as taxpayers, but only if admission policies are structured to address the needs of an aging society.

This chapter summarized the discussion surrounding labor mobility in North America that took place at a roundtable in which leading experts from Canada, Mexico, and the United States participated. The report does not purport to conclusively summarize the research literature on the topic or to offer definitive projections of population growth and labor mobility, because there are no definitive projections of labor mobility and its economic impacts over the long run. Even the workshop participants did not agree on all particulars about historical migration patterns and their relationship to economies—much less the best policies for optimizing the management of future labor mobility. Rather, the participants examined various scenarios and assumptions that policymakers can take into account.

Having made this obvious disclaimer, it should be noted that most researchers and the roundtable participants agree about the value of projections for policy formulation. And most agree in principle on several policy principles regarding the need for better projection methods. In addition, they understand that immigration is part of the toolkit used for addressing aging populations; that Mexican migration—especially unauthorized migration—requires realistic and timely solutions; and that efforts to boost economic development are the best medium- to long-term solution to the challenges North America faces form migration or population growth.

IMPROVING POPULATION PROJECTIONS

Projecting population growth, labor force mobility and demand, and economic outcomes is a notoriously problematic undertaking. Most, if not all, available projections—no matter how complex their details—are little more than extensions of historical trends or best assumptions about future trends. The projected outcomes are subject to unforeseen shocks and unanticipated sea changes in behavior.

Refining projection methods and the accuracy of projections requires constant and iterative research, workshops such as the one summarized in this report, and financial support. This academic call for "more research" has become irksome in many arenas, but projections are one of the most basic inputs to good policymaking. Regular iterations in the execution of projections are, in fact, an integral part of improving their accuracy.

MIGRATION AS A SOLUTION TO SLOW-GROWING AND AGING POPULATIONS

No matter how problematic projections are, all observers agree that population growth will continue to slow substantially in North America and that the aging of each country's population creates serious challenges to its productivity, Social Security system, and labor mobility. Even if the fertility rate were to increase suddenly—despite all trends to the contrary—it would take a couple of decades for those new births to increase the size of the population in the country's labor force that is of working age.

The slowing rate of population growth and the aging of the population will generate a latent demand for international labor mobility—latent because the magnitude of the demand is unknown and could be offset by increases in the retirement age or female labor force participation, to say nothing of unforeseen changes in technology. However, and absent strong changes in such factors, the demand for and number of international migrants are more likely to remain high and could even increase. Therefore, the following recommendations can be proposed:

- Policymakers should not view migration as a magic bullet to the growing relative size of the elderly population and its potential drag on the Social Security system or productivity; migration policy cannot substantively ameliorate the dependency ratio of elderly persons to those of working age. The magnitude of migration required to offset the declining relative size of the working-age population is beyond what is politically feasible and would itself have serious repercussions on a country's economic growth.

- Migration can, nevertheless, be an important policy tool used for addressing future population trends insofar as all projections indicate that immigrants and their children will be the major source of labor force growth in Canada and the United States. Furthermore, the latent demand for migrants will be stronger in some sectors than in others—for example, in rapidly growing high-tech jobs or in those involving care of the elderly. Policies that target sectors with labor shortages can be an effective force for economic growth.

THE SPECIAL CASE OF MEXICAN MIGRATION

The discussions in the workshop that are reported on in this chapter lead to general statements about current and future migration policies but cannot comment on the many details and nuances of those policies. Broad-brush agreements emerged regarding immigration to Canada and the United States; but the sizable level of emigration from Mexico necessitates special consideration:

- Whether or not unauthorized Mexican migration has been driven by migrant networks, failed U.S. policies, disregard of the rule of law, or more prosaically by employer demand, the sheer number of illegal residents creates significant economic inequities and undermines workers' rights.

- Resolving those problems requires policymakers to negotiate their differences so that they can realistically address the existing population and its inevitable growth if controversial policy solutions are not implemented. The problem will only continue to worsen if it is not addressed in the near future.

- Regularization of the status of the existing migrant population, through phased legalization or amnesty earned through a period of work, is a necessary policy solution. Fourteen million U.S. households have at least one illegal resident who will not simply return home even if worksite and border enforcement is enhanced.

- Regularization of the status of the existing population will improve the labor market by evening the playing field between employers and improving the long-run productivity of workers.

- Legal guest worker programs, which were originally designed as a way to enable workers to return to their home countries, can substitute, to some degree, for unauthorized migration. However, the design of guest worker programs must be carefully considered. Some observers believe that long-term stays and automatic rights to permanent residency can make it easier for the worker to contemplate regular returns to Mexico. Other observers believe that those rights would, conversely, foster a growing permanent immigrant population.

- Guest worker programs should be designed to target sectors with cyclical or long-term shortages of domestic labor as well as jobs that are either seasonal or temporary. Otherwise, programs that supply workers for permanent, year-round positions may foster employer dependency and unauthorized employment.

TRADE AND ECONOMIC POLICIES AFFECTING MIGRATION

NAFTA has boosted economic growth and, in the process, has led to an increase in the demand for labor in all three nations on the North American continent. However, the relationship between freer trade and migration in the short run is debatable; clearly, free trade has not reduced emigration from Mexico in the dozen-plus years since NAFTA was enacted. At the same time, enforcement policies at the border and in the interior have not been able to entirely control illegal migration, and it is likely that they will never be able to do so. Therefore, policies need to be enacted that address migration by increasing long-run employment growth.

- Free trade may stimulate migration in the short run or, in the case of Mexico, at least will not reduce migration, but it remains a significant policy for increasing mid- to long-term economic growth, which, in turn, will reduce future migration.

- The United States should invest in Mexico's economic development in order to manage and reduce migration. The NAFTA partnership offers a rationale for increased investments in Mexican infrastructure designed to boost the country's growth and to strengthen its role in the North American economy. Bilateral agreements could trigger such investments and should include steps the Mexican government can take to improve its institutions.

ADVANCING THE DIALOGUE ON LABOR MOBILITY AND NORTH AMERICAN INTEGRATION

Looking beyond NAFTA, the topic of labor mobility acquires particular relevance in the global context, where labor mobility and human capital are increasingly central in shaping the competitiveness of nations and regions alike. Of course, any debate of whether or not the North American countries should formally open their borders to the free movement of labor is still pending. The three nations are a long way from the level of integration that preceded the freeing of labor mobility in the European Union. Neither is the political discourse remotely open to the possibility of that level of integration by the year 2025.

Nevertheless, ongoing North American integration raises many possibilities for the future of labor mobility. First, the role of labor mobility in the future of North America cannot be fully understood without acknowledging the complex linkages that exist between labor mobility and the movement of goods and capital. It is important to know more about how these flows contribute or do not contribute to economic growth and development and thereby foster regional integration and competitiveness. Research on these topics, as described above, surely needs to continue and should also address new possibilities. For example, several questions should be answered:

- Does the aging of the population offer particular opportunities for Mexican migration to contribute positively to the U.S. or Canadian labor force?

- Do Mexican workers make contributions to the demand for services generated by an elderly population?

- Which jobs in Canada and the United States are likely to generate the greatest demand?

- What would it take in terms of human capital investment and skill development for Mexican workers to actually be able to replace retiring baby boomers in the United States and Canada?

- Is Mexico prepared to provide the right supply of labor to fill these gaps?

The aging of populations in Canada and the United States may even prompt less migration if the three North American countries decide to implement effective investment policies in order to profit from Mexico's "demographic dividend." It would be helpful to have the answer to two questions: (1) Are there any policies that could result in Mexicans providing services to U.S. and Canadian citizens from their own home country instead of migrating to the north? (2) What kind of policies in Mexico could help substitute migration for investments?

The future may also see the increasing movement of people from north to south as a result of older people's search for cheaper health services or a better climate. Perhaps seeing the aging of a population in a context of economic integration and labor market interdependence can help start a discussion about how Canada, Mexico, and the United States could turn their demographic future into a positive dynamic that has benefits for all three countries.

NOTES

1. Conference Board of Canada, *Canadian Outlook, Long-Term Forecast 2007: Economic Forecast* (Ottawa, 2007).

2. Ibid.

3. Jeffrey S. Passel, "U.S. Population and Labor Force, 2025: Two Projections of the Future of North American Labor Mobility, 2025," Pew Hispanic Center, Washington, D.C., 2007, Presentation to the Labor Mobility Roundtable, Future of North America, 2025, Project, Center for Strategic and International Studies, Washington, D.C., 2007

4. United Nations, Population Division, *Replacement Migration: Is It a Solution to Declining and Aging Populations?* (New York, 2001), http://www.un.org/esa/population/publications/migration/migration.htm.

5. Ibid., p. 4.

6. Serge Feld, "Active Population Growth and Immigration Hypotheses in Western Europe," *European Journal of Population* 16, no. 1 (2000): 3–40; Axel Boersch-Supan, "Labor Market Effects of Population Aging," Working Paper 8640, National Bureau of Economic Research, Cambridge, Mass., 2001; D.A. Coleman, "'Replacement Migration,' or Why Everyone's Going to Have to Live in Korea: A Fable for Our Times from the United Nations," Department of Social Policy and Social Work, University of Oxford, Oxford, England, 2001, http://www.apsoc.ox.ac.uk/Oxpop/wp03.pdf.

7. Roderic Beaujot, "Effect of Immigration on the Canadian Population: Replacement Migration?" Discussion Paper No. 03-03, Population Studies Centre, University of Western Ontario, London, Canada, 2003, http://www.ssc.uwo.ca/sociology/popstudies/dp/dp03-03.pdf.

8. Conversely, in terms of dependency ratios, declining fertility means fewer children to educate, which, in turn, frees up resources to care for the elderly (see Virginia Deane Abernethy, "Comment on Bermingham's Summary of the UN's Year 2000 Replacement Migration: Is It a Solution to Declining Population and Aging?" *Population and Environment* 22, no. 4 [2001]: 365–375). Along these lines, it is pointed out that immigrants' children increase the current and future school-aged population (see Frederick A.B. Meyerson, "Replacement Migration: A Questionable Tactic for Delaying the Inevitable Effects of Fertility Transition," *Population and Environment* 22, no. 4 [2001]: 401–409).

9. John R. Bermingham, "Immigration: Not a Solution to Problems of Population Decline and Aging," *Population and Environment* 22, no. 4 (2001): 355–363.

10. Jonathan Grant et al., *Low Fertility and Population Aging: Causes, Consequences and Policy Options* (Santa Monica, Calif.: RAND Corporation, 2004). Only France has had much luck with pronatalist policies and those designed to increase the fertility rates; however, the complexities involved in making such policies work have thus far not generated French fertility rates that meet replacement rates.

11. Peter McDonald and Rebecca Kippen, "Labor Supply Prospects in 16 Developed Countries, 2000–2050," *Population and Development Review* 27, no. 1 (March 2001): 1–32.

12. Michael Cichon, Florian Léger, and Rüdiger Knopp, "White or Prosperous: How Much Migration Does the Ageing European Union Need to Maintain Its Standard of Living in the Twenty-First Century?" Prepared for the Fourth International Research Conference on Social Security, "Social Security in a Long Life Society," Antwerp, May 5–7, 2003.

13. Generally speaking, most European nations are, like Canada or the United States, unlikely to experience significant declines in the working-age population through about 2020 (see Feld, "Active Population Growth and

Immigration Hypotheses"). This makes labor force participation policies even more fundamental and makes it clear that the role immigration role becomes more critical in the years beyond 2020.

14. James P. Smith and Barry Edmonston, eds., *The New Americans: Economic, Demographic, and Fiscal Effects of Immigration* (Washington, D.C.: National Research Council, 1997).

15. Donald R. Davis and David E. Weinstein, "Technological Superiority and the Losses from Migration," Working Paper 8971, National Bureau of Economic Research, Cambridge, Mass., 2002.

16. Manon Domingues Dos Santos, "Is the Unskilled Workers Immigration Necessarily Harmful for the Unskilled Natives?" EPEE-Université d'Evry Val d'Essonne and CREST-INSEE, 2000, http://www.crest.fr/pageperso/lma/manondds/manondds.htm.

17. George J. Borjas, "The Labor Demand Curve Is Downward Sloping: Reexamining the Impact of Immigration on the Labor Market," *Quarterly Journal of Economics* 118, no. 44 (2003): 1335–1374.

18. B. Lindsay Lowell, "The Foreign Temporary (H-1b) Workforce and Shortages in Information Technology," in *The International Migration of the Highly Skilled: Demand, Supply, and Development Consequences in Sending and Receiving Countries,* ed. Wayne Cornelius (San Diego: University of California, 2000), pp. 131–162.

19. AnnaLee Saxenian, *Local and Global Networks of Immigrant Professional in Silicon Valley* (San Francisco: Public Policy Institute of California, 2002).

20. Hans Fehr, Sabine Jokisch, and Laurence Kotlikoff, "The Role of Immigration in Dealing with the Developed World's Demographic Transition," Working Paper 10512, National Bureau of Economic Research, Cambridge, Mass., 2004.

21. See the recommendations made by the U.S. Commission on Immigration Reform, *Legal Immigration: Setting Priorities* (Washington, D.C., 1995).

22. Nevertheless, temporary workers may draw Social Security upon retirement abroad, depending on whether or not they paid into the system and whether or not there are bilateral agreements to facilitate payments. For an initial estimate of the tax consequences of temporary workers, see Davesh Kapur and John McHale, *The Global War for Talent: Implications and Policy Responses for Developing Countries* (Washington D.C.: Institute for International Economics/Center for Global Development, 2003).

23. Jeffrey G. Reitz, "Immigrant Employment Success in Canada, Part II: Understanding the Decline," *Journal of International Migration and Integration* (2007).

24. Heather Antecol, Deborah A. Cobb Clark, and Stephen J. Trejo, "Immigration Policy and the Skills of Immigrants to Australia, Canada, and the United States," McMaster University, Ontario, April 1999.

25. Chris Hawley, "Canada Is Wooing Mexican Immigrants," *The Arizona Republic*, Mexico City Bureau, May 3, 2005.

26. The estimates through 2004 are taken from Elena Zúñiga and Paula Leite, "Estimaciones de CONAPO con base en INEGI, Encuesta Nacional de la Dinámica Demográfica (ENADID), 1992 y 1997 y Encuesta Nacional de Empleo (ENE) Módulo Sobre Migración, 2002," Mexico City, 2004; and these are, in turn, taken from U.S. database estimates made by the Binational Study Group, *Binational Study: Migration Between Mexico and the United States* (Washington D.C.: U.S. Commission on Immigration Reform, 1997), http://www.utexas.edu/ lbj/uscir/binational.html. The estimate for the latter 1990s is made by CONAPO, Mexico's lead statistical agency.

27. Jeffrey Passel, "Unauthorized Migrants: Numbers and Characteristics," Report of the Pew Hispanic Center, at http://pewhispanic.org/files/reports/46.pdf, 2007.

28. Douglas S. Massey and Rene Zenteno, "The Dynamics of Mass Migration," *Proceedings of the National Academy of Sciences* 96, no. 8 (1999): 5325–5335.

29. Binational Study Group, *Binational Study*.

30. Total fertility rates represent the average lifetime fertility of a woman. A replacement level for total fertility rates is about 2.05–2.1.

31. One researcher notes that some 400,000 long-term residents of Los Angeles left during the 1990s (pre-1990 arrivals from all countries, not just Mexico). Despite the significant growth of the Mexican population, he characterizes Los Angeles as an "ebbing gateway" city, which means some lessening of poverty and increasing homeownership for the average foreign-born resident (see Dowell Myers, "The Impact of Ebbing Immigration in Los Angeles: New Insights from an Established Gateway," Paper presented to the Population Association of America, Philadelphia, April 2005).

32. Binational Study Group, *Binational Study*.

33. Raul Hinojosa Ojeda, Robert McCleery, and Terrie Walmsley, "North American Competitiveness and Labor Market Interdependence," Roundtable Presentation, North American Future, 2025, Project, Center for Strategic and International Studies, Washington, D.C., 2007.

4

OUTLOOK FOR COMPETITIVENESS

SIDNEY WEINTRAUB

This chapter focuses on policies to promote competitiveness in Mexico, Canada, and the United States as well as in North America as a whole. Defining competitiveness at the national level requires examining overall and sectoral productivity and productivity growth in the three countries and comparing these data with what is taking place in other countries. In addition to data on productivity, it is necessary to compile and examine comparative data on technological innovation, the ability to attract foreign direct investment, the training and quality of human resources, appropriateness of exchange rates, and trade outcomes. The analysis requires a close look at macroeconomic policies (budgets, balance of payments, and monetary matters) and structural issues (the educational system, labor markets, the justice system, the tax structure, and others); the strength of national institutions; the effectiveness of antimonopoly policies; and the ability of the governance structure to make timely changes that upgrade the nation's competitiveness. The comparative positions in key sectors—such as communications, transportation, and finance—are highly relevant to this analysis.

Assessing competitiveness in the predominantly market systems that dominate economic activity in North America also requires examining how different business entities in the same sectors fare in the regional and global marketplace. Some companies in comparable situations succeed under national policies that are in place; other companies do not. Antimonopoly practices, by definition, are significant factors that can foster or impede competitiveness.

This chapter will present recent (from 1990 forward) economic trends in comparative quantitative form for the three countries of North America. The economic issues that will be covered are productivity, budgets, balance of payments, investment, and trade. The comparative data point out the challenges each country will face in upgrading these competitive indicators not only for regional comparisons but also as an indication of the global challenges that will need to be confronted.

The discussion of challenges—relatively low productivity growth, large current account deficits, structural shortcomings, and others— will be set forth by focusing on governance rigidities that impede corrective action. This report will offer projections about the global competitive situations the three countries will face in 2025. Data on competitive accomplishments in the recent past are useful because they provide indicative guidance about likely future governance patterns in the three countries.

It is also important to look at challenges to deepening the structure of North American integration. Many regional problems are related to transportation issues, such as delays in bringing merchandise across borders because of heightened security concerns and the inability thus far to work out a single trucking system to be used throughout North America. Delays at the border impede the establishment of effective just-in-time inventory systems for production that is shared in several countries within North America, especially between Mexico and the United States. Checking the security clearance of containers when they reach ports may slow the speed of delivering the merchandise inside. Accreditation problems accompany the delivery of many professional services from one country to another in North America. Canada and the United States have integrated electricity delivery systems, but a comparable system between Mexico and the United States is largely lacking. These are just some examples of the need for a more competitive integration of North America.

The variables chosen for detailed examination in this report are critical to the analysis of North American competitiveness. Other chapters in this overall report of the North American Future, 2025, project cover other important variables—namely, energy, the environment, labor mobility, infrastructure, and security. Because a separate report on demographic trends was not commissioned for this project, these will be noted in the discussion that follows.

COMPETITIVENESS DATA FOR NORTH AMERICAN COUNTRIES

The graphs in the appendix to this chapter provide background on competitiveness indicators as they have manifested themselves since 1990 in the three countries that make up North America.

Figure 4.1 shows comparative annual labor productivity growth in the three countries since 1990. The data shown for Mexico show dramatic shifts rather than gradual changes from one year to the next; apparently these data are deeply affected by annual changes in Mexico's gross domestic product (GDP). Figure 4.1 shows that, between 2001 and 2004, the United States had higher productivity growth than Canada did, but in 2005 U.S. productivity declined, whereas Canada's rose. Indeed, in 2005, Canada's productivity growth was higher than that of the United States. It is hard to predict if the lower recent productivity growth in the United States will be durable or if it can be explained by what is expected to take place after a long period of economic growth begins to show signs of slowing down. It is also difficult to determine whether the recent increase in productivity growth in Canada is an indication of the start of new overall economic growth, with plants beginning to operate at full, or nearly full, capacity.

Figures 4.2, 4.3, and 4.4 show productivity growth in manufacturing in the three countries. Figure 4.4, which presents the U.S. data, is interesting because it shows clearly that, even with a slightly declining labor force, manufacturing output has increased since 1990. In Canada and Mexico, the labor used for manufacturing grew essentially at the same rate as the real output of manufacturing. Figure 4.5 shows productivity growth in the service sector in the three countries since 1990. Over the entire period, productivity growth in the United States has been consistently higher than the growth in Canada. However, the productivity growth figures for Mexico are much like those for productivity growth in manufacturing and largely coincide with annual changes in GDP; therefore, the figures may not be reliable.

Figure 4.6 shows that the U.S. budget moved from a large deficit in 1990, to a surplus in 1997, to a deficit again in 2002, and then to a diminution of the deficit in 2005 and 2006. By contrast, the Canadian budget deficit was erased in 1997, and the surplus has increased since then. The Mexican budget deficit has been reasonably modest and constant since about 1997.

Figure 4.7 shows great disparities in the current account balances of the three countries over most of the period since 1990. The current account balance of the United States has deteriorated consistently since 1991, with the deficit reaching more than 6 percent of GDP in 2005. Canada's current account balance has shifted over the selected time period but shows a surplus since 1999. Mexico's account balance showed a deficit of 7 percent of GDP in 1995, improved remarkably in 1996, then suffered another decline after 1997; since 2005, Mexico has been running a modest deficit of less than 1 percent of GDP. The trade provisions included in the North American Free Trade Agreement (NAFTA), which came into effect on January 1, 1994, appear to have had an impact on Mexico's account balance: Mexico faced a severe financial crisis at the end of that year, suffered through a severe depression in 1995, and recovered in 1996.

Figures 4.8, 4.9, and 4.10 show the export performance of the three countries from 1990 through 2006. The data are clear: all three countries show upward trends in their nominal exports throughout the period. The United States has had a larger decline in annual exports than Mexico or Canada has, both of which show an upward trend. The downturns for Mexico and Canada correspond to years of relatively lower GDP growth in the United States.

Figures 4.11, 4.12, and 4.13 show exports of the three countries by destination in 2006. The fact that 82 percent of Canada's exports and 77 percent of Mexico's exports that year went to the United States makes it evident why U.S. economic growth is critical for its two NAFTA partners. Both Mexico's and Canada's substantial reliance on the U.S. market has long been a fact of life; indeed, Mexico's dependence on the U.S. market for 77 percent of its exports in 2006 is relatively low. A key reason for the modest decline in the percentage of Mexican exports to the United States that year was the increase in Mexico's exports to Canada—a trend that has been more dynamic since NAFTA went into effect than the percentage of Canada's exports to Mexico.[1]

Figures 4.14, 4.15, and 4.16 show absolute levels of foreign direct investment (FDI) into Canada, Mexico, and the United States, respectively, from 1990 through 2005; the three graphs also show the three countries' growing stock of FDI. The value scales on the vertical axes of the three graphs differ. The increase in FDI inflows into Mexico shows the marked increase that took place after 1994; attracting these increased flows was an important incentive for Mexico to sign NAFTA.

Figure 4.17 shows FDI inflows into the three countries between 1992 and 1996 as a percentage of each country's GDP. This presentation shows markedly different performances than the graphs based on absolute levels of inward FDI into the three countries. The best performance of FDI inflows in relation to GDP over this period has been in Mexico, followed by Canada, with the United States last. FDI performance according to this measurement is precisely the reverse of performance using absolute dollar levels of FDI inflows. Mexico has been an attractive destination for foreign investors—who come mainly from the United States—since the implementation of NAFTA. Foreign investors have demonstrated that they are confident that Mexico's solid financial policies during the past 15 years will continue in the future.

The foregoing competitive indicators show data for the three countries that are geographically part of North America, but it is difficult to make direct comparisons among the three. Mexico compares better in terms of global competitiveness with other large emerging countries, such as Brazil, Russia, India, China, and South Africa. Mexico's performance on this score will be taken into account later in this chapter.

The United States is an advanced industrial country, and the size of its economy makes it unique in North America. Canada can be compared with other countries that are members of the Organization for Economic Cooperation and Development (OECD), but Canada's GDP is roughly 10 percent the size of that of the United States. This 10:1 ratio should be kept in mind when comparisons are made between the two countries.

Nevertheless, comparisons can be made among the three countries for the variables highlighted in this report. A summary of these comparisons is presented in the concluding section. The central variable is productivity—that is, getting the most from the labor force and other factors used in production processes. Without trying to define precisely what policies contribute what portion of increases in productivity, we do know that productivity depends on the skills of the country's labor force and the government's ability to adapt investment and trade policies to meet the challenges of the global economy. The nation's fiscal framework, monetary policies, and regulatory structures influence the willingness of both domestic and foreign investors to risk their resources in a given country. Along with year-by-year macroeconomic policies, sectoral policies (such as those related to education, employment, monopolies, and the justice system) play an important role in fostering or hindering growth and equality in a country. National institutions—their efficiency and adaptability or rigidity—play a substantial role in either attracting or repelling investors. All these variables influence a nation's productivity; they are all noted, when appropriate, in the discussion of individual countries and regions that follows.

COMPETITIVE CHALLENGES

The North American Future, 2025, project was designed to look ahead to 2025. The undertaking requires examining what challenges to competitiveness each of the three countries faces and then providing an assessment of the extent to which these challenges will be addressed.

CANADA

Canada has undergone considerable self-reflection in recent years about its competitive position both with respect to the United States (keeping in the mind the 10:1 ratio) and with comparable high-income OECD member countries. It is necessary to first present some assessments of Canada's competitiveness vis-à-vis the United States. The growth in the number of Canadian exports to the United States was substantial following the negotiation of the Canada-U.S. Free Trade Agreement (CUSFTA) that went into effect in 1989, and this growth continued after NAFTA went into effect in 1994. Most of the relevant years for Canada's trade growth under CUSFTA are shown in figure 4.8. It is worth noting that, after 2003, Canada's exports to countries outside North America were proportionately higher than they had been earlier. The Canadian dollar was relatively cheap at the beginning of 2003 (according to the Bank of Canada, the exchange rate was 64 Canadian cents to the U.S. dollar), and this fact surely stimulated Canada's exports. This situation has changed: in September 2007, the Canadian dollar was worth roughly US 95 cents. Canadian productivity must increase to compensate for the stronger Canadian dollar. Large exports to the United States, which account for about 25 percent of Canada's GDP, are crucial for the Canadian economy.

Even taking into account the favorable growth figures for 2004 and 2005, Canadian productivity still lags behind that of the United States (as does the productivity of many OECD countries, as will be shown below). In 2005, Canada's productivity was 105.4 compared with the U.S. index figure of 113.2, both on a base of the year 2000.[2] Consequently, Canada's per capita income is now about 85 percent that of the United States.[3]

One immediate reaction of the United States to the terrorist attacks that took place on September 11, 2001, was to close its border with Canada in order to protect national security. The closure did not last long, but it sent a red alert to Canadian industrialists. One significant consequence of the free trade agreement between Canada and the United States was growth in co-production by firms in the two countries. Many of the firms cooperating across the border are affiliated with one another; one analyst has estimated that about 40 percent of bilateral trade between the United States and Canada today is of items produced by the same firm operating in each of the countries.[4] Consequently, a great deal of the trade between the two countries consists of inputs needed for production as opposed to final completed products. Because of the relative proximity of the firms, coupled with the ability to ship goods back and forth without tariffs or other protective barriers, a sophisticated system of just-in-time delivery of inputs needed for production was developed in order to minimize the cost required for maintaining large inventories. This is especially the case for automotive production, where the distance between Windsor, Ontario, and Detroit, Michigan—where the parts are produced and assembled— makes the trip not much greater than crossing the Friendship Bridge. These arrangements were disturbed when the United States closed its border with Canada, putting into question the reliability of the just-in-time delivery system. One way for producers to overcome the risk of border closure is to move all production to the U.S. side; this has not happened, but it could occur if the border were closed again, which would be costly for Canada and would raise questions about the value of its free trade agreement with the United States.

In January 2007, the Conference Board of Canada issued the final report of what it called the Canada Project, a three-year research exercise entitled "Sustainable Prosperity for Canada: Mission Possible Executive Summary."[5] The report included several recommended steps for improving Canada's performance in the global economy, summarized as follows:

- adoption of a national productivity strategy;

- creation of a single Canadian market;

- improvement of the immigrant selection process in order to address skill shortages;

- revitalization of international investment and trade; and

- increased focus on the foreign policy priorities on the United States, China, and key developing countries.

Much of the analysis in the Canadian study and, hence, the focus of many of its recommendations is the need to strengthen Canada's major cities—or, more precisely, the country's 27 central metropolitan areas. The study zeroes in on 10 of these: Vancouver, Calgary, Edmonton, Regina, Saskatoon, Winnipeg, Toronto, Ottawa-Gatineau, Montreal, and Halifax. These urban centers received attention because, according to the Conference Board of Canada, they are caught in a fiscal pincer from the cost of providing major services that the federal government gradually unloaded on these urban centers and their constrained ability to raise the necessary revenues. The bedrock of the analysis is that these urban centers are the driving force of Canada's economic growth, whereas the central government's approach is to provide funding to provinces and municipalities based on the principle of "equal treatment for all." The report asserts that the "success of hub cities boosts the economic performance of surrounding smaller communities."[6]

A separate study by the Conference Board of Canada—"How Canada Performs: A Report Card on Canada," issued in May 2007—provides considerable detail on the country's problems related to competitiveness.[7] In this report card, Canada is compared with 16 peer OECD member countries in six broad domains, with the following results:[8]

- innovation: Canada is rated fourteenth of the 17 countries and received a grade of D;

- economic performance: Canada ranks eleventh and receives a grade of B;

- environment, Canada ranks fourth and receives a grade of D;

- education and skills: Canada ranks third and receives a grade of A;

- health care: Canada ranks eighth and receives a grade of B; and

- society: Canada ranks tenth and receives a grade of B.

Some of the considerations taken into account in areas that received low grades were the following:

- Canada ranked twelfth in the proportion of graduates with degrees in science and technology;

- Canada is rapidly becoming a country with an aging population and will have to rely increasingly on immigrants to provide needed skills;[9]

- Canada is not meeting its potential in attracting FDI;

- the country's taxation rate of capital is high;

- the country's productivity growth has lagged in relation to its GDP and is below the average growth of all 17 countries that were compared;

- Canada's public and private investment in research and development is relatively low; and

- the country's carbon dioxide emissions per capita are high—fifteenth of the 17 countries (ahead of only the United States and Australia).

Using studies done by the country's official and private institutions, including universities and research institutes, Canada probably merits a grade of A for self-evaluation. The problems impeding its competitive position have been well publicized and are being confronted to a considerable degree. One example of this has been the measures that have been taken to reduce the difference between Canada's GDP per capita and that of the United States. The gap is driven by two factors: differences in the labor productivity of the two countries and the number of hours worked. In the 1990s, the difference in productivity accounted for one-third of the gap in GDP per capita, and the difference in hours worked accounted for two-thirds of the gap. The hours worked in Canada from the mid- to late-1990s were about 88 percent of those in the United States; by 2005, the number of hours worked in Canada reached 94.7 percent of the U.S. level. By then, Canada's lower productivity accounted for two-thirds of the per capita income gap with the United States. As indicated in figure 4.1, Canada's productivity growth was equal to or exceeded that of the United States in 2004 and 2005.[10]

Canada's provinces often have different regulations and purchasing provisions that restrict bidding by companies from other provinces.

Professional associations in the provinces often do not recognize professional credentials from other provinces. Point-to-point trucking within Canada is restricted to Canadian companies, and there are trade barriers between provinces.[11] All these practices impede national competitiveness.

Canada is going through an important change under which economic power is shifting from Ontario, Quebec, and other provinces that rely heavily on manufactured exports for their well-being to those provinces in western Canada that are benefiting from high prices for their commodity exports, especially oil. Alberta, the hub of Canada's oil production, has a population of 3.3 million, whereas Ontario and Quebec together have a population of more than 20 million (12.5 million and 7.6 million, respectively); thus, the trend in export dynamics is shifting from the more highly populated provinces of central Canada to a region that is relatively sparsely populated. This trend could stimulate a profound shift in Canada's governance, depending on how long the economic shift lasts, how deep it becomes, and what corrective actions are taken. Canada is already experiencing demands for greater contributions to the federal budget from the faster-growing provinces (that is, Alberta) in order to achieve something approaching the equal distribution principle of federal allocations in Canada. Canada may be undergoing a version of "Dutch disease"—namely, that receipts from high-priced commodity exports are driving up the value of the Canadian dollar to the detriment of manufactured exports with higher value added.[12] Unless addressed, a structural change of this kind could affect Canada's competitiveness in the years to come.[13]

MEXICO

In Mexico, the growth in GDP per capita has averaged 1.5 percent a year since 1990, based on constant 2000 U.S. dollars.[14] Before assuming the presidency on December 1, 2000, Vicente Fox spoke about creating at least 600,000 jobs a year over his six-year term. In fact, the number of jobs created during Fox's term in office was between 1.2 to 1.3 million.[15] About 60 percent of Mexico's labor force works in the informal sector.[16] With 1980 equal to 100, in 2006, per capita GDP in Mexico was 126, compared with Chile's GDP of 216, South Korea's 431, and China's 857—all in 2006.[17] Growth in productivity in Mexico over the past 45 years has been half of that observed in Chile and a quarter of that seen in South Korea.[18] These three realities—the relatively low growth in income per capita, the inadequate creation of formal jobs, and the inability to increase productivity to any great extent—provide a useful shorthand description of Mexico's substandard economic performance since 1982—a year in which Mexico defaulted on its external debt.[19]

Mexico has had important economic successes in the period since 1980. Perhaps the most significant is the reduction of inflation, which is now running at an annual rate of 3–5 percent. This reduction is the result of Mexico's conservative macroeconomic policy of avoiding large budget deficits, following a cautious monetary policy, and generally allowing the peso to float rather than protecting an overvalued exchange rate vis-à-vis the U.S. dollar by market intervention. The largely fixed exchange-rate policy was the principal reason for Mexico's financial crisis at the end of 1994 and the devastating depression that followed in 1995.[20] The stringency of Mexico's macroeconomic policy is what prompted key U.S. credit agencies to rate Mexican government debt instruments as investment-grade instruments. Confidence that this stringency will continue in the future has also stimulated the relatively high level of foreign direct investment that Mexico has received in recent years; the dramatic increase over 15 years is shown in figure 4.15.

Mexico has also pursued a successful policy to curtail excessive population growth. In 2004, the country's fertility rate was 2.2—just above the replacement rate of 2.1—compared with 7.3 in 1960 and 4.7 in 1980.[21] The decline in the fertility rate starting in the 1960s was the result of conscious policy implemented by the government. Life expectancy in Mexico is now 75 years. In addition, Mexico still has a relatively young population, and the number of children per 100 working-age adults has fallen—from 147 in 1975 to 77 in 2005. The total dependency ratio—that is, the ratio of children plus elders to working-age adults—is now 87 and is projected to decline to 65 in 2030. This trend provides a "demographic dividend" of working-age adults that can be exploited until 2030, when the dependency ratio is expected to start rising. A graph showing the age of the population of Mexico today would have a wide base and a pyramidal form that narrows from the bottom upward. By 2050, based on current projections, a similar graph will look much like that of the United States—largely wide from the top down, reflecting an older population. The demographic dividend is now also showing up in the migration of large numbers of working-age Mexicans to the United States, rather than working at home and increasing national output. The eventual disappearance of the demographic dividend also means that, at some point in the not-too-distant future, the United States will no longer have to be concerned about mass unauthorized emigration from Mexico.

Mexico has managed its macroeconomic policy variables well during the past 10 years, but the same cannot be said about structural issues. The word "structural" refers to underlying systemic issues that transcend year-to-year policies. Correcting deficiencies in structural policies is a highly controversial effort, because some of these policies are rooted in history (such as energy policy); others must overcome deep-seated vested interests (such as labor unions' opposition to altering labor policy or many business leaders' opposition to entrenched monopolies); and still others involve reducing government spending (which is replete with subsidies) or raising more government revenue (which means collecting more taxes). For the most part, structural deficiencies have remained in place over the years, despite a consensus of economists that changes are necessary.

Mexico is a country in which there are great inequalities in the income and wealth of its citizens, and these inequities are not being corrected. Poverty is high, but valuable palliatives are in place, such as the *Oportunidades* program that deals simultaneously with welfare, health, and nutrition issues; rather than "eliminating" poverty, this program "alleviates" some of the consequences of poverty. Mexico has a reputation as a country in which corruption is widespread, and despite each successive presidential administration's promise to deal with the problem, over the years little has changed on this score. In recent years, trade in narcotics has grown, and Mexico is now a producer of many drugs (methamphetamines, marijuana, and opium poppies) as well as the passageway for drugs coming from other countries and destined for the U.S. market. Compounding the problem are the conflicts between drug traffickers over control of the market, which have led to a great deal of unrest and a high murder rate in many parts of Mexico— some of which, such as the area around Monterrey, were previously considered safe—and this situation has prompted the federal government to use military troops to deal with the problem. There is also evidence that drug usage within Mexico has increased.

When the conditions are good, Mexico can reach 4 percent GDP growth, as it has today—sometimes even a bit higher than 4 percent— whereas other countries with emerging economies exceed 6 and 7 percent. In a good year, Mexico may create as many as 400,000 jobs—although job creation at such a substantial level has been rare in recent years—but the country probably needs closer to double that number if the government wants to fully exploit the demographic dividend. Most Mexican migrants to the United States worked in Mexico before deciding to emigrate but usually earned little on the job, worked part-time, or had informal jobs. The issue, therefore, is not just job creation, but creation of jobs that pay reasonably good wages. This problem may become worse in the near future if the United States is able to curtail unauthorized immigration and thereby cut off Mexico's emigration escape valve.

The solution to Mexico's problems related to economic growth and jobs requires many structural changes; it is hard to figure out where to begin. Perhaps the best place to start is education, because correcting deficiencies in the country's educational system takes much time and is a necessary precondition for dealing with other structural problems. Mexico's development plan for 2007–2012, which was produced by the presidential administration, notes that more than 30 percent of persons who are more than 15 years of age never complete primary and secondary school. Persons between the ages of 15 and 24 spend an average of 9.7 years in school; the goal of the development plan is to raise this number to 12.5 years by the end of 2012.[22] The educational system attended to 73 percent of the demand in 2006—an increase from 60 percent in 1992. The biggest deficiencies are in rural and poor areas, where schools show the greatest number of deficiencies. (It should be noted that most of the poverty in Mexico is found in rural areas, and this is a major reason for migration to urban areas within Mexico or out of Mexico and into the United States.) According to the National Development Plan, in 2006, 25 percent of the population was enrolled in higher education institutions, but the plan also notes that this number is much lower than the number enrolled in other OECD countries.[23]

In its reports, Mexico's National Science and Technology Council (CONACYT) has pointed out that Mexico can no longer rely on low wages to be competitive in international markets, including the United States, because other emerging economies, such as China, pay even lower wages than Mexico does. CONACYT's conclusion is that, if Mexico is to be competitive, much more capital must be allocated to Mexico's manufacturing sector, including the assembly plants near the U.S. border (the *maquiladoras*); this step calls for more educated workers.

Mexico's labor laws are rigid in terms of benefits that must be paid to full-time workers, including large payments based on time worked when employees are dismissed from their jobs. In light of these regulations, employers protect themselves by limiting the number of full-time workers they hire and, instead, using prospective employees as independent contractors on a part-time basis. Official unemployment figures for Mexico are low—in the area of 5–6 percent in major cities—but part-time workers are not included in the unemployment figures. The labor statistics are not meaningful; official unemployment is low, but actual employment on a full-time basis is also low. Full-time workers who are members of labor unions benefit from this system, whereas the overall labor force does not. This structure also partially explains the reason a majority of the workforce in Mexican cities is informal. Labor reform will be hard to accomplish. Some are concerned that workers will be exploited under a more flexible system, but there is also a high probability that more full-time jobs can be created under a flexible system than under the rigid structure that is in place. It will be hard to work out a compromise between the current rigid structure and a more flexible approach; therefore, any attempt to change the labor laws would have to involve bargaining between the Mexican government, unions, and employer associations.

Oil, gas, and energy policy in Mexico needs drastic changes. The state-run oil company, Petroleos Mexicanos (PEMEX), has a monopoly on upstream oil exploration and production as well as on retail sales of gasoline and diesel. PEMEX also has a monopoly on exploration and production of natural gas. Two government-owned electricity companies, the Comisión Federal de Electricidad and Luz y Fuerza del Centro, have near monopolies on the generation and distribution of electricity in Mexico. Private equity investment in oil and gas is prohibited in Mexico, and electricity generation by private companies is largely prohibited; private companies that generate their own power can sell any excess power to the two government-owned power companies. Mexico is an importer of natural gas and petroleum products but is still a major exporter of oil. The country's proven reserves are declining rapidly: absent new discoveries, at the current rate of oil production, proven oil reserves can last for only about 10 years.

PEMEX is heavily taxed on its gross revenues in order to provide about one-third of the revenue needed to finance the central government's budget, leaving little for PEMEX's own investment in exploration and production. The central government does try to provide funds for PEMEX operations, but public financing depends on total government receipts in any given year. Government receipts in the past year have increased because of high prices for Mexico's oil exports. Other than this source of funding, PEMEX has to depend on loans to undertake exploration and production, and the company's debt today is quite substantial, making it difficult to get more loans for the time being. PEMEX has had few successes in its exploration in recent years and—to add to the company's problems—oil production at Cantarell, Mexico's largest oil field, has been declining. Permitting private equity investment in oil exploration and production apparently requires a constitutional amendment—something that is not now possible.

There are good prospects for finding oil and gas in the deep waters of the Gulf of Mexico, and U.S. and foreign oil companies are already demonstrating the potential on the U.S. side of the gulf. Drilling in the deep waters of the gulf is costly, however, and PEMEX lacks the funds for this risky investment. Moreover, PEMEX has no experience in deepwater drilling because of its lack of funds. Petrobras, the Brazilian national oil company, has a structure that permits joint ventures with private and other national oil companies and has entered into many of these partnerships, including one for deepwater drilling in the part of the Gulf of Mexico that is controlled by the United States. The price of structural stagnation in Mexico's oil and gas sector could be high. In addition, the inability to generate more electricity could leave Mexican business short on power and could also worsen Mexico's competitive position.[24]

The federal government of Mexico normally collects tax revenue that accounts for about 10–11 percent of GDP but spends about 18 percent of the GDP. The difference is made up mostly from the high taxes imposed on PEMEX's gross revenues. Even in comparison with those of other Latin American countries, Mexico's tax collections are low. (The U.S. federal government's revenue from taxes is about 18 percent of GDP.) The current administration of President Felipe Calderón has proposed tax reforms that would raise federal tax revenues by an estimated 2 percent of GDP and raise state tax collections by an estimated 1 percent of GDP by 2012. The reform has three elements: a business flat tax of 16–19 percent, principally tax on income from sales of goods and services; a 2 percent tax on cash deposits in banks that exceed 20,000 pesos a month, aimed at capturing revenue from persons in the informal job sector; and a 20 percent excise tax on lottery and gambling fees. If the reform is enacted, as is likely, the additional tax collections could ease the tax burden on PEMEX's gross revenues by a modest amount.

Earlier in 2007, President Calderón was successful in his effort to have the Mexican Congress enact legislation to alter the structure of pensions for about 2.8 million active and retired federal workers. The government estimated that, over time, this change would result in a 20 percent savings for the Institute of Social Security for Government Employees. These two pieces of legislation—tax reform and government pension reform—will be discussed further below, because they demonstrate that President Calderón, who is still in the early stage of his six-year administration, is prepared to address complex structural issues.

Mexico suffers from the existence of monopolies that impede competitiveness and from special (subsidized) tax regimes for powerful companies and sectors. Government monopolies in the oil, gas, and electricity sectors have already been noted. The monopolies and oligopolies in the communications sector—fixed-line telephones, cellular telephones, and television—are particularly onerous. President Vicente Fox showed a reluctance to tackle these issues, and the Calderón administration's National Development Plan 2007–2012 is largely silent on this issue.

Finally, there is no equal justice under law in Mexico, nor is the justice system efficient and transparent. These have long been sore points, and there have been repeated promises to correct the problems—but, thus far, there have been more promises than actions. The interplay between the judicial structure and competitiveness is discussed in some detail in a report issued recently by the Executive Council of an organization representing the 28 largest global companies operating in Mexico.[25]

Reaching a conclusion about the state of competitiveness in Mexico in 2025 requires making some judgments and contemplating several questions, including, but not limited to the following:

- Will the current administration address issues left unattended until now?

- Will the government make structural changes to enhance competitiveness as a way to avoid a crisis, say, in the energy field, or will action be taken only after there is a crisis?

- Will Mexico deal with its monopolies and oligopolies or continue to temporize?

One positive sign has been President Calderón's willingness to address some difficult structural issues seriatim—on taxes and government pensions—at a time that he believes is appropriate. Based on some of his actions along these lines—many of which are discussed in his administration's National Development Plan 2007–2012 and were handled with considerable political skill—it is reasonable to conclude that the process will continue. In June 2007, Mexico reached an agreement with the OECD to evaluate the cost and time involved in the legal procedures required for opening a new business and increasing productivity. In addition, CONACYT is devoting a great deal of time and energy to promote innovation in Mexico.[26]

The National Development Plan also shows that Mexico is embarrassed that it is generally behind its counterparts in the OECD on critical indicators of productivity, GDP growth per capita, and innovation; therefore, national pride may overcome the political positioning that often dominates policymaking. Mexico's competitive position is apt to improve by 2025 over what it is today, perhaps stimulated by economic crises on which political leaders tend to focus. This was the pattern after the crises of 1982 (when import substitution gave way to export promotion) and 1995 (when the fixed exchange rate gave way to a floating currency).

UNITED STATES

From 1990 through 2005, annual growth in GDP per capita in the United States in constant 2000 dollars was 1.86 percent—higher than Mexico's rate of growth, despite the higher U.S. base. Productivity growth in the United States has been lower since 2004 than it was from 2001 through 2004, as shown in figure 4.1. In addition, in August 2007, the U.S. Department of Labor revised U.S. productivity growth in 2004 through 2006 downward, as follows:

- down to 2.9 percent from 3.1 percent in 2004,

- down to 2.0 percent from 2.1 percent in 2005, and

- down to 1.0 percent from 1.7 percent in 2006.

In its press release announcing these revisions, the Department of Labor explicitly pointed out that the 1.0 percent increase in productivity in 2006 was low compared with the level in previous years.[27] It is too soon to say whether this is a temporary slowdown in productivity growth coming at the end of period of sustained GDP growth, when plant production is at nearly full capacity, or the start of a new trend of relatively low productivity growth.

In addition to the uncertainty about productivity growth in the near future, the United States faces other major problems related to competitiveness in the global economy. The issues that must be confronted include ways to deal with the large deficit in the current account balance (shown in figure 4.7); confusion about trade policy (dealing with both the protection of imports and the effects of outsourcing); inadequate maintenance of national infrastructure (as evidenced by the collapse of the bridge over the Mississippi River in Minneapolis on August 1, 2007); and, of course, the continuing drain on resources caused by the mounting costs of health care and the war in Iraq.

The current deficit in the U.S. account balance is being financed by capital flows into the United States—many of which come in the form of foreign central bank purchases of U.S.Treasury debt instruments. China, whose foreign reserves now exceed US$1.3 trillion, is particularly important as a major purchaser of these instruments. However, China has indicated its desire to diversify its future reserve accumulations by purchasing nondollar assets, including attractive private investments, to increase its returns. China has not been divesting current dollar instruments that it holds, partly because such withdrawals would result in actual investment losses as a consequence of the decline in the value of the dollar. In addition, China may not want the U.S. dollar to depreciate precipitously because this would affect its exports to the United States.

Since 2000, the U.S. dollar has depreciated by one-third of its value on a trade-weighted index; the dollar is down to half the level it had in the 1980s. A commentary by two researchers at the Federal Reserve Bank of New York argues that dollar depreciation by itself is unlikely to eliminate the trade deficit because the pass-through in higher prices of goods imported by the United States is relatively modest. Based on data from 1975 to 2003, the authors estimate the pass-through in import prices after one year from a 1 percent change in the exchange rate to be 0.42 for the United States, compared with 0.81 for the euro and an average of 0.64 for OECD countries. However, it is important to note that the value of U.S. exports increases more sharply from lower prices for foreign buyers after the devaluation of the dollar.[28]

If dollar depreciation is not the complete solution, the United States should look at other ways to reduce or eliminate the deficit in the U.S. current account balance. A slowdown in U.S. economic growth would reduce demand for foreign goods and services, just as higher growth in foreign markets would stimulate demand for U.S. products. If the United States were unable to borrow from foreign sources, by definition, the current account deficit could not exist. This outcome seems unlikely, but it is a possibility, and it would result in a hard landing, as opposed to a soft landing over time. The latter obviously is preferable for the United States; a hard landing would adversely affect the rest of the world as well.

Analysts and legislators disagree about U.S. trade policy. As of September 2007, President Bush does not have the authority to negotiate trade agreements under what used to be known as "fast track authority" and is called trade promotion authority today. Under fast track authority, the U.S. Congress must either approve or reject agreements submitted by the executive branch, based on a rigid timetable, without amending them—or, in practice, mostly without amending them. Bilateral trade agreements already negotiated with Peru, Panama, Colombia, and South Korea are meeting with resistance in Congress. A successful conclusion of the Doha Round of trade negotiations by the World Trade Organization is uncertain; even if an agreement is concluded, it is likely to be less comprehensive than contemplated earlier.

There is also disagreement about what benefits the United States gains from outsourcing, that is, producing all or part of a final product or rendering services outside the United States, where wages are lower—a practice that is common under globalization. For the manufacturing firm or service agency, outsourcing should increase its competitiveness. Even though workers in the United States lose their jobs, job creation in the United States as a whole may increase because of improved competitiveness. The outsourced jobs can be low-tech jobs, such as jobs in assembly plants; modestly complex, such as jobs at call centers; or more advanced, such as jobs in the sciences, computer programming, radiology, and the like. In addition, analysts disagree about the number of U.S. jobs that may be lost over time as a result of outsourcing. Alan Blinder, a respected economist, has stated his concern publicly, writing that the number of jobs that will be lost will be considerable—perhaps even in the millions.[29] Jagdish Bhagwati, another respected economist, particularly for his analyses of trade, is largely optimistic about the effects of globalization, including offshore production.[30] Globalization is undoubtedly here to stay, although impediments may be placed in its way, such as measures taken to penalize U.S. companies that move production processes offshore and provide services that can be rendered more cheaply from locations outside the United States. Company-based provision of health insurance adds considerably to the cost of production of many goods, such as automobiles and trucks, compared with the costs companies bear in all other industrial countries where health insurance costs are borne by the government (that is, the taxpayers).

The competitiveness problems faced by the United States and discussed in this report are being actively debated. This report does not examine other problems that could affect U.S. competitiveness, because they would have other effects as well, some of which would be quite important, for example—

- a shift to a value-added tax system, under which taxes paid before a product or service is exported can be rebated, unlike the prevailing practice for income taxes;

- imposition of taxes on consumption of goods and services as opposed to investment;

- changes in immigration laws to attract skilled professionals, especially in science and technology, as opposed to the primary immigration policy emphasis on reuniting families; and

- an increase in financial assistance to students specializing in science and technology.

A report on competitiveness in Canada, Mexico, and the United States issued by the North American Competitiveness Council also includes many recommended measures that would facilitate the movement of goods within North America and elsewhere.[31]

The issue of U.S. competitiveness in a global economy is high on official and private agendas. Therefore, given the nature of U.S. governance and society, the issue will undoubtedly lead to changes many times over between now and 2025. The results of some of these changes are likely to be good, some bad, and others indifferent.

North American Integration

The report produced by the North American Competitiveness Council cited above is directed to the three governments of North America as part of the Security and Prosperity Partnership, which is designed to deepen North American economic integration beyond what now exists—creating a "NAFTA plus," as it has been called. The benefits accruing from this partnership thus far have been quite modest.[32]

There are real problems with North American integration that are adversely affecting the region's competitive position. An example from the transportation sector clearly illustrates the problem. Despite the provision in the original agreement permitting Mexican trucks to provide service throughout the United States after January 1, 2000, Mexican trucks have not been allowed to do so, allegedly on safety grounds. Mexican trucks must now stop at the U.S. border, go through inspection at both Mexican and U.S. posts, and, if approved on security grounds, transfer the containers from a Mexican tractor to a U.S. tractor. This entire process adds to the cost of shipments. As another example, a pilot program designed to move toward full implementation of NAFTA was compromised in September 2007 by the U.S. Congress, which eliminated appropriations for the trial program.

Even though there has been much talk of harmonizing product standards and eliminating differences in regulatory procedures affecting trade in North America, steps still need to be taken to achieve this goal. The Security and Prosperity Partnership is probably the best venue in which to discuss these issues. Antiterrorism measures add to the cost of cross-border shipments. Many of the rules of origin used to define what goods are eligible for free trade in North America were devised with protectionist motives in mind. In short, even though the system has improved, many problems remain.

Despite its success in achieving its main objectives to increase trade and investment in North America, NAFTA remains controversial—at least in Mexico and the United States. In Mexico, the agreement is blamed for the country's lackluster economic growth since the agreement went into effect, and many critics in the United States assert that NAFTA has led to overall job losses. Some critics claim that NAFTA has accelerated Mexican emigration from rural areas into cities and into the United States.[33]

CONCLUSIONS

A summary of the main conclusions of this report on competitiveness is presented in tabular form in table 4.1.

Table 4.1. Looking Ahead to 2025

	Canada	Mexico	United States
Productivity	Needs to sustain economic growth at a rate of 2–3 percent, especially if the currency remains strong.	Must raise overall economic growth and diminish volatility.	Must reverse the recent lower rate of economic growth to sustain high per capita income.
Budget	Must continue sound fiscal policy related to its account balance and make modest variations as required by rises and falls in the GDP.	Its overall fiscal policy is sound, but tax collections must be increased in order to deal with the needs of society and the infrastructure.	The current deficit is modest as a percent of the GDP, but the uncertainty about tax policy needs to be resolved.
Current account balance	Needs to sustain the trend of the last five years and achieve modest surpluses in the years ahead.	Has moved from large deficits to a balanced position, and this trend must be sustained.	The deficit is exploding and is the basis for today's global imbalance; the country's position needs gradual but sustained improvement.
Trade	Export growth has been satisfactory in recent years, including diversification outside the United States, but this may become more complex as the Canadian dollar gains strength.	Must improve the technology inherent in production and diversify markets beyond North America.	Manufactured exports have held up well in recent years, but service and agricultural exports will depend heavily on growth outside of North America.

(continued next page)

Table 4.1. *(continued)*

	Canada	Mexico	United States
Foreign direct investment	The absolute level of new FDI inflows seems to be picking up after sharp declines; this trend will have to continue for the country to meet its investment needs by 2025.	Net FDI has been substantial since the mid-1990s in both absolute terms and as a percent of GDP; this result stems from stringent financial policies.	FDI, along with portfolio investment, has helped finance the deficit in the current account balance; however, meeting competitiveness goals in 2025 requires rectification of the large current account deficit.
Structural problems	Must deal with financing health care and emphasize the need to increase funding on technology research.	Must deal with labor policy, tax collections, declining oil and gas reserves, education, justice, and internal security—areas in which Mexico faces gaps compared with the United States and Canada.	Needs to resolve growing income disparities and availability and cost of health care and make adjustments to Social Security and other pension systems.
Competitiveness gaps in 2025	Innovation and overall productivity.	Wide disparities in GDP per capita and technology development.	Savings and reliance on foreign financing for the deficit in the balance of payments of the current account.

Some key points should be highlighted in a projection of the competitive position in which Mexico, Canada, and the United States are likely to find themselves in the future:

- Each of the three North American countries faces challenges to upgrading its competitive position.

- The three countries are markedly heterogeneous. Most Americans and Canadians live in reasonable comfort, whereas about half of all Mexicans live under harsh circumstances. Competitive failures, therefore, would be particularly unfortunate in Mexico. Table 4.1 shows the challenges for comparable variables in the three countries.

- The impediments to meeting future competitive challenges in all three countries are largely vested interests in the status quo, historical determinants (such as oil in Mexico), conflicts among political parties (which are now fierce in both Mexico and the United States), and a tendency to take steps only after proper analysis is made of the problems that need correction (such as education, trade, and migration policy in the three countries).

- Meeting competitive challenges requires reconciliation of two opposing objectives: increasing security (which slows down the movement of goods, services, and people across borders) and deepening economic integration (to speed and expand the movement of goods, services, and people). Thus far, however, no formula has been accepted for accomplishing the two objectives.

- The most encouraging aspect related to improving competitiveness is the amount of self-examination that all three countries have been conducting.

As stated earlier, some variables that affect competitiveness have been omitted from this chapter, because they are examined in other reports that are part of this project—those dealing with energy, the environment, labor mobility, infrastructure, and security. The United States' failure to enact comprehensive legislation dealing with immigration in 2007 and, instead, the country's focus on restrictions against undocumented immigrants could affect the competitiveness of several U.S. industries in the years ahead: for example, in construction, where about 40 percent of recent employees have been immigrants; and in agriculture, where there is a need for workers to move from place to place for different planting and harvesting activities. The restrictive U.S. actions—including building fences along the common border with Mexico—will impose a need for Mexico to improve job creation by cutting off the emigration escape valve. Looking ahead to 2025, it is almost certain that Congress will enact new U.S. immigration legislation between now and then—although there is no certainty as to what form (or forms) this legislation will take over the next 17 years.

By 2025, Mexico's demographic picture may show enough aging to diminish the supply of potential migrants to the United States.

Other changes are possible in North America—and some are even necessary if economic integration is to deepen. The most important of these changes are simplification of customs procedures and facilitation of trade; better harmonization of product standards, especially for intermediate product inputs; and compatible industrial and service regulations among the three countries. There may be greater coordination of monetary policies, possibly even efforts at monetary integration, but these are issues that require extensive analysis in their own right.

APPENDIX

Sources are provided for each of the charts shown in the following appendix. For the most part, databases available on the Internet were used to construct them.

Figure 4.1. Total Labor Productivity Growth, NAFTA Countries, 1990–2005

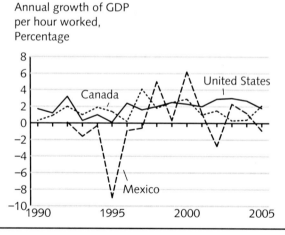

Source: Organization for Economic Cooperation and Development, Productivity Database, September 2006.

Figure 4.2. Productivity Growth in Manufacturing, Canada, 1990–2005

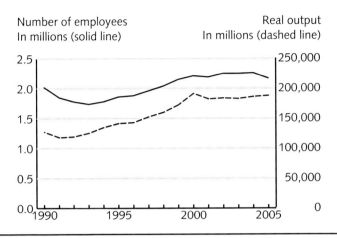

Sources: Organization for Economic Cooperation and Development, Annual Labor Force Statistics
Database, September 2006; Organization for Economic Cooperation and Development,
Productivity Database, May 2007.

Figure 4.3. Productivity Growth in Manufacturing, Mexico, 1990–2005

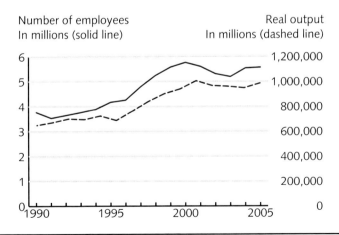

Sources: Organization for Economic Cooperation and Development, Annual Labor Force Statistics
Database, September 2006; Organization for Economic Cooperation and Development,
Productivity Database, May 2007.

Figure 4.4. Productivity Growth in Manufacturing, United States, 1990–2005

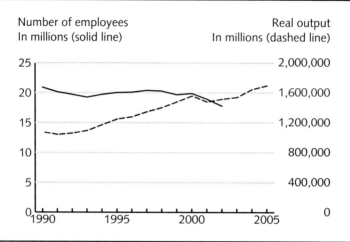

Sources: Organization for Economic Cooperation and Development, Annual Labor Force Statistics Database, September 2006; Organization for Economic Cooperation and Development, Productivity Database, May 2007.

Figure 4.5. Productivity Growth in Services, NAFTA Countries, 1990–2005

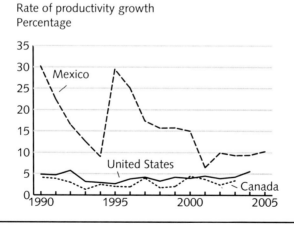

Sources: Groningen Growth and Development Centre 10-Sector Database, June 2007; Groningen Growth and Development Centre, 60-Industry Database, February 2005 and September 2006.

Figure 4.6. Budget Surplus/Deficit, NAFTA Countries, 1990–2006

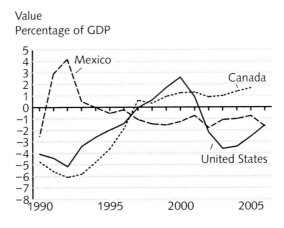

Sources: International Monetary Fund, International Financial Statistics Database 2007; World Bank, World Development Indicators Database 2006.

Figure 4.7. Current Account Balance, NAFTA Countries, 1990–2005

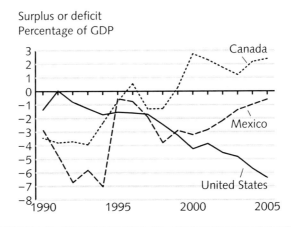

Source: World Bank, World Development Indicators Database 2006.

Figure 4.8. Canadian Exports by Destination, 1990–2006

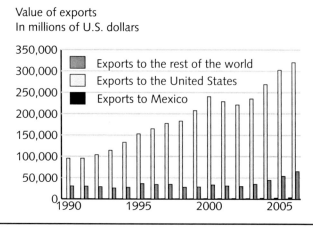

Value of exports
In millions of U.S. dollars

Source: International Monetary Fund, Direction of Trade Database 2007.

Figure 4.9. Mexican Exports by Destination, 1990–2006

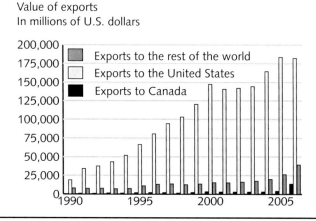

Value of exports
In millions of U.S. dollars

Source: International Monetary Fund, Direction of Trade Database 2007.

Figure 4.10. U.S. Exports by Destination, 1990–2006

Value of exports
In millions of U.S. dollars

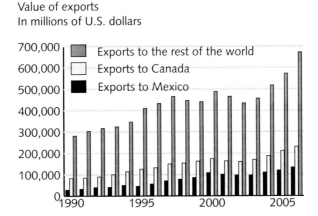

Source: International Monetary Fund, Direction of Trade Database 2007.

Figure 4.11. Canadian Exports by Destination, 2006

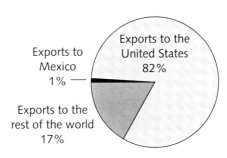

Source: International Monetary Fund, Direction of Trade Database 2007.

Figure 4.12. Mexican Exports by Destination, 2006

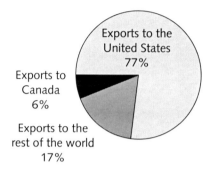

Source: International Monetary Fund, Direction of Trade Database 2007.

Figure 4.13. U.S. Exports by Destination, 2006

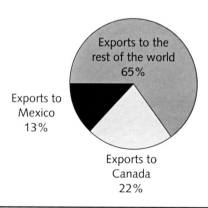

Source: International Monetary Fund, Direction of Trade Database 2007.

Figure 4.14. Foreign Direct Investment, Canada, 1990–2005

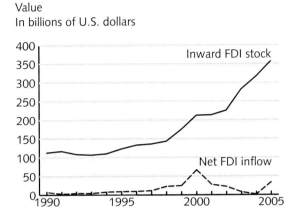

Source: United Nations Conference on Trade and Development, Foreign Direct Investment Database 2006.

Figure 4.15. Foreign Direct Investment, Mexico, 1990–2005

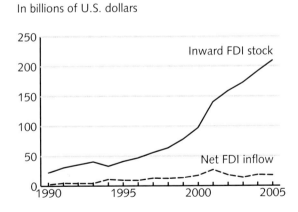

Source: United Nations Conference on Trade and Development, Foreign Direct Investment Database 2006

Figure 4.16. Foreign Direct Investment, United States, 1990–2005

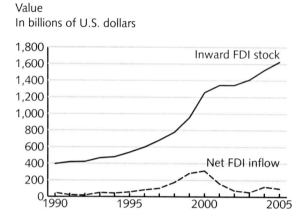

Value
In billions of U.S. dollars

Source: United Nations Conference on Trade and Development, Foreign Direct Investment Database 2006.

Figure 4.17. Net FDI Inflows as Percentage of GDP, NAFTA Countries, 1992–1996

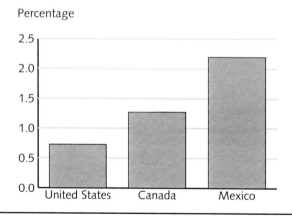

Percentage

Source: World Bank, World Development Indicators Database 2007.

NOTES

1. This may overstate the case, because Canada's exports to Mexico may show up as exports to the United States that are later reshipped to Mexico. Canadian trucks are permitted to operate throughout the United States; Mexico's trucks are still limited to border areas in the United States, despite NAFTA's explicit provisions allowing movement of Mexican trucks throughout the United States starting in 2000.

2. Organization for Economic Cooperation and Development, Productivity Database, September 2006.

3. Glen Hodgson, "Canada-U.S. Competitiveness: The Productivity Gap," Woodrow Wilson International Center for Scholars, Washington, D.C., June 2007.

4. Ibid.

5. Conference Board of Canada, "Sustainable Prosperity for Canada: Mission Possible, Executive Summary," *The Canada Project, Final Report,* vol. 4 (Ottawa, January 2007).

6. Ibid, p. 36.

7. Conference Board of Canada, "How Canada Performs: A Report Card on Canada," Ottawa, May 2007. The copy of the report used in this study is labeled "draft" because the manuscript had not yet gone through a quality check.

8. The 17 countries are Australia, Austria, Belgium, Canada, Denmark, Finland, France, Germany, Ireland, Italy, Japan, the Netherlands, Norway, Sweden, Switzerland, the United Kingdom, and the United States.

9. According to the Conference Board of Canada, immigration has been responsible for more than half of Canada's growth since 1991 (see Conference Board of Canada, "How Canada Performs," p. 27).

10. The information in this paragraph came from an e-mail sent by Statistics Canada.

11. These examples come from the Conference Board of Canada, "If We Can Fix It Here, We Can Make It Anywhere: Effective Policies at Home to Boost Canada's Global Success," Ottawa, March 2007.

12. The author of a preliminary paper asks if Canada is suffering from the Dutch disease and concludes that it "quite possibly" is (see Richard Harris, "Canadian Competitiveness: Remarks," John Deutsch Institute Conference, Queens University, June 23, 2006).

13. Ibid. Harris states in his paper that the manufacturing sector has so far adjusted quite well to the increase in the exchange rate vis-à-vis the U.S. dollar.

14. World Bank, *World Development Indicators* (Washington, D.C.: World Bank, 2007).

15. The author of a newspaper column gives a figure of 1.4 million jobs cre-

ated over the Fox *sexenio*—about 230,000 new jobs a year. There was a spurt in job creation in 2006, President Fox's last year in office (see Joel Kurtzman, "Mexico's Job-Creation Problem," *Wall Street Journal*, August 3, 2007). Sergio Sarmiento reported that 725,686 jobs were created during the first five years of the Fox administration, according to the official records of the Instituto Mexicano de Seguro Social. Of these, Sarmiento noted that 595,000 were temporary positions (see *Reforma*, January 9, 2006). These differences should not be belabored, because the main point remains that formal job creation in Mexico has been insufficient to absorb all willing workers. Moreover, most of the jobs that were created paid low wages.

16. This percentage comes from subtracting the number of workers who are formally registered in various social security registries from the total figure of the labor force.

17. Poder Ejecutivo Federal, *Plan Nacional de Desarrollo 2007–2012* (National Development Plan), (Mexico City, 2007), p. 82.

18. Ibid, p. 83.

19. The reference is to *a* year, not *the* year, because Mexico was also unable to meet its debts in 1995.

20. Sidney Weintraub, *Financial Decision-Making in Mexico: To Bet a Nation* (Pittsburgh, Pa.: University of Pittsburgh Press, 2000).

21. Richard Jackson, "Building Human Capital in an Aging Mexico," Report of the U.S.-Mexico Binational Council, Center for Strategic and International Studies, Washington, D.C., and Institúto Tecnólogico Autónomo de México, Mexico City, July 2005. Subsequent comments in this paragraph on demographic trends in Mexico come from this source.

22. Poder Ejecutivo Federal, *Plan Nacional de Desarrollo*, p. 175.

23. Ibid., p. 176. The figure given for the United States is 82 percent; 57 percent for Canada in 2006.

24. For more detail on the energy situation in Mexico, see Sidney Weintraub, "Mexico," in *Energy Cooperation in the Western Hemisphere: Benefits and Impediments*, ed. Sidney Weintraub, Annette Hester, and Veronica Prado (Washington, D.C.: Center for Strategic and International Studies, 2007), pp. 106–131.

25. Consejo Ejecutivo de Empresas Globales, "Reflexiones Sobre la Competitividad en México," Mexico City, 2006.

26. See James A. Lewis, "National Policies for Innovation and Growth in Mexico," Center for Strategic and International Studies, Washington, D.C., June 2006.

27. U.S. Department of Labor, "Productivity and Costs, Second Quarter 2007," Preliminary Report, Washington, D.C., August 7, 2007.

28. Linda Goldberg and Eleanor Wiske Dillon, "Why a Dollar Depreciation

May Not Close the U.S. Trade Deficit," *Current Issues in Economics and Finance* (Federal Reserve Bank of New York) 13, no. 5 (June 2007). For the uninitiated, if the value of the dollar declines vis-à-vis a particular foreign currency, U.S. importers have to pay more dollars for a product or a service priced in that foreign currency, thereby reducing demand for those foreign products. A foreign buyer of a U.S. product or service may be induced to buy more because the cost goes down in the foreign currency. The three reasons given in the article as to why this pass-through from dollar depreciation is relatively low are: (1) much trade between foreign countries is invoiced in dollars but remains fixed in the foreign currency, (2) foreign exporters are prepared to shave their profit margins to retain market share in the United States, and (3) dollar costs to distribute goods are high after they reach the United States.

29. Alan Blinder summarizes his thinking in his article, "Free Trade's Great, but Offshoring Rattles Me," *Washington Post*, May 6, 2007, sec. B, p. 4.

30. Jagdish Bhagwati, *In Defense of Globalization* (New York: Oxford University Press, 2004).

31. North American Competitiveness Council "Enhancing Competitiveness in Canada, Mexico, and the United States: Private Sector Priorities for the Security and Prosperity Partnership of North America," Initial Recommendations, 2007.

32. There is also vociferous opposition to the Security and Prosperity Partnership in the United States, with critics arguing that it is designed to reduce U.S. sovereignty in such areas as immigration and homeland security. An example of this position is James R. Edwards, Jr., "The Security and Prosperity Partnership: Its Immigration Implications," Center for Immigration Studies, 2007. Edwards' paper reads more like conspiracy theory than solid analysis of the purposes of the partnership. An example of conspiratorial thinking appeared in a *New York Times* report of Republican presidential candidates' responses to a question about secret plans to build a NAFTA superhighway from Mexico to Canada, stopping off in Kansas City. Rudolph Giuliani said he had never heard of the plan; Mitt Romney answered that he did now know about it but added "I'll stop it" (see "Road or Rumor, They're Against It," *New York Times*, July 31, 2007, sec. A, p. 13). The Security and Prosperity Partnership was launched at a summit meeting of the three North American governments held in Waco, Texas, in March 2005; the three principals met in Cancún, Mexico, a year later and in Montebello, Canada, on August 21–22, 2007. The spawning of far-out thinking may be related to the lack of transparency in the working-level negotiations under the aegis of the Security and Prosperity Partnership, but this explanation should not be overdrawn; opponents of the agreement also dislike NAFTA, whose workings are far from secret.

33. I do not want the body of this paper to be polemical, but a few points can be made here. The inadequate growth of the Mexican economy and

of job creation can be amply explained by failures in Mexican policies, as described in the section on Mexico in this chapter; people are leaving rural areas of Mexico to escape from poverty, which antedated NAFTA. Overall U.S. employment growth is a function of GDP growth and macroeconomic policy, not of trade.

OUTLOOK FOR INFRASTRUCTURE

NORMAN F. ANDERSON

North America—the individual countries and the region as a whole—is faced with the problem of steadily losing its competitiveness because of low and inconsistent investment in the region's infrastructure. To address this problem, which is an urgent priority, North America needs to find a compelling vision for the creation of strategic infrastructure projects for the future—a competitiveness vision—that can provide a clear view of where the region wants to be in 2025 and also prioritizes the projects that are critical for each country to achieve the goals set for that future.

The region is in the midst of an infrastructure crisis. The problem of deteriorating infrastructure (or nonexistent infrastructure) has been a leading political issue for a generation and is a key cause of North America's lack of competitiveness, declining quality of life, and ugly public policy debates (about such issues as shrinking wages and illegal immigration). The way forward involves creating a new vision of how the United States—along with the North America as a whole—should address the opportunities presented by today's globalizing economy. The solution proposed in this chapter is evolutionary rather than revolutionary, focusing on bringing existing expertise to bear in new ways—most likely through newly invigorated institutions.

The problem is great, because without a clear vision—similar to the one that gave rise to the U.S. Interstate Highway Act or the much earlier American System of Henry Clay—the United States, Mexico, and

Canada run the risk that they will continue to muddle through the crisis into the future and fail to see, let alone seize, the great opportunities that exist for North America in a rapidly changing world. The new vision must, for the first time, include Canada and Mexico as intimate partners of the United States in developing an overall vision of North American competitiveness. Creating this North American powerhouse by stitching together the strengths of the economies of all three nations, while mitigating their weaknesses, is a task that will require a generation of sustained effort. The task will also require a robust financing structure across three countries that only rarely think in terms of the strategic economic advantages that a well-designed, optimized, and well-maintained infrastructure system will offer to the 450 million residents of the region.

This chapter will assess the infrastructure of North America and the outlook from today to 2025. The aim is to present the current state of North American infrastructure "by the numbers" and to use a series of forward-looking scenarios to assess the strengths and weaknesses in each of the three countries; to suggest a vigorous path forward for North America, because globalization makes a noncoordinated approach both costly and self-defeating; and to set forth a set of concrete action items that should be taken to select, finance, build, and maintain the kind of high-quality infrastructure that will allow North America to create and sustain long-term competitiveness and economic growth.

It should be noted that this analysis does not focus on North American *integration*, but on the critical strategic economic importance for the region to build world-class infrastructure within each country and to do so to such a degree that the region's overall competitiveness improves, new businesses are created, opportunities throughout the income spectrum multiply, and overall global economic performance is dramatically enhanced. Thus, the driving concept is not integration but a vision of a North American system—consisting of the United States, Canada, and Mexico—that works together for growth. Just achieving the required levels of investment needed for infrastructure projects will add nearly 4 million direct jobs and 8 million indirect jobs to the region *each year for the next 17 years*.[1]

THE CURRENT STATE OF NORTH AMERICA'S INFRASTRUCTURE

Today the infrastructure systems in place in Canada, the United States, and Mexico are generally thought to be inadequate to meet the demands of the global economy. Rates of investment are no more than one-third of the amount needed for critical requirements. What is worse is that many of the investments made today are focused on the upkeep of old systems that were designed and constructed when—in the case of the United States—the economy was internally integrated, rather than a "just-in-time" importer and exporter of goods and services from around the world. Investments are too small, they are focused on the wrong projects, and there is no agreement about the way forward and no agreement about priorities. Investments that are made respond to political considerations and local political needs in all three countries rather than to the more urgent demands of global competitiveness. The region as a whole needs to reach a clear agreement on how the three economies can complement one another to increasingly seize opportunities to assume global leadership in the economic, political, cultural, and even social arenas.

The size of the problem is substantial and it compounds with every year of underinvestment in the region's infrastructure. For Canada, Mexico, and the United States, it is generally accepted that there is a *yearly* underinvestment in the range of US$250 billion; the region invests roughly US$150 billion annually in infrastructure but should be investing US$400 billion. Each country underinvests not only in new infrastructure but also in the maintenance of existing infrastructure. This lack of attention creates direct economic costs, examples of which abound: US$54 billion for U.S. motorists because of poorly maintained highways; US$2 billion in greater Toronto because of delays caused by traffic congestion; and untold billions of dollars in Mexico, which, among other crippling problems, processes only about 20 percent of its wastewater and has to operate a modern economy with only 4 percent of its cargo containerized (as compared with more than 40 percent in the United States).[2]

Three facts stand out:

- All three countries show a tendency toward inaction. Despite the crisis, there is no current sense of urgency about the issue and no compelling argument for addressing it.

- There seems to be no place at the table for Mexico. Mexico is the odd country out. There is no consensus about, and little energetic discussion of, how Mexico might fit into a competitive North America.

- The three nations are simply muddling through the crisis and are doing so separately. None of the North American countries—let alone the region as a whole—has a vigorous organizing vision for the future. Canada is furthest along on this score, and Mexico has announced a strong program, but none of the current arguments will generate the tripling of investment that is required.

Any single one of these issues is what infrastructure project developers call a "fatal flaw," and the presence of all three in the calculus suggests the difficulty of building the infrastructure required for a North America that urgently needs to become increasingly competitive.

From the point of view of North America's infrastructure in 2025, the most striking fact is the lack of any aggressive discussion of a way forward. The old model clearly does not work, and a new model is somewhere over the horizon. A substantial part of the solution lies in the technical realm: (1) finding a financial arrangement robust enough to mobilize an additional US$250 billion per year in new financing; (2) creating a system that productively brings together all the critical actors—engineers, financiers, public decisionmakers, business leaders, and private citizens—to investigate and adopt a new model; and (3) sustaining that system through the inevitable start-up problems as it gets up and running. But the issue that comes before all of these considerations is how to take the enormous expertise that is available and—through evolutionary change—identify, finance, and build the infrastructure projects that will result in a competitive North America. After all, the talent is available and the funds can be found. But what is the vision that will allow North America to close the gap, which has left the continent with an accumulated infrastructure deficit greater than US$1 trillion?

DEVELOPING A STRATEGIC COMPETITIVE VISION

A country's—or a region's—infrastructure is made up of discrete, well-designed, clearly imagined, and quickly financed projects that have a long life expectancy. The projects designed today will be operational in 2025 and, indeed, will be critical to the region's competitiveness for at least 20 years—and perhaps for as long as 50 years. It is also useful to combine the system-focused and project-focused idea of infrastructure with a global strategic approach, which might be called "strategic infrastructure." This concept recognizes the unique economic nature of infrastructure—that infrastructure is generally a public good that can serve the region's competitiveness interests for 20 to 30 years.

The strategic view leads to the conclusion that for a country to achieve and sustain high levels of investment in its infrastructure it is helpful to have a national consensus on a nation's strategic priorities. In the United States, the Interstate Highway Act reflected such a consensus—that this is a requirement that involves vision and implies a leading role for the central government, built around a clear sense of a country's immediate need to be competitive, such as low-cost broadband access, 33 percent reduction of traffic congestion in major cities, 50 percent fewer detentions of ships at ports, and so forth. The vision also requires a consensus about the country's future needs, including, for example, developing world-class systems for transmission of electricity to support an increasingly high-tech manufacturing base, better light rail systems to facilitate decentralized work and to reduce traffic congestion, and the like.

Once infrastructure is viewed in terms of a country's competitiveness—that is, as a strategic plan for the country's success—and is no longer considered a system that simply provides public services, then there is a powerful logic in matching the value of that particular infrastructure (a power plant, a port, or a pipeline, for example) over its projected life span with the term of the debt required to build and maintain it. This way of thinking is critical for Mexico, where long-term financing was not available in the past, but it is also important for the United States and Canada, where pension funds and other institutional investment enterprises would be logical investors in long-term assets. Currently, nearly US$14 trillion is managed by U.S. pension funds (60 percent of the world's total), nearly US$500 billion is managed by Canadian pension funds, and nearly US$50 billion is managed by Mexico's pension funds.

DIAGNOSING THE PROBLEM AND MAKING THE RIGHT CHANGES: CREATING INFRASTRUCTURE

The term "infrastructure" actually refers to a system of systems—highways; railways; electricity generation, transmission, and distribution;

digital systems; water and water treatment facilities; logistics; and so forth—that creates the conditions for economic productivity, business creation, and equity. These are not the only systems that lead to economic success; less visible systems—taxation, education, justice, and labor, for example—are just as critical, but infrastructure systems are physically visible and symbolically important. If modern and optimized, infrastructure systems allow firms as well as individuals to be as productive and as creative as anyone in the world is; if the systems are not modern and are not optimized, if they are crumbling or simply nonexistent, then these systems serve as constant—and invisible—barriers to economic success.

This chapter deals with the infrastructure systems that North America needs to have in place by 2025 if the region's economy is to be broadly competitive in terms of global leadership. The key to solving the problem does not involve bringing about any kind of creeping integration of systems but developing and reaching a very high level of complementarity—that is, designing infrastructure systems that lead to regional competitiveness while generating increased global competitiveness *within* North America's countries over a life cycle of 20–30 years.

In this context, the questions Mexico, Canada, and the United States must address involve how best to improve their own internal infrastructure systems while identifying the specific projects—as well as the types of projects—that will get North America moving. Given that the countries' resources are not unlimited, policymakers in the public sector as well as the market need to answer several questions:

- What projects should have priority? The answer to this question lays the groundwork by explaining the financing that is required and the period of time that will be needed to bring about a dramatic increase in the region's competitiveness. Projects that have priority are by no means limited to those that involve interconnections between the countries. How quickly the United States can build freight infrastructure projects matters as much to Mexico as Mexico's own internal projects, like Punto Colonet, matter. And how quickly Canada can develop its petroleum resources and transport networks is in the interest of not only U.S. energy planners but also investors in long-term production facilities (that rely on the North American price of oil, natural gas, and electricity).

- How should these projects be designed and sized? The answer to this question determines where and how decisions are made—at the local level, at the national level with local input, or at the national level with an eye to North American competitiveness. In a sense, this is the major question, involving the locus of the decision, which is—in the case of infrastructure as in the case of everything else—a dramatically political issue. One does not need a central government authority making local decisions, and one certainly does not need a transnational authority making these decisions. At the same time, locating decisions that affect the global capacity of Mexico, the United States, and Canada to compete at the local level is a recipe for the kind of disorganized, underperforming, and underfunded infrastructure project creation that is the case today. The challenge is to bring local knowledge together with national financial and technical capacity in order to build the right projects based on an overall vision of competitiveness.

- How should priority projects be built? The answer to this question describes the repertoire of financial options within each country and across North America. The current model, at least in the United States, is largely a municipal finance model, with a shrinking level of federal transfers. On the highway side, according to the National Chamber Foundation "between 2006 and 2015 annual Highway Trust Fund (HTF) revenues will fall US$23 billion short of maintaining highway and transit systems, and US$48 billion short of the federal share needed to improve the systems."[3] Where will the additional monies come from? Canada and Mexico are experimenting with public/private partnership models, allowing greater private participation in the process, and the United States has recently had some success in this area with the Alameda Corridor project, among others. The challenge is to catalyze the evolution of a model that increases both the capacity of federal funding and the role that private sector financing and management plays in the process.

Infrastructure forces decisionmakers to think in the long term. The infrastructure projects designed today will be operational in 2025 and, indeed, will remain critical to the region's competitiveness for as long as 50 years. At the same time, many of today's investments are focused on maintenance of an old system that was designed and constructed when—in the case of the United States—the economy was internally integrated, rather than a just-in-time importer and exporter of goods and services from around the world.

The magnitude of the problem makes it a first-tier policy issue in terms of competitiveness, jobs, immigration, energy, growth, and opportunity. The United States needs to invest on the order of US$250 billion additional dollars annually in projects to improve roads, rail, water, ports, logistics, digital systems, and the like. Mexico, whose investment in infrastructure projects rarely exceeds US$10 billion annually and, as a developing country, is in catch-up mode with the rest of the region, must invest between US$35 billion and US$40 billion more each year.[4] Canada invests approximately US$12 billion in infrastructure per year, whereas a vigorous public debate suggests that this figure could be six to ten times higher—and should be at least three times higher. In each case, it is clear that the previous model through which infrastructure projects were proposed, coordinated, and financed at the direction of the majority in each nation's central government direction is neither strategically nor financially responsive to current needs.

MODELS FOR FUTURE ALTERNATIVE INFRASTRUCTURES
It is clear that North America's future success in the global economy—in terms of job creation, wage enhancement, technological leadership, and quality of life—will depend on an infrastructure system that is modern and well designed. It is also clear that creating that future must begin now.

This section will look at three alternative infrastructure scenarios for the countries of North America. The first scenario, called the "Business as Usual" scenario, is a base case that assumes maintenance of the status quo—continued problems with new investment and project selection and design as well as financing of existing infrastructure. This scenario describes the muddling through process that characterizes the region. The second scenario, which might be called the "Spanish Gambit," assumes that the United States and Canada will continue along the same path of project selection and infrastructure investment, but that Mexico—the emerging market laggard, with an investment-grade credit rating—will take advantage of available institutions in order to generate new investments in infrastructure, tripling Mexico's investment levels by 2010 and maintaining that pace through to 2025. The third scenario, called the "New Model," focuses on building infrastructure in North America aggressively within each country, with an active eye to complementarity, and creating a North American platform for explosive growth. (The three scenarios are graphically depicted in figure 5.1; the graph in the lower right-hand corner shows the increase in job creation under the New Model scenario, as compared with the Business as Usual scenario.)

Figure 5.1. Comparison of the Costs of Three Scenarios and Job Creation, North American Countries, 2007–2025 (in billions of U.S. dollars)

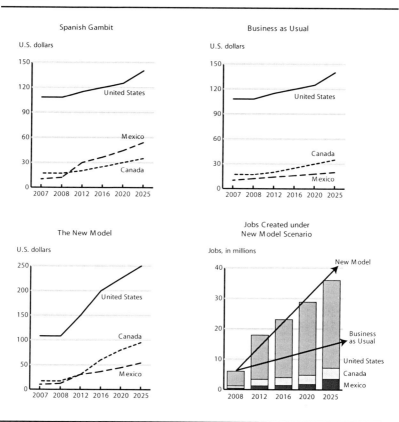

Source: Calculations by CG/LA Infrastructure, LLC, from various sources, Washington, D.C., 2007.

It is important to recognize that the current infrastructure crisis is real. There is little evidence, aside from political rhetoric, to suggest that Mexico, let alone North America as a whole, will be able to break out of the current approach. And there is mounting evidence—for example, lower revenue from property taxes, rising costs of infrastructure inputs, overall lack of an alternative vision—to suggest that the region could well be stuck in a Business as Usual scenario through to 2025 and beyond.

SCENARIO 1: BUSINESS AS USUAL

The Business as Usual scenario describes what North America will look like in 2025 if it continues along the current path. This is a view of the future in which existing infrastructure is barely maintained; new infrastructure is occasionally built with substantial financial effort; and the increasing problems that result—including congestion, public health issues, and more expensive electricity—render North America increasingly uncompetitive at an increasing velocity. The problem would be particularly acute in Mexico; without new jobs, immigrants would continue to flee to the United States and Canada looking for opportunities in an economic environment in which wages are declining and hostilities are increasing. Under current conditions—in which levels of investment in infrastructure have been declining in all three countries for 25 years or more—the probability that the Business as Usual scenario will prevail in 2025 is at least 60 percent.

Under this scenario, no new guiding vision emerges—one whose impact is similar to that of the U.S. Interstate Highway Act, the Clean Water Act, or even Kennedy's promise to land a man on the moon in the 1960s. Instead, there would be occasional, and perhaps increasing, problems that would cause loss of life and loss of income; there would also be occasional increases in effort—such as crises to overcome or Olympic Games to organize—that would lead to the creation of new projects. In general, federal, state, and local officials would continue to do the best that they can in an environment of artificial constraints (an outmoded infrastructure investment model) and real constraints (lower property taxes for funding projects following declining competitiveness) as they work through a political Darwinian fight for scarce resources. Under this scenario, well-managed and politically connected entities would thrive.

Figure 5.2. Accumulated Infrastructure Deficit, United States, 2025 (selected sectors) (in billions of U.S. dollars)

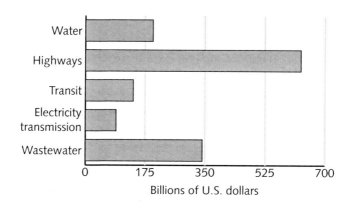

Billions of U.S. dollars

Source: Calculations by CG/LA Infrastructure, LLC, from various sources, Washington, D.C., 2007.

The Business as Usual scenario makes two critical assumptions about the process by which major decisions are made about North American infrastructure. First, there will be no "game changing" visions. The traditional system, which is highly political and dominated by the local public sector, will monopolize the activity and resources needed for the region's infrastructure. Much of the private sector's expertise will continue to be used only on the margins of projects based on a fee-for-services arrangement with public entities. Second, the traditional financial system in Mexico, Canada, and the United States will continue to have real trouble mobilizing resources, and this will affect the rate and quality of project development. "New" projects would be more akin to remedies to the old system than to major developments addressing the opportunities presented by globalization. This measurable under-investment would exacerbate existing problems; for example, annually the United States would invest only US$11 billion for drinking water, US$35 billion for highways, US$8 billion for mass transit, and US$19 billion for sanitation. Investment to "fix" old problems—such as congestion at the Port of Long Beach, Mexico City's wastewater problem, and Toronto's urban highway congestion—would consume most of the region's financial and professional resources. New projects would be scarce and would be tied to legacy problems, with no resources available for competitiveness initiatives—for example, the logistics projects required to tie ports to rail, or new natural gas import projects, or even simple cross-border projects to alleviate trade congestion.

As shown in figure 5.2, according to the Business as Usual scenario, in 2025, the United States would have an accumulated infrastructure deficit of US$1.4 trillion. Canada's accumulated deficit would be of a similar magnitude, although it would have a smaller absolute value (some sources calculate Canada's *current* infrastructure deficit to be as high as US$125 billion). In the case of Mexico, this lack of performance would be truly catastrophic. Continued investment at the levels invested in 2001–2006—roughly US$10 billion per year—with virtually no new investments outside of the electricity generation sector and occasional investments in highways would simply exacerbate the deterioration of an already fragile quality of life that Mexicans currently find unacceptable.

For Mexico's poorer citizens, the situation would be unbearable. Maintaining the status quo would lead to water and wastewater problems, which would create a massive drag on Mexico's health care system; wage erosion, which would result from persistent inefficiencies in the transportation system; and general economic stagnation, which would launch immigrants into the only labor market available to them—the United States and Canada.

In short, Canada and the United States can muddle through at present levels, but doing so would be costly in terms of competitiveness and wages as well as lost economic opportunities. Continuing very low levels of investment in infrastructure investment would be catastrophic for Mexico's citizens and could ultimately lead to the failure of the Mexican state.

It should be noted that, under this scenario, the reigning public finance model continues to dominate the actions taken as well as the outcome. That model has a number of obvious weaknesses, but three are critical:

- Public-private confusion: Projects are often behind schedule and result in cost overruns that must be paid by the public, indicating a clear mismatch of public and private responsibilities.

- Market weakness: The worldwide infrastructure market is weak in terms of real market activity, and this is particularly true in the case of the United States, Mexico, and Canada, where project design and finance are largely crowded out by the public sector's decisionmaking.

- Strategic drift: Aside from the lack of a strong thrust toward competitiveness within countries, the public sector's responsibility for guaranteeing the best product for the best price is seriously undermined by a system that both hides transaction costs (such as the costs for project development) and is very slow in initiating required innovative projects.

SCENARIO 2: THE SPANISH GAMBIT

The Spanish Gambit scenario describes what North America would look like in 2025 if Mexico (like Spain in the 1990s) were brought up to the developed world's infrastructure standards. Beginning this process is the stated goal of President Felipe Calderón's six-year administration. According to this scenario, the United States and Canada—acting in the interests of North American competitiveness, much as the European Union (EU) acted in the interests of European competitiveness when making roughly US$100 billion available to Spain for its infrastructure projects over the last 10 years—would facilitate the creation of a robust, well-designed, and ambitious system of modern infrastructure in Mexico. The estimated probability that the Spanish Gambit scenario will be realized by 2025 is 25 percent.

According to this scenario, the overall objectives would be to quadruple investment in infrastructure in Mexico, to raise Mexico's gross domestic product (GDP) to a sustained annual growth rate of 6–7 percent, and to double the GDP per capita within the next 15 years. As shown in figure 5.3, investment levels would go from roughly US$10 billion per year in 2007 (excluding investments in the oil and gas sector), to US$30 billion per year by 2012, and to nearly US$50 billion per year by 2025. The regional aim would be to create a strong strategic partner for the United States and Canada in terms of manufacturing and labor absorption.

Replacing the current rather anemic vision of "border competitiveness" would be a hard focus on assisting Mexico in building world-class infrastructure, which is designed to catalyze strong internal growth, a rapid increase in global competitiveness, and creation of opportunities. This aggressive vision would ultimately complement U.S. and Canadian competitiveness. In this scenario, which assumes substantial

Figure 5.3. Growth in Infrastructure Investment under the Spanish Gambit Scenario, Mexico, 2007–2025 (selected sectors) (in billions of U.S. dollars)

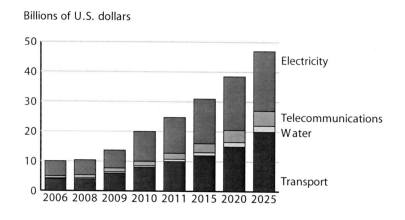

Source: Calculations by CG/LA Infrastructure, LLC, from various sources, Washington, D.C., 2007.

investment in a specific number of highly competitive geographic regions, the Spanish model, which is anchored by the globally competitive greater Madrid region, is a useful guide for how the United States and Canada might contribute to strong Mexican growth. It might even be possible to build a series of superior national firms that specialize in infrastructure projects in Mexico, as Spain did with its world-class engineering/construction firms (such as ACS and OHL energy companies (Iberdrola, Endesa, and Repsol), equipment firms (CAF and Gamesa), and others.

Generating this increased level of investment is likely to require something more aggressive than the current plan and budget strategy. Spain, for example, did not build up its border with the European Union but focused from the very beginning on the creation of a globally competitive economy *within* the EU. In this same sense, Mexico would have to develop a strong set of policies that move the action from the border to internal regions and from a *maquiladora* culture (which has largely moved to China) to one in which Mexico competes at an increasingly high level.

The Spanish Gambit scenario focuses on increasing investment in Mexico's infrastructure in all sectors and recognizes the time required to ramp up investment levels, including the time needed to conduct feasibility studies for strategic projects, to develop the public sector's analytic and decisionmaking capacity,[5] and to create and incorporate the private sector's professional expertise (and, after nearly 15 years of little demand, the required increase in the number and quality of engineering and construction firms would be significant). Essentially, a ramp-up in expertise would be required and, given the very local nature of Mexico's infrastructure market, this "expertise creation" would be built on a Mexican engineering and construction base that was largely decimated during the Tequila Crisis of 1995.

Projects—and the scarce but necessary resources to support those projects—might be focused on economic competitiveness zones that would, in effect, dramatically change the nature of the infrastructure game. One frequently discussed idea, for example, involves developing the agriculturally rich and economically depressed southern part of Mexico through the twin developments of large-scale irrigation and the classic arrival of a logistics system (road and rail, containerization, and refrigeration) that would allow produce to reach Mexico City, northern Mexico, and the United States rapidly (and could easily extend to Europe and Asia, thus resulting in Mexico's joining the global trade in long-haul fresh produce pioneered by Chile).[6] This type of project would be a tremendous boon to the development of Oaxaca and the surrounding states of Guerrero, Veracruz, and Tabasco. Other key projects might include the following:

- deepening the development of the Guadalajara region as a first-class technological center, combined with ready logistics to Asia, the United States, and the rest of Latin America;

- supporting the further development of the Monterrey region as a truly cutting-edge manufacturing center, thereby creating, as a powerful by-product of the center, much-needed strategic manufacturing depth for Mexico's northern partners; and

- revolutionizing greater Mexico City's infrastructure in terms of roads, urban mass transit, water, sanitation, and so forth, so that the centrally located city could develop and sustain its Latin American leadership position in business, finance, and culture (Madrid is an excellent example of this outcome, although Mexico City is roughly a millennium older than the capital of its former colonial power).

An approach of this kind does not ignore other regions (or other sectors, like water and wastewater). Rather, this approach selects strategic projects based on a long-term vision of competitiveness and prioritizes projects that are initially critical and then—as those projects get up and running (in 24 to 30 months) and as the public and private sectors develop expertise—allows projects in less economically critical regions to develop more rapidly than would have been possible otherwise. The outcome of efforts along these lines would include (1) massive investments and job creation in Mexico; (2) significant depth for the U.S. and Canadian manufacturing and service sectors (as Mexico's economy begins to complement those economies); and (3) a strong likelihood of increased investment in logistics and digital infrastructure located north *and* south of the Rio Grande, as the intensity and quality of manufacturing, service, and produce logistics systems develop.

For Mexico to achieve these goals to increase investment in infrastructure, four requirements would have to be met. First, Mexico would need to develop a focused infrastructure strategy—one that is built on global competitiveness, rather than on simple access to the ever changing U.S. market. Second, North America would need to recognize that bringing Mexico up to world-class infrastructure levels is profoundly advantageous to the United States and Canada. Both of these requirements involve political decisionmaking, leadership, and risk taking, for which there is little alternative.

The next two requirements are somewhat more technical but no less important. Something has to be done about the ineffectiveness of the financial institutions that oversee and facilitate the creation of infrastructure projects. It is critically important to either re-tool these institutions so that they can accomplish their missions or to create new institutions that can get this job done. Mexico's two internal development banks—BANOBRAS and NAFINSA—are bureaucratically run and inefficient; they are incapable of lending the amounts needed to bring Mexico's infrastructure up to world-class levels. Between 2001 and 2006, for example, BANOBRAS provided only a bit more than US$2 billion in loans for infrastructure projects, leveraging total investments in the range of US$7 billion (at a time when Mexico invested US$60 billion but needed to invest an amount more on the order of US$180 billion).[7] To achieve the goals assumed in the Spanish Gambit scenario, Mexico would need to pursue aggressive funding for normally hidden transaction costs for project preparation, structuring, loan

Figure 5.4. Diagnostic Model Used to Assess Creation of Infrastructure Projects

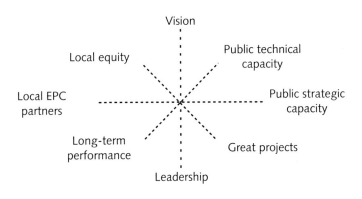

Source: Diagnostic Model developed by CG/LA Infrastructure, LLC, Washington, D.C.

disbursals, and monitoring. This kind of new vision always requires the development of new institutions.

Finally, a quick diagnosis of Mexico's internal capacity to generate and support the creation of infrastructure projects identifies areas that need rapid improvement.[8] CG/LA Infrastructure LLC, a firm that focuses on infrastructure strategy and development, has created an eight-point diagnostic model to assess a country's capacity to develop infrastructure projects, pinpoint a country's weaknesses, and suggest areas for improvement. (See figure 5.4.) On a 10-point scale (with 10 indicating the highest score), Mexico's performance in eight categories has been rated as follows:

1. Vision: Mexico scores quite high on vision (7) because of President Calderón's decision to make this the *sexenio* of infrastructure. (Canada would score at a similar level, and the United States' score would be much lower.) The issue is a high priority and is front and center in all areas of political discourse.

2. Public Sector's Technical Capacity: Mexico scores extraordinarily high (7) for its public sector's technical capacity. (Canada's score would be as high or higher, as would the U.S. score, but, for a developing country, Mexico has a capability that is extraordinary.) The only country in Latin America that approximates this level is Chile. Even though Mexico's capacity in this area is on a par with

that of the United States and Canada, Mexico does not have the number of technical experts that its northern neighbors have, and talent falls off dramatically in the states.

3. Public Sector's Strategic Capacity: This is an area of significant weakness for Mexico (3). (Canada would score much higher, whereas the United States, like Mexico, also lacks a bias for action on the part of executives in the public sector.) Mexico's score in this category is low not only because of technical professionals' minimal experience in getting things done but also because of the litigious nature of reactions to government activity in Mexico. As one former official reported in a private conversation, "The problem is that you are sued *personally,* even one year after leaving office, for *professional* actions taken while you were in office."

4. Great Projects: Mexico is rated as very weak in this area (3), and the lack of a well-prepared project pipeline is extremely harmful for the country's infrastructure. (Canada's score is in the 5–6 range, and the United States' score is somewhat lower; apparently, after years of underfinancing, government executives no longer "think big.") An overarching vision of competitiveness would address this weakness, because the vision would lend authority to project development as a national priority.

5. Leadership: Mexico does not get a particularly high score in this area (5). (Canada scores higher, but the United States is famously inept in this area.) Aside from basic issues of vision, technical capacity, and strategic capacity, a government must have the simple ability to push decisions about infrastructure along, and to do so consistently. The decentralized management of Mexico's infrastructure—much like the case in the United States—is plagued by project delays and cost overruns. The lack of a single agency with executing authority is a significant flaw in this process.

6. Long-term Performance: Mexico gets a low score in this area (4, which is a rough score, indicating both problems and potential). (Canada and the United States would rank 8 and 9, respectively, in this category—a tremendous advantage.) One of Mexico's key issues in mobilizing high-level resources for

investing in infrastructure is the spotty performance record of those projects—particularly in the mid-1990s. Mexico is an investment-grade country, but because of past performance problems, it is difficult to give Mexico a generous score in this area. (In CG/LA's diagnostic model, virtually all eight categories lend themselves to rapid improvement, but it is only in the long-term performance category that improvement is a long-term proposition. Mexico needs a majority of infrastructure projects to perform well over a period of four to five years in order to improve its rating in this key category.)

7. Local Engineering Procurement Construction (EPC) Partners: Mexico scores very low in this category (2). (Canada and the United States, which are both weak internationally, are very strong locally in this category, and would received scores of 8 and 9, respectively.) Local EPC firms tend to have a strong sense of the design, sizing, and execution required for the creation of first-class, long-term infrastructure; after all, these firms will have to live and conduct business in the country for the term of the projects (typically 20–30 years). Mexico's weakness in this area, like that in the Long-term Performance category, stems from the Tequila Crisis of 1995, when most EPC firms suffered mortal financial wounds. Currently, Mexico does not have enough local EPC firms that can put their balance sheets to work for strong project initiatives. Mexico urgently needs to address the scarcity of viable local EPC firms—much as Spain did with its national champions project.

8. Local Equity Participants: Mexico received a very low score in this category (3). (Both Canada and the United States received the highest score—10—because of the endless amounts of equity available for good infrastructure projects.) It is critical to have a strong group of local investors ready to invest in infrastructure and to have projects structured in a way that allows these investors to make those investments with relative ease. For Mexico, the low availability of equity from local pension funds is a significant weakness. Pension funds in Mexico hold roughly US$70 billion in assets (10 percent of GDP, compared with Chile's figure, which is six times larger), and these funds are not significant players in the project development market. At the same time, Mexico has

an emerging class of infrastructure equity entrepreneurs who are interested in this market and in the supposedly high returns that can be captured through investments in infrastructure projects.

Given this initial assessment, if Mexico is to reach world-class infrastructure levels by 2025—and to achieve the kind of immediate and abrupt increase promised over the next few years—not only will the government need to make rapid conceptual and policy changes, but it will also need to implement aggressive institutional reforms. The country could also benefit from significant support from the United States and Canada—principally from the private sector in these countries but also including assistance from the public sector in terms of risk mitigation and debt facilitation. Spain did not develop into a world-class economy without strong institutional support and guidance from the European Union (specifically in the form of the European Investment Bank and its hand-in-glove relationship with Spanish public sector project developers); similarly, dramatic increases in sound infrastructure projects in Mexico are not likely to happen without strategic, aggressive, and patient support from its North American neighbors. The Spanish Gambit scenario would triple infrastructure investment; support sustained growth in the range of 6–7 percent; and address the contentious issues that cause friction between the United States and Mexico and, to a lesser extent, between the United States and Canada.

SCENARIO 3: THE NEW MODEL

The New Model scenario focuses on addressing the backlog in North America's infrastructure—from deferred maintenance to visionary new projects—and to do so within five years. Observers from other countries now comment regularly on how "old" the U.S. infrastructure is, and this is also a constant refrain in and about Canada. The U.S. share of a robust North American infrastructure market would be a little more than 75 percent.

The New Model scenario describes what North America could look like if available expertise and resources could be reorganized in a way that would enable the creation of cutting-edge infrastructure. The New Model scenario describes the massive new investments needed for infrastructure projects in the United States, Canada, and Mexico—three times the level of regional investment. The timing is right for an initial ramp-up through to 2012, given that the U.S. economy would

Figure 5.5. Comparison of Infrastructure Growth Under Three Scenarios, **North America** (in billions of U.S. dollars)

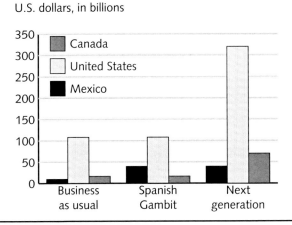

U.S. dollars, in billions

Source: Calculations by CG/LA Infrastructure, LLC, from various sources, Washington, D.C., 2007.

be the motor for the New Model process (because heavy U.S. investments in infrastructure would improve the returns of similar programs in Canada and Mexico). The scenario focuses on aggressive steps to increase funding for infrastructure projects in the United States and Canada while making the idea of bringing Mexico up to world-class levels a specific objective. According to this scenario, by 2012, the North American infrastructure market would be greater than US$400 billion—a level that would be roughly 25 percent of global infrastructure demand, as compared with the current level of 12–15 percent.[9] (Figure 5.5 shows a graphic comparison of the growth that would be achieved under all three scenarios.) The probability that the New Model scenario would be adopted by 2025 is 15 percent.

The driving vision behind the New Model scenario is that of U.S. infrastructure that not only propels growth regionally (that is, in North America, specifically including Mexico and Canada) but also builds the capacity to use technology, logistics, and services to drive a strong and highly interconnected global economy. Under this scenario, the tripling of investment in infrastructure in the United States is motivated by intense responsibilities at the local level combined with intense recognition of global commitments and opportunities.

The New Model's vision of more than an additional US$250 billion invested in North American infrastructure also addresses a strong symbolic element of creating infrastructure in a number of ways—moving from old and tired systems to young and vigorous ones. Infrastructure that is consistently and efficiently designed, financed, and constructed tells citizens a great deal about themselves and their public institutions: it principally addresses the issue of competence but also relates to the nation's probity and vision. Conversely, infrastructure that is poorly designed, slow to get financing and undergo construction, and prone to cost overruns delivers a numbingly depressing message to citizens. (Figure 5.6 presents a graphic comparison of cost overruns in North America and Europe.) In this area of modeling competence, the United States and Canada send much the same message to their citizens as does Mexico—particularly in terms of new projects but also in terms of maintenance of existing infrastructure. In its best possible light, that message is: "In this most visible area of our economic machinery we are simply not very good at what we do." And, in the larger cities of Mexico, Canada, and the United States, this message is drilled into citizens in large and small ways—from power outages, to bridge collapses, to traffic and transit congestion—day after day, hour after hour.

Another feature that this scenario takes into account is "high architecture." The scenario is based on a model of a society's view of itself and of its ambitions and aspirations. In contrast, the model that prevails today has a strong tendency to focus on systems that have the lowest cost in terms of function—bridges, power plants, wastewater treatment systems, and the like. These are systems that consistently miss the opportunity to involve society and motivate its highest ambitions and aspirations. This is not a negligible issue, because the opportunity to build soaring, beautiful, and motivating infrastructure—compare, for example, the Golden Gate Bridge with the bridge in Minnesota that collapsed in September 2007—is something that defines a culture to others as well as to its own citizens. The term "old" goes hand in hand with terms like "unimaginative" when describing North American infrastructure. In fact, infrastructure is one of the most imaginative of society's physical products, symbolizing the ambitions and goals of citizens as well as their sense of the future and their place in it.

The New Model scenario focuses on three areas: renewing existing infrastructure, revitalizing the infrastructure base, and revolutionizing the North American infrastructure matrix. According to this sce-

Figure 5.6. Average Cost Overruns in Transportation Infrastructure Project, North America and Europe, 50-Year Sample

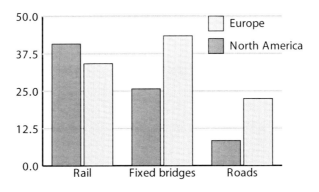

Billions of U.S. dollars

Source: Bent Flyvbjerg et al., "How Common and How Large are Cost Overruns in Transport Infrastructure Projects?" *Transport Reviews* 23, no. 1 (2003): 71–88.

nario, the largest and most important portion of new funds— roughly US$175 billion annually (targeted at US$100 billion for the United States, US$35 billion for Mexico, and US$40 billion for Canada)— would be dedicated to radically transforming the North American infrastructure matrix. The focus in the United States and Canada would be on next-generation infrastructure—projects that are not even considered today, not only because of the difficulty of conceiving and financing them (not to mention the increasing difficulty of containing cost overruns) but also because of the depressing weight of existing requirements. Projects might include fast-track development of high-speed rail systems (to relieve airport congestion and to provide for an alternative mode of transportation in the event of a crisis); new electricity transmission systems; massive upgrades to the nation's water and sanitation systems; and a new system of electricity generation, specifically including offshore terminals that receive natural gas as well as safe small-scale nuclear power plants.

The New Model specifically treats Mexico as part of the North American system and sets a high priority on catalyzing Mexico's development of a fast-growing and internally healthy job-creating economy by 2025. Essentially, the New Model scenario adopts the European

Union's approach to Spain—as the Spanish Gambit scenario does—and modifies that according to North America's political realities. The assumption is not made for purposes of stealth integration; rather it is designed to optimize North America's utilization of Mexico's resources (much like North America uses Canadian and U.S. resources) to create strategic options and opportunities that, given current low infrastructure capacities and low levels of investment, cannot even be glimpsed today.

Of the new funds that would be made available under this scenario, roughly US$50 billion would be targeted for Mexico's needs. An annual amount of US$35 billion would be used for new infrastructure projects in Mexico, preferably next-generation projects, in order to allow Mexico to bypass old infrastructures and use the funds for the projects (irrigation systems, rail systems, knowledge cities, and logistics corridors, for example) that would supercharge its economy. Mexico might target US$5 billion of the total funds for rebuilding and maintaining existing infrastructure and another US$10 billion for developing the kind of traditional infrastructure that is not currently in place—that is, the "missing" infrastructure that hobbles most developing countries, especially systems for water and sanitation as well as highways used for long hauls. (Figure 5.7 depicts the breakdown of funding allocated to each country for old and new infrastructure projects.)

The scenario assumes the same rough breakdown for Canada and the United States. Under the New Model scenario, the overall result would be a significant increase in North America's competitiveness by 2025. In addition, according to this scenario, North America would be placed in a position that would allow joint development of new technologies and new productive systems. If the New Model scenario were to be realized, by 2025 North America will have created nearly 40 million new, high-paying jobs that would be directly and indirectly related to investment in infrastructure.

FINANCING NORTH AMERICAN INFRASTRUCTURE THROUGH 2025

For the New Model scenario to be realized and the required improvements to North American infrastructure—in both concept and design—to be made, the New Model would need to be powered by

Figure 5.7. Allocation of Funding for Repair, Maintenance, and Construction of Infrastructure under the New Model Scenario, North America (in billions of U.S. dollars)

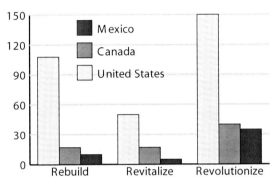

Source: Calculations by CG/LA Infrastructure, LLC, from various sources, Washington, D.C., 2007.

a financing model that would couple the enormous engineering and financial expertise available with new ways of thinking about project financing, ownership, and management. This section discusses mechanisms for building the New Model scenario through 2025.

There is an infrastructure crisis in North America: the region's obviously "crumbling" infrastructure is a hindrance to competitiveness, and a series of other issues, including undocumented immigration and weakening wages, are attributable to the region's weak and economically ineffective infrastructure. Critically, one peculiar reality about infrastructure is that the effects of crisis in this area will unfold over time; however, because projects take so long to conceive, finance, and build, the results of current inaction will be felt for a generation. Therefore, action must be taken now to address this issue; this demands strong political leadership.

Dealing with the infrastructure crisis in North America requires a new model for infrastructure investment. At the same time, nothing is more challenging than creating a new and, for the sake of argument, "more modern" model for financing the infrastructure investments that North America needs. In the absence of a clear crisis, wrenching change is politically difficult. This is another issue that requires political leadership.

A successful model that would be capable of consistently supporting North American investments in infrastructure in the range of US$400 billion per year would need to have four characteristics:

- The model would need to be motivated by an overall vision of global competitiveness; local advantages, pork, and earmarks are political realities, but they do not add up to the visionary leadership that is required.

- Project selection along with a significant financing component would need to be organized—planned and overseen, but not managed—by the federal governments of the United States, Canada, and Mexico.

- The financing mechanism for each country would need to be "strategic"—that is, substantial enough to support massive financial investments and visionary enough to support those projects that would generate sustained competitiveness.

- Very significant decisionmaking power, along with risk capacity, would be assigned to the private sector, whose role would be that of a linchpin in the process: structuring, executing, and managing projects (with significant financing coming from firms that put their balance sheets to work for these projects).

The key to the success of this model is recognition not only that enormous expertise is available but also that it is necessary to gradually experiment with new ways for the private and public sectors to participate in infrastructure project conception, development, and maintenance. The model traced out below is not designed to tilt power from either the private sector or the public sector, or from the state level to the national level; rather, the model is designed with an eye toward North America's need to rapidly build the right infrastructure for a rapidly globalizing and interdependent world.

NATIONAL VISION

The key requirement for achieving the New Model scenario is a national vision of the specific infrastructure requirements needed to gain sustained competitiveness. The vision needs to be developed within the three countries and—what is even more challenging—it needs to be developed across the three countries in the context of competitive complementarity. Thus, if Mexico were to build a major new port—for example, Punta Colonet on the Pacific Coast, which would double Mexico's container capacity—the United States would need to sequence an investment in the logistics systems required to make that new capacity successful.

The vision that underlies the New Model provides a blueprint for action that results from a discussion among the citizens and political leaders in each North American country that clearly recognizes the need for massive new investments in the all three countries' infrastructure. At the same time, the discussion must also set forth a sense of how those projects will address critical issues of both global competitiveness and local quality of life.

While searching for their own vision, however, Canada, Mexico, and the United States cannot lose sight of the fact that the region needs an overall North American vision about its infrastructure and its effect on regional competitiveness. This quest for a regional vision is not a smokescreen for integration. It is increasingly clear that the driving concept in each country must be the aggressive development of its own resources (natural, human, imaginative), vision, and standard of excellence. Moreover, it is inevitable and fundamental that the direction for the New Model come from each national or federal government. The model requires coordinating decisionmaking—not initiative. Nevertheless, without an overall vision of how the three countries of North America will be competitive, there is little chance of creating and sustaining an aggressive infrastructure model.

PROJECT SELECTION: THE LOCUS OF DECISIONMAKING

The New Model requires an overall level of planning, coordination, and strategic action that is currently absent. In the area of infrastructure, decentralized decisionmaking is not practical, because the power of arguments for national competitiveness is weak when lined up against the immediacy of local needs. This is particularly the case when an increasing amount of financing is generated locally. A national vision—and the discussion surrounding that vision—requires coordination, prioritization, and action. There is no doubt that local voices in Mexico, Canada, and the United States will remain powerful, but organization on a national level is fundamental if new investments are to drive competitiveness systematically.

What is required is an institutional focus on the aspects of infrastructure that are related to long-term competitiveness. In this sense, North America's current governing machinery has not caught up with globalization; the mechanisms are based on the old logic and language of public works, public finance, and short-term construction contracts. Canada seems to have moved the fastest in terms of modernizing its governing machinery and establishing a ministerial level department—Infrastructure Canada—in 2002 as a way to coordinate the country's infrastructure initiatives. (It is important to note that Infrastructure Canada publishes its own budget.) In Mexico, President Calderón's government established a presidential-level infrastructure coordinating position when the president took office at the end of 2006; the administration has given that office the power to organize the priorities of each of the cabinet-level agencies focused on Mexico's infrastructure: the National Water Commission and the powerful Energy and Transport and Communications Ministries. In contrast, the United States has had no similar recognition of what might be called the strategic importance of infrastructure; rather, each government department has its own budget, its own priorities, and its own congressional constituency, and each department bureaucratically engages in full-scale battles against its rivals for attention and funding.

PROJECT FINANCING: BRINGING FEDERAL GOVERNMENTS AND THE PRIVATE SECTOR INTO THE EFFORT

Money is the critical component in the New Model scenario, and organizing the kind of strategic effort that is required is clearly a national function. In fact, the linchpin of the New Model for each of the three countries would have to be a centralized infrastructure bank that has the sovereign backing required to raise money from the capital markets and to invest in projects and systems that are a priority. This is not a particularly radical idea; entities to carry out this kind of function have always existed in the central governments of the three countries and have been used to transfer revenues. For example, in the United States, the Federal Highway Administration carries out this function under the U.S. Interstate Highway Act; in Europe, the European Union chartered the European Investment Bank to raise funds for, and to invest in, infrastructure projects that were considered a priority for member countries as well as for the EU as a whole.

Given the sums required for infrastructure investments it is essential that an infrastructure bank be established.[10] In each country, this bank would be tasked with four functions:

- raising funds;

- generating a robust and systematic pipeline of projects consistent with increasing the country's global competitiveness;

- disbursing funds to priority projects; and

- monitoring the design, construction, and especially long-term performance of these projects.

Establishing an infrastructure bank would not require the creation of large bureaucracies in each country for two reasons: (1) Many of these functions are already well staffed in various departments in Canada, Mexico, and the United States, thus duplication would be eliminated. (2) The private sector would perform much of the actual work, as it does now, and there would be increasingly venturesome experiments with public-private partnerships. The challenge would be to take on the leadership that is needed to inject a sense of the urgency of the mission to make the specific investments the New Model requires and especially to achieve performance goals nationally as well as regionally.

PRIVATE ACTION: GIVING RESPONSIBILITY TO THOSE
WITH EXPERTISE

If financing is the linchpin of the New Model, then a gradually expanded role for the private sector would be the motor not only for increased investment in North America's infrastructure but also for improved decisionmaking on projects and better management of public investments. Currently, the private sector in Mexico, Canada, and the United States participates in infrastructure projects mainly on a risk-free, fee-for-services basis. This arrangement creates a fairly limited role for the private sector as well as for the market in terms of initiative, risk-taking, and responsibility. In fact, responsibility is simply not aligned with expertise: the public sector develops projects, generates financing (through tax-exempt bonds, federal government transfers, and the like), and structures bidding processes; private firms respond to requests, are awarded contracts, and submit invoices (with multiple change orders) as the work is completed. The fairly sterile division of labor walls off infrastructure investments from free market energy, initiative, and creativity. (Given that cost overruns, which characterize the current system in all three countries, *average* between 10 percent and 40 percent of the original amount of contract awards and plague the operation and maintenance of projects after they have been completed, it would make sense that new ways of doing business need to be explored).

The new model for financing infrastructure projects would experiment with redistributing fundamental tasks between the private and public sectors, improving the velocity of project creation, making funding available for projects, and working vigorously to ensure the efficient execution and management of projects. Moving toward this approach—broadly termed a public-private partnership—the public sector would ideally focus on what it does best: conceive of long-term projects and care for the public's interest. The private sector would do what it does best: find ways to develop, finance, and execute projects efficiently and within strict (and strictly monitored) guidelines that are established by the public sector. (Figure 5.8 graphically compares the way responsibilities for financing infrastructure tasks are distributed today with the way that the New Model proposes.)

The firms in the private sector that have healthy balance sheets would be given a level of responsibility that is not typical in the protected public infrastructure market that is in place in North America today. Executives of firms in the private sector would be responsible for initiating projects; guaranteeing costs (on their balance sheets); raising funds, based on the project's value and on their balance sheets; and, in some cases, operating those projects for a period of 20–30 years. The basic trade-off is that the private sector would play a much bigger role—and assume much more risk—while taking responsibility for significant new monies injected into the system as well as for making sure that projects are executed and managed quickly and profitably. Thus, private stakeholders would receive reasonable returns on their contribution to what is, in essence, massive public value creation.

In sum, under the New Model, authority for creating and completing infrastructure projects would remain with the public sector, whereas tasks would be rationalized and shifted to the private sector. As a result, there would be a very strong set of public sector executives

Figure 5.8. Distribution of Financing Responsibilities for Infrastructure Tasks, Current Model versus New Model

	Originate	Finance	Bid	Construct	Operate	Maintain	
New Model	public	public	public	private	public	public	Decision
	local	local (2/3)	local	local	local	local	Action
Current Model	public & private	public & private	public	private	private	private	Decision
	national/ local	national/ local	national/ local	national/ local	national/ local	national/ local	Action

who would think through the country's future and a very restless and innovative set of private sector executives who would balance aggressive business development with a long-term appreciation of risk and reward.

CONCLUSION: MAPPING THE WAY FORWARD

If infrastructure is a system of systems, then it is clear that North America needs to create a new model for developing and maintaining its infrastructure. The New Model proposed in this report has two urgent strategic purposes:

- The New Model will finance efficient, modern, and robust infrastructure projects in all three countries.

- It will oversee rational and consistent decisions on infrastructure projects that have a high priority not just by financing projects but by financing the right projects to ensure that the systems in each North American country generate internal competitiveness as well as a rapid increase in competitiveness for the region as a whole.

Creating a new model for selecting infrastructure projects and financing them is an extraordinary challenge that will require real leadership in all three countries. The biggest problem—and one that is likely to be most deeply manifested in the United States—is resistance to change on the part of the many people who have substantial expertise in the current system. This group includes chief executive officers of construction firms, who have spent their entire careers in a relatively risk-free, fee-for-services environment; financial officers in municipal bond investment firms, who benefit from an essentially captive US$70 billion annual market; and executives in the public sector as well as those in public sector unions, who exercise enormous control (one might easily call it a stranglehold) over the nation's infrastructure. The situation is not very different in Canada and Mexico. As figure 5.8 clearly shows, the challenge lies in transitioning public sector executives from responsibility for action along the infrastructure value chain to responsibility for management throughout that chain and for action mainly at the point when the project is designed and the contract for its completion is put out for bids. At the same time, the private sector will need to increase its sphere of activity in a number of areas—specifically in the areas of finance and project delivery guarantees.

Implicit in this discussion is the notion that a similar model would emerge in all three countries. This need for congruence is probably a requirement, because the vast increase in necessary funding would come from a "grand bargain" between the public and private sectors. On the one hand, new investments would be catalyzed by a new funding source located at the heart of each country's central government; on the other hand—the piece that makes the whole idea work—the private sector would complete the equation by providing both equity and debt financing for projects. Getting the model right and creating a relatively similar structure across the entire continent will have the added value of creating shared learning across all three countries as well as a shared set of the rules of the game that will theoretically allow the most efficient infrastructure-related companies to work in each country.[11]

As North America moves forward in the face of the current infrastructure crisis, perhaps the key requirement is for the three countries to begin to think in terms of regional competitiveness, tripling the annual investments in infrastructure that the United States, Mexico, and Canada currently make while keeping a sharp eye on competitive complementarity. Although the Business as Usual scenario seems to be the most likely outcome for the future of North America's infrastructure (which would be catastrophic for Mexico) and the Spanish Gambit scenario offers a minimal way to secure North America's future, it is the investment targets proposed in the New Model (an annual investment of US$300 billion in new funds) that should galvanize the attention of North America's political leadership.

The road forward needs to begin with a rapid ramp-up, similar to the one provided by the U.S. Interstate Highway Act or even by President Kennedy's stated goal to put a man on the moon. The current situation, with North America simply muddling through the crisis, presides over the festering of old problems and the creation of ugly new ones. Mapping the New Model involves a series of changes—in terms of vision, institutions, financing, and the roles of the private and public sectors—that recognizes the enormous availability of expertise and merely experiments with rearranging that expertise in a way that will rapidly meet the challenges and opportunities of globalization.

Creating world-class infrastructure is a strategic measure, which defines and describes a country's ability to compete; decisions made today generate results over a 20–30 year period. Including—or simply viewing—the challenge in terms of the North American map builds a capacity for adopting a deeper strategy in depth, moving away from the export/import and high wage/low wage paradigms and beginning to think in terms of new possibilities. And those possibilities—for example, southern Mexico's production of food for the world, northern Mexico's ability to host world-class manufacturing enterprises, the capability of U.S. and Canadian markets to power *regional* competitiveness, or the ability of US$14 trillion in U.S. pension fund assets (60 percent of the world's total) to increase North America's value—are feasible.

If the region is to have the capacity for world leadership in 2025—in terms of world-class industry, services, and quality of life—it is critical for Canada, Mexico, and the United States to accept the strategic challenge and to quickly and intelligently build world-class infrastructure throughout North America. In so doing, in 2025, North America—a region consisting of three sovereign states and nearly 500 million citizens and one that has the ability to invest US$400 billion annually to design, build, and manage first-class infrastructure—should be the most competitive region in the world.

SOURCES

GENERAL

Doshi, Viren, Gary Schulman, and Daniel Gabaldon. "Lights! Water! Motion! Strategy + Business." Booz, Allen and Hamilton, McLean, Va., May 2007.

Fay, Marianne, and Mary Morrisson. "Infrastructure in Latin America: Recent Developments and Key Challenges." Washington, D.C.: World Bank, August 2005.

Flyvbjerg, Bent, et al. "How Common and How Large are Cost Overruns in Transport Infrastructure Projects?" *Transport Reviews* 23, no. 1 (2003): 71–88.

Organization for Economic Cooperation and Development. "Infrastructure to 2030: Telecom, Land Transport, Water and Electricity." Paris: OECD, June 22, 2006.

———. "Infrastructure to 2030: Mapping Policy for Water, Electricity and Transport." Paris: OECD, August 30, 2007.

Urban Land Institute and Ernst and Young. "Infrastructure 2007: A Global Perspective." Washington, D.C., 2007.

World Bank. *World Development Report 1994: Infrastructure for Development.* New York: Oxford University Press, 1994.

CANADA

Cannon, Lawrence. "2007–2008: Report on Plans and Priorities." Ottawa: Infrastructure Canada, 2006, http://www.infrastructure.gc.ca.

Government of Canada, Ministry of Finance. "Annual Financial Report of the Government of Canada: Fiscal Year 2006–2007." Ottawa, 2007, http://www.fin.gc.ca/afr/2007/afr2007e.pdf.

Harchaoui, Tarek M., Faouzi Tarkhani, and Paul Warren. "Public Infrastructure in Canada: Where Do We Stand?" Ottawa: Statistics Canada, Micro-Economic Analysis Division, November 2003.

Leckie, John. "The Top 10 Infrastructure Projects in Canada." Toronto: Renew Canada, January 2006, http://www.renewcanada.net.

Toronto Dominion Bank Financial Group. "Mind the Gap: Finding the Money to Upgrade Canada's Aging Public Infrastructure." Toronto, May 2004, http://www.td.com/economics/special/infra04.pdf.

MEXICO

Anderson, Norman F., and Patricia Pietravalle. "Infrastructure Rankings in Latin America," Second Annual Report. Washington, D.C., November 2007.

Calderón Hinojosa, Felipe. "Programa Nacional de Infraestructura." Mexico City, July 2007, http://www.infraestructura.gob.mx.

CG/LA Infrastructure, LLC. "The Top 40 Infrastructure Projects in Mexico," Report prepared for the Second Annual Mexico Leadership Forum, Guadalajara, Jalisco, Mexico, October 24–25, 2007.

Robles Ferrer, Daniel. "Créditos Estructurados en Infraestructura: Detonadores de Inversión," BANOBRAS, Mexico City, December 2006, http://www.banobras.gob.mx/BANOBRAS/CasosdeexitoRevistayEventos/Revista/4toTrim2006/creditosestructurados.htm.

Eggers, William D., and Tiffany Dovey. "Closing America's Infrastructure Gap: The Role of Public Private Partnerships." A Deloitte Research Study, Deloitte Development LLC, Washington, D.C., 2007.

UNITED STATES

American Society of Civil Engineers. "Report Card for America's Infrastructure." Reston, Va., 2005.

Anderson, Norman F. "Dramatically Improving Infrastructure Competitiveness: The Eight Key Policy Requirements." Report presented by CG/LA Infrastructure LLC, Washington, D.C., May 2007.

Eggers, William D., and Tiffany Dovey. "Closing America's Infrastructure Gap: The Role of Public Private Partnerships." A Deloitte Research Study, Deloitte Development, LLC, http://www.deloitte.com/dtt/cda/doc/content/us_ps_PPPUS_final(1).pdf.

National Surface Transportation Policy and Revenue Study Commission. "Transportation for Tomorrow." Washington, D.C., January 15, 2008.

Rohatyn, Felix, and Warren Rudman. "It's Time to Rebuild America: A Plan for Spending More—and Wisely—on Our Decaying Infrastructure." *Washington Post*, December 13, 2005.

U.S. Congress, Congressional Budget Office. "Trends in Public Infrastructure Spending," Washington, D.C., May 1999.

U.S. Government Accountability Office. "U.S. Infrastructure: Funding Trends and U.S. Agencies' Investment Estimates," Report no. GAO-01-986T. Washington, D.C., July 2001, http://www.gao.gov/cgi-bin/getrpt?GAO-01-986T.

AUTHOR INTERVIEWS

Alfredo Elias Ayub, director general, Comisión Federal de Electricidad, Mexico City, August 3, 2007.

Oscar de Buen, undersecretary, Secretariat of Communication and Transportation, Mexico City, August 3, 2007.

Isabel Martín Castellá, former vice president (2000–2006), European Investment Bank, Madrid, September 3, 2007.

Mortimer Downey, chairman, Coalition for America's Gateways and Trade Corridors, and president, PB Consulting, Inc. Washington, D.C., October 17, 2007.

Antonio M. Lopez Corral, director general (1995–2003), Programación Económica del Ministerio de Fomento, currently a private consultant and professor at the Polytechnic University of Madrid, Mexico City, September 10, 2007, and Washington, D,C., September 15, 2007.

Arturo Olvera, managing director, Hermes Infraestructura (formerly on the staff of BANOBRAS), Mexico City, July 13, 2007.

NOTES

1. The World Bank uses a figure of 15,000 jobs created for each US$1 billion invested in developing countries' new infrastructure, with a total figure for jobs creation three times as large; thus, for each US$1 billion invested, roughly 45,000 jobs are created; see World Bank, *World Development Report 1994: Infrastructure for Development* (New York: Oxford University Press, 1994). For developed countries, the Massachusetts Infrastructure Investment Coalition estimates the investment of 57,400 new jobs for each US$1 billion invested in infrastructure; see "Infrastructure Status Report: Massachusetts Drinking Water," May 2007.

2. William D. Eggers and Tiffany Dovey, "Closing America's Infrastructure Gap: The Role of Public Private Partnerships," A Deloitte Research Study, Deloitte Development, LLC., Washington, D.C., 2007, http://www.deloitte.com/dtt/cda/doc/content/us_ps_PPPUS_final(1).pdf; Toronto Dominion Bank Financial Group, "Minding the Gap: Finding the Money

to Upgrade Canada's Aging Public Infrastructure, Toronto, May 2004, http://www.td.com/economics/special/infra04.pdf; author interview with Oscar de Buen, Undersecretary, Secretariat of Communication and Transportation, Mexico City, August 3, 2007.

3. National Chamber Foundation, "Future Highway and Public Transportation Financing, Phase II," Washington, D.C., 2005.

4. As an emerging market, Mexico needs to make investments in infrastructure that are equivalent to about 5 percent of its gross domestic product. Currently the country's annual investment rate in infrastructure is about 1.5 percent of its GDP (when the oil and gas sector is excluded); whereas China invests 9 percent of its GDP in infrastructure each year, and India and Chile invest in the 5 percent range. CG/LA figures taken from Norman F. Anderson and Patricia Pietravalle, "Infrastructure Rankings in Latin America," Second Annual Report, Washington, D.C., November 2007.

5. The requirement for using expertise in infrastructure projects is significant. In Spain, for example, the public sector entity that drove this process, FOMENTO, was headed by a group of highly qualified—and even visionary—professionals from the moment of Spain's entry into the European Union, and this was further facilitated by a very tight relationship (based on expertise) between these professionals and the European Investment Bank.

6. The initiative bears no resemblance to the ill-fated Plan Puebla Panama, which was simply an integration scheme without economic substance.

7. Private communication with Arturo Olvera, formerly of BANOBRAS and currently working for Hermes Infraestructura, a local private equity firm, Mexico City, July 13, 2007.

8. The diagnostic for both the United States and Canada shows significant overall weakness on a par with Mexico's; all the areas of strength and weakness differ.

9. CG/LA Infrastructure estimates that the global market demand for infrastructure is US$1.1 trillion per year; Macquarie, an infrastructure investment firm, estimates a slightly larger global market of US$1.3 trillion annually; and two other studies, which focus on demand rather than historical performance, see the market requiring nearly US$2 trillion per year, according to the study published by Viren Doshi, Gary Schulman, and Daniel Gabaldon ("Lights! Water! Motion!" *Strategy + Business,* Booz Allen Hamilton, McLean, Va., Spring 2007), or US$3 trillion per year, according to the Organization for Economic Cooperation and Development in "Infrastructure to 2030: Mapping Policy for Water, Electricity and Transport" (Paris: OECD, August 30, 2007). The global infrastructure market is large and demand is robust, but there is significant debate about how investment matches demand, particularly in the areas of water and wastewater.

10. Felix Rohatyn and Warren Rudman have called for a National Infrastructure Corporation to exercise this catalytic investment role; see Felix Rohatyn and Warren Rudman, "It's Time to Rebuild America: A Plan for Spending More—and Wisely—on Our Decaying Infrastructure," *Washington Post,* December 13, 2005.

11. This will also allow North America to create infrastructure champions who would be capable of operating in the rest of the world. Currently, there are no North American local engineering procurement construction firms with the ability to develop large infrastructure projects around the globe; in effect, the North American infrastructure model excludes North American firms from leading major efforts in the global market that is worth an estimated US$41 trillion (through 2030).

6

OUTLOOK FOR SECURITY

ARMAND B. PESCHARD-SVERDRUP
ROBERT S. SHAW

The security of North America in 2025 will be determined by the ability of Canada, Mexico, and the United States to manage a wide array of emerging challenges, which may include terrorism, intercontinental missile attacks, threats to public security, economic shocks, the scarcity of the energy supply, environmental pressures, natural disasters, and the spread of diseases and pandemics. Not many conceivable situations would seriously challenge North America's fundamental governing institutions, but the security threats of the coming decades have the potential to test the capacity of these institutions and also pose a serious risk to the public welfare of the countries' residents. Despite the diverse views of the three countries' governments about the severity of the threats and the levels of response required, the need for cooperation is great and reflects the shared interests of all North Americans.

The United States redefined its North American agenda in response to the terrorist attacks that took place on September 11, 2001. The actions of a few individuals, supported by the Al Qaeda terrorist network, demonstrated an ability to cause massive destruction and loss of life in major population centers in North America. The attacks caused a degree of fear among the general public, created conditions that exacerbated slow growth in Canada and an economic recession in Mexico and the United States, and had a dramatic impact on perceptions of security threats and challenges. Preventing future terrorist attacks became the cornerstone of a new U.S. national security agenda: the government created the U.S. Department of Homeland Security, established a North

American military command, placed unprecedented focus on border security, and emphasized preventive measures to keep threats from materializing. Terrorism now dominates the North American security agenda, and Mexico and Canada have actively supported a wide array of measures pushed for by the United States, including intelligence sharing and increased border security.

Nevertheless, measures to combat terrorism are only one element of a comprehensive strategy North America must undertake to mitigate threats to the public in the coming decades. In order to manage the safety of North America's population effectively, it will be critical to expand the traditional view of security and to consider a broad array of issues and threats that have the potential to have a detrimental impact on the population's way of life. As the region moves toward 2025, a comprehensive North American security agenda should take into account disasters such as future terrorist attacks on cities that can have a serious effect on human life, infrastructure, electronic communications, and public health. The strategy should also include measures for protecting the countries from natural disasters, environmental catastrophes, and water shortages as well as diseases and illnesses that threaten public health and contaminate the food supply or create shortages in the supply. In addition, the governments of all three nations will need to take steps to secure the supply of energy and to prepare for major energy disruptions as well as economic crises. Finally, North America's comprehensive security strategy should renew emphasis on confronting violence perpetrated by transnational organized criminal organizations and nonstate actors, such as gangs, drug and human traffickers, and extremist radicals or terrorists.

Even though some of these threats may appear more regional or country-specific, if and when they materialize, the negative effects on public welfare, the economy, and political stability will be shared in various degrees across the North American community. In the year 2025, all indications point to the need for deeper integration and interdependence among Canada, Mexico, and the United States. In today's context, security threats do not respect traditional political borders, and the transnational impact of threats will be even more pronounced in the future. North America will be far better positioned to meet the emerging challenges to its security in the coming decades by coordinating prevention efforts and methods of response.

Complicating this task are significant differences in security emphasis and priorities held by Canada, Mexico, and the United States. North America has yet to truly identify a shared security agenda; in fact, there is even inconsistency in the way policymakers and the general public conceptualize the basic meaning of the word "security." In Mexico, the term has traditionally been applied to domestic conditions related to public safety. In fact, the notion of security carried with it a negative connotation for many years, although a recent survey of Mexican public opinion conducted jointly by the Centro de Investigación y Docencia Económicas and the Consejo Mexicano de Asuntos Internacionales suggests that Mexicans have increasingly been thinking of security in more global terms.[1] The U.S. public is far more inclined to view security within a global context and, in the past, has accepted policies intended to meet threats abroad and to preserve the world order. In Canada, the governments have gradually made peacekeeping and humanitarian operations the primary focus for the country's military since 1956. This focus has had widespread public support despite the Canadian government's more combat-oriented role in Afghanistan—under both Liberal and Conservative governments—since early 2002, where, as of January 2008, there had been a total of 76 Canadian combat fatalities. Overall, the Canadian government has security priorities that differ even more from those held by its neighbors.

The differences are reflected in each country's military strategy and position in world affairs. Even though it is important to bear this divergence in mind, the differences are not great enough to prevent policymakers from focusing on shared challenges facing the region and beginning to develop comprehensive prevention strategies and to plan for coordinated responses to threats. Despite the differences separating the North American community on issues of security, each country is working to find ways to improve management of its borders, respond to natural disasters, combat organized crime, ensure economic stability, and protect its residents and economies. Leaders of the three countries must focus on shared values in other areas and recognize that the current relationship rests on far more than the simple fact that the three countries happen to share borders.

This chapter begins with a discussion of specific threats that may challenge North America's security in the coming decades. The first section will examine changing dynamics in the geopolitical situation of the world, consider the range of threats to North America's security, and end with a discussion of various vulnerabilities that leave North America's public welfare exposed. The second section of the chapter will look at North America's current security architecture, including the bilateral security relations between each country, the current border agreements and their attention to security, and the current trilateral framework for cooperative efforts to assure North America's security. The authors of this chapter conclude that the continent's current security framework is inadequate to effectively mitigate and respond to the broad spectrum of threats and challenges facing the region in the twenty-first century and that policymakers in each country must encourage organizational and cultural changes in order to protect the welfare of their citizens in the coming decades. The final section of this chapter will offer various recommendations for a new North American security architecture in the face of the threats and challenges that the region is likely to face in 2025.

CHALLENGES FACING NORTH AMERICA'S SECURITY

STATE AND NONSTATE ACTORS: A 2025 WORLD ORDER

The world in 2025 will be different in fundamental ways from the unipolar system that emerged following the Cold War. The dominance of the United States in both "hard" and "soft" power that defined the 1990s is already being challenged. In 2025, economic, military, and political power will be diffused among a greater number of state and nonstate actors than it was at any time in the modern era. Barring some cataclysmic event, globalization will continue to interconnect countries and societies as the world moves toward a truly multipolar system. The nature of the changes in the world order that are occurring today and are bound to become even more dramatic in the future makes it problematic to predict the types of security challenges the region will need to address in 2025. As opposed to conjuring up future security scenarios, which may or may not develop, it might be more helpful to look at current trends and fast-forward to the way they may conceivably evolve by the year 2025.

The Rise of Global Powers: China, India, Russia, and Brazil

The rise of China and India as economic powers will make these countries drivers of the world's economy, playing one of the most significant roles in the shifting balance of global power. Russia's vast energy resources and recent economic growth position the country to be among the most powerful states in 2025, although achieving this status will require Russia to overcome serious domestic problems. Brazil also faces many internal challenges, but its rise as a regional economic power is likely to continue; in the decades to come, Brazil will join the most powerful economic states in the world. China's ability to maintain its fast-paced economic growth could depend on several key variables, including the evolution of the country's political and legal institutions and the government's ability to manage economic growth in its rural and urban centers. India's sound democratic governing institutions, its functioning legal system, its free press, and the members of its workforce who are educated and English-speaking all provide the country with considerable advantages for its long-term growth potential. Increases in China, India, Russia, and Brazil's share of the world's economy in the coming decades will create geopolitical opportunities that will expand these nations' sphere of influence.

Current trends indicate that these four countries will be powerful state actors in 2025. In some areas, such as technologically advanced weapons systems, the power of the United States will remain unmatched in 2025, but U.S. economic influence and power are likely to diminish in many ways. Any change in the status of the United States on the world stage will have both direct and indirect consequences for Canada as well as Mexico. It would be in the best interest of North America and the international community as a whole to focus on deepening integration and economic interdependence and on encouraging the peaceful resolution of disputes in order to minimize conflict among countries that are part of the changing world order.

Equally important will be the ability of international institutions to accommodate the shifting realities of global power; their success or failure to do so is likely to determine their future relevancy. To further both these ends, the countries of North America should take the lead in reinvigorating global trade talks and in advancing meaningful reform of the United Nations.

The Middle East, East Asia, and Nuclear Proliferation

The political conditions in the broader Middle East are of national importance not only to the United States but also to its North American

neighbors. In the coming decades, Iraq's internal situation, Iran's nuclear program, and the Palestinian issue will have serious consequences for the security of the Middle East. The region's large share of the
world's energy supply makes stability in the region of vital importance
to the international community. Nationalism, religious extremism,
political instability, and the prospect of nuclear proliferation together
pose serious challenges for the future of the region.

Instability in Iraq and the United States' attempt to improve the
situation in that country has drained U.S. resources, diverted attention
away from other potential problems, and also limited U.S. maneuver-
ability on other issues. The U.S. commitment in Iraq has had major
implications for Canada and Mexico. Even with international involvement, stabilizing the political situation in Iraq could take a decade or
more, and some of the actors who have been inflamed by the conflict
not only pose a danger to the security of the greater Middle East but
also can be propelled to take steps to strengthen international terrorist
networks.

Iran's relations with many of its neighbors are tense, and its relationship with the United States is perceived as hostile—and it currently
seems to be deteriorating even further. Similarly, Iran perceives the
United States as antagonistic. Iran's conventional military power may
be the greatest potential military threat to many states in the Middle
East and to U.S. interests in the region. There is a very real possibility that by 2025—or even earlier—Iran will have developed a nuclear
weapon and the means to attach it to a ballistic missile. This ability
would seriously threaten the stability of the region because of the
likelihood that Egypt and Saudi Arabia would race to develop their
own nuclear capability and Israel could attempt to launch a preemptive strike. Iran has taken measures to prevent economic isolation, and
even though the international diplomatic community has been effective in temporarily halting Iran's attempts to develop nuclear capability,
the threat is likely to be present in 2025.

In 2025, Iran may be one of several new members to the so-called
"nuclear club," especially if the United Nations or other key international players fail to develop and prioritize a more effective nonproliferation strategy. Even though most countries without nuclear weapons
capabilities abide by the Nuclear Non-Proliferation Treaty and are not
likely to develop these weapons, proliferation remains a major threat to
world security. Some argue that proliferation brings stability because

no one would dare to initiate a nuclear attack in light of the realization that the target's counterattack would destroy them as well, but this theory is dubious at best and rests on the assumption that rational actors control nuclear arsenals. The argument fails to consider terrorist organizations' stated desire to acquire and use these weapons. Even among states that currently have nuclear capabilities, avoiding future conflict may not be an easy task, and effective diplomacy will be required on the global stage for many years to come.

North Korea successfully tested a nuclear bomb in 2006. The international community condemned the action, and the six-party talks led by the United States were reinvigorated in an attempt to encourage North Korea to abandon its nuclear program. Despite reaching a major international deal in February 2006, whereby North Korea was to take steps to disarm, the situation now has many similar characteristics to a previous arrangement made in 1994 between the United States and North Korea, which was subsequently broken. North Korea's political future is extremely difficult to predict, but the future of the country's nuclear program will have implications on proliferation in the rest of East Asia and possibly on the diffusion of nuclear technology to other states or to nonstate actors.

It is possible that the United States will accelerate its efforts to develop a missile defense system as a way to protect itself against increased proliferation. But the threat level would have to increase dramatically for Canada or Mexico to agree to join such a program. The technology needed for a missile defense system is still in its infancy; however, if the program remains a priority for the United States, it may be realized by 2025.

The Western Hemisphere

Approaching 2025, the governing institutions and free market systems in many Latin American states will come under increasing pressure. Various factors could lead to instability in certain parts of the region; these include a rise in crime rates, gang violence, drug-related violence, a failure to address substantial social inequalities, and general disillusionment with democracy and the neoliberal economic system. Latin American governments must promote policies that will encourage long-term economic growth, regional competitiveness, and poverty reduction in order to mitigate these threats. It is in the best interest of North America to support and encourage these efforts. Canada,

Mexico, and the United States will be most concerned with the region's overall ability to manage emerging pressures and overall stability in the hemisphere, particularly in Central America and the Caribbean.

The future strength of Latin America's governing institutions hinges on economic growth and a reduction in the poverty level in the region. Recent statistics along these lines are encouraging. Following five years of economic stagnation that started in 1998, the region is now enjoying its fourth consecutive year of economic growth, averaging a healthy annual growth rate of 5 percent. According to the *Economist,* inflation is low, the region's exports are stronger than its imports, and several Latin American economies are benefiting from broad-based growth in exports.[2] In addition, the United Nations estimates that poverty in Latin America fell from 48.3 percent to 39.8 percent between 1990 and 2006.[3] However, the vast majority of economic growth in the region is commodity-driven and is not based on Latin America's global competitiveness. It is doubtful that the region could maintain the current rates of growth if the U.S. economy cools or those of China and India slow down. Compared to the rising economic powers and even to Eastern Europe, Latin America has a significant disadvantage when it comes to the education of its population, technology, and foreign investment.[4]

During the current period of economic strength driven by the high demands in commodities, it is critical for Latin American governments to address the many internal impediments to growth and poverty reduction. The countries of North America should make it a priority to support Latin America's efforts to resolve these problems. In the absence of a better educational system, a more advanced transportation infrastructure, and more efficient regulation of business, Latin American economies will fail to grow and will become more vulnerable to crisis and instability. Regional polling data by *Latinobarometro,* a Chilean organization that works with the *Economist,* suggests that the population of Latin America will not easily revert to authoritarianism and that a majority of the public agrees that democracy is still the "least bad" system of government.[5] Nevertheless, in 2006, a majority of respondents in every Latin American country—except Uruguay, Venezuela, and Argentina—indicated dissatisfaction with the way democracy is working in their own countries. It is in the interest of North America and the Western Hemisphere as a whole to consolidate the democratic institutions in the region and to reduce the pressures facing Latin American governments today.

Serious crises and instability in Central America would have a direct impact on Mexico's southern border, on Mexico's internal security situation, and on migration to the United States. Drug trafficking, transnational gangs, and organized crime have bred instability and violence in Guatemala, El Salvador, and Honduras. The murder rates in these countries are nearly three times as high as the rates in the rest of Latin America. Violence is also directly affecting elections in the region, with the number of campaign-related murders—primarily targeted at local candidates—on the rise. Areas of these countries may prove to be ungovernable and could develop into safe havens for gangs and drug traffickers. The possibility exists that the fundamental governing institutions of these Central American countries may be challenged as a result of dissatisfaction among their populations or because of the violence perpetrated by gangs or drug traffickers. The impact on the region and on Mexico could be devastating. To manage this situation, North America will need to support Central American efforts to control violence and to govern their societies effectively, and this is one of the objectives of the Mérida Initiative, which is discussed in more detail later in the chapter.

The potential for instability in Cuba in the coming decades is a concern for U.S. national security, given the size of the Cuban population and Cuba's proximity to southern Florida. The nightmare scenario for the United States would be a transition marked by massive violence and a humanitarian crisis, leading to a high level of Cuban migration into the United States. This possibility seems unlikely, however, in light of the peaceful and stable interim transition of power that already occurred in Cuba in 2006, when Fidel Castro, dictator for 50 years, transferred power to his brother, Raul Castro, who assumed the position of acting president. This transition progressed further in February 2008, when Fidel Castro formally stepped down as president because of ailing health, setting the stage for that nation's presidential succession. Although Raul Castro was ultimately named the successor, it remains to be seen whether the transition of power brings about generational change by preserving certain aspects of the Cuban Revolution while also overseeing the gradual reform process that the country needs. After all, even China has demonstrated that the two models are not mutually exclusive—at least thus far. However, even if Cuba's leadership remains in the hands of Raul Castro, it is highly unlikely that he would be in power in 2025, given that he would be 94 years of age. This presidential succession may provide the opportunity for the United States to ease the economic and travel restrictions imposed on the current regime and develop a much more constructive relationship in the future.

Weak and Failing States

A country becomes a failed state when its central governing authority essentially loses control over a significant portion of its territory and can no longer provide security and basic services to its population. Conflict is a critical factor that can result in state failure, but a variety of internal conditions can threaten a state's internal stability, making it a weak state.[6] Instability and violence within a failed state can result in massive humanitarian disasters, human rights violations, and regional strife. Moreover, some failed states could pose a serious threat to the economic stability of the world. Finally, territory that falls out of the control of a central governing authority in a failed or weak state can become a safe haven for terrorist cells or other nonstate actors that could threaten Western and North American security. Failed states and ungoverned territories pose serious risks to global security and should be of concern to all three countries of North America.

Strengthening institutions and the rule of law and ensuring stability throughout the Western Hemisphere is a priority that the governments of all three North American countries share. In the past decade and a half, the international community intervened in Haiti in an attempt to strengthen its democratic institutions and to provide an atmosphere of security for Haiti's population. The consequences of instability in that country were, for the most part, contained within its borders because of Haiti's relatively small size, economic isolation, and lack of military capability. The projected impact of state failure would be far greater if instability were to develop in Cuba or Central America. Preventing pockets of ungoverned territory from emerging in the Caribbean region and Central America, as well as in Mexico, should be a critical priority. North America must support efforts to mitigate the threat posed by criminal organizations, drug trafficking, and violence in Central and Latin America while focusing on reducing corruption, strengthening democracy, and reinforcing the rule of law in the countries in those regions.

The international community has spent billions of dollars on humanitarian assistance and peacekeeping in failed states. Inside and outside of the failed state's area, there are costs that are attributable to disruptions of trade and investment. Organized crime can flourish within a failed or weak state; trade in conventional weapons, precious metals, diamonds, and narcotics is likely to proliferate. Preventing the emergence of weak states in the Western Hemisphere is clearly of vital importance to North America, but Canada, Mexico, and the United States will need to consider the implications of state failure on a broader scale. North America's geographic isolation no longer provides a guaranteed buffer against instability in other parts of the world.

The consequences of state failure are most evident at the regional level, but at times these developments can have serious global implications. Two of the world's weaker states, Pakistan and North Korea, have developed nuclear weapons; thus, state failure in those countries could have disastrous implications for international security. Future instability among international energy suppliers—such as Nigeria, Egypt, or Venezuela—could have severe repercussions on the global economy. Weak states have already provided an area of operation for international terrorist organizations—as is evident from Al Qaeda's presence in Afghanistan, Somalia, Sudan, Iraq, and some of Pakistan's tribal regions. In addition, it is believed that the triborder region in South America is providing a safe haven for Hizballah cells, and it is possible that Al Qaeda and other terrorist groups could seek to exploit ungoverned territory in the Western Hemisphere.

Even though the risks of humanitarian disasters and human rights violations should be enough of an impetus for the international community to undertake actions meant to prevent state failure, protecting regional stability and international security may demand action in many cases as well. As the world further integrates and the availability and lethality of weapons increase, the global consequences posed by weak and failing states are amplified dramatically.

Nonstate Actors

In the context of globalization, the ability of nonstate actors to influence a nation's behavior, international markets, and world events has grown to an unprecedented level. Increased market integration, the ease of global travel, and international communication networks allow corporations, nongovernmental organizations, and individuals to influence world events directly—in both positive and negative ways. Nonstate actors have had profound implications on security in today's world, and the actions of groups and individuals who are independent of governments will be among the most important determinants of the state of the world in 2025.

The diffusion of power that will lead to a multipolar world in 2025 will not be limited to state actors. As multinational corporations grow in size, so too do their influence and interests. Nongovernmental organizations—including international aid groups and advocacy organizations—have the power to affect the development and political future of countries around the world. International terrorist groups have dramatically affected state behavior, and most conflicts today involve at least one nonstate actor.[7] Globalization acts as a force that can transfer power directly to individuals. In his recent book, *The World Is Flat*, Thomas Friedman, a columnist for the *New York Times* and champion of globalization, captured this aspect of power diffusion in what he terms "super-empowered individuals." Individuals in the 1990s demonstrated the ability to change the course of world events for the positive; as an example, Jody Williams received the 1997 Nobel Peace Prize for her efforts to advance an international treaty banning the use of land mines. But individuals can bring about negative changes as well, as demonstrated by various terrorist acts across the globe orchestrated by Osama bin Laden and his agents.

Technology is a critical component of the power held by nonstate actors in today's world. The Internet allows global communication, international money transfers, and the dissemination of ideas and information with lightning speed and at minimal cost. Technology and globalization could make it possible for future attacks by a few individuals to cause the deaths of thousands or perhaps even millions of people. Chemical, biological, radiological, and nuclear weapons are lethal technologies that may no longer be under the strict control of state actors. Moreover, recipes for making conventional weapons are widely available, and their destructive capabilities will undoubtedly increase in the years to come.

Clearly, the substantial change in the world order, which will undoubtedly be more dramatic in the future, will be accompanied by changing and often unpredictable threats to the security of North America as well as other nations of the world. The challenge for Canada, Mexico, and the United States will be to adapt to the realities of the changing world order and to be prepared to respond to transnational events in order to counter the threats to North America's security that can emanate from external sources.

TERRORIST THREATS

The possibility of future terrorist attacks in North America poses a very real danger for Canada, Mexico, and the United States alike. From the very worst of imaginable catastrophes, such as the detonation of a nuclear device in a North American city, to less destructive acts, such as the detonation of improvised explosive devices on transportation infrastructure or tourist destinations—all three North American countries will be forced to face the economic and political consequences of terrorism equally. For Canada and the United States, radical Islamists are the primary terrorist threat. And even though Mexico may not be immune to the terrorist acts fueled by hatred of the United States and the Western world, as espoused by many extremist Islamic groups—particularly Al Qaeda—to date, the primary terrorist threat facing Mexico has come from the country's own leftist extremists as well as from transnational criminal organizations, such as drug cartels. The countries of North America all have a vested interest not only in preventing foreign fighters from entering the region but also in taking steps to halt the emergence of home-grown terrorists motivated by similar ideologies. It is also important for North American governments to avoid the disenfranchisement of other elements of their societies that might use terrorist acts to advance their cause. All these eventualities can be fostered clandestinely within the country—over and above the ability of these groups to use information technology to disseminate their message; for example, Iranian diplomats and intelligence operatives in Mexico have been seeking out and engaging members of the radical Left.

The United States has made fighting and winning the war on terror the single most important priority in U.S. foreign policy today. The 2006 National Security Strategy of the United States characterized the specific threat facing the country as the "rise of terrorism fueled by an aggressive ideology of hatred and murder; fully revealed to the American people on September 11, 2001."[8] The war on terror, which is, in fact, a battle against Al Qaeda and an effort to prevent any future terrorist attacks on the United States, has had dramatic implications for both Mexico and Canada.[9]

After the September 11 attacks, preventing international terrorism dominated the North American agenda, diverting focus and energy from progress on other critical issues. The war on terror redefined the relationship between the United States and Mexico; for example, immigration reform and economic development moved from the centerpiece of the partnership between the nations' two presidents. Moreover, in the aftermath of the attacks, trading activities in North America were redefined as new security policies were implemented to ensure greater levels of confidence about the people and goods crossing the various borders of all three nations.[10] Certainly, the most tragic cost of the terrorist attacks was the loss of life in the World Trade Center towers, the Pentagon, and the ill-fated United Airlines Flight 93, which crashed near Shanksville, Pennsylvania. The United States had to bear the economic costs of the attacks as well, including billions of dollars in lost property and cleanup efforts as well as a reduction in international and domestic air travel, a dramatic fall in consumer confidence, and the creation of a more risk-averse investment climate—all of which exacerbated recessive growth in the United States, which has had a negative impact on the economies of Canada and Mexico.

Since fall 2001, North America has drastically changed its approach to countering terrorist activity. In December 2001, the United States and Canada signed the Smart Border Declaration and Action Plan to secure their shared border with the aim of creating a border that is "open for business, but closed for terrorists." The action plan involved securing border infrastructure, ensuring and facilitating the movement of documented goods and people, and sharing information. Mexico and the United States signed a similar agreement—U.S.-Mexico Smart Border Partnership Action Plan—in March 2002. Although there remains room for much improvement, the three North American countries have developed a defensive strategy for preventing a future attack by foreign terrorists through measures designed to protect borders and to share information.

Although Al Qaeda's most sought-after targets seem to be located in key cities in the United States, the threat that the organization might conduct terrorist attacks in Canada and Mexico is real, but the probability of attack varies. In an attempt to increase pressure on the United States to withdraw its troops from Afghanistan and Iraq, Al Qaeda called on its members to disrupt the flow of oil to the United States.

An unsubstantiated report by the Saudi arm of Al Qaeda referred to more specific attacks on facilities in Canada, Mexico, and Venezuela. Although the threat has yet to materialize, the statements highlight the shared nature of the international terrorist threat. A sting by law enforcement agents that took place in Canada in 2006, which resulted in the arrest of 17 individuals accused of planning acts of terror, showed that a home-grown terrorist cell was developing in Canada. The group was heavily influenced by Al Qaeda, and some of its members reportedly had links to international terrorist organizations. The incident reinforced the need for Canada to work even more closely with its diverse cultural communities in light of its growing immigrant population.[11]

Looking ahead to 2025, it is unlikely that Al Qaeda will conduct another terrorist act until the group is confident that the attack will meet or exceed the destructive or disruptive impact of the attacks perpetrated on September 11. Al Qaeda's leadership will adopt this approach as a way to counter the perception that the group may have been weakened as a result of the counterterrorism measures that have been undertaken. Simultaneous attacks are likely to occur again, as the group looks to strike symbolic structures, financial centers, and critical infrastructure in Los Angeles, New York City, and Washington, D.C.; peripheral threats exist in Boston, Seattle, and Chicago as well. The group may employ suicide tactics and use conventional weapons, including improvised explosive devices, rocket-propelled grenades, wire-guided missiles, or drones. If Al Qaeda can gain access to chemical, biological, radiological, or nuclear weapons, the attacks could have even more devastating consequences. The material for such attacks would probably be obtained on the international black market and transported to the United States in shipping containers. Ultimately, time is likely to be in the terrorists' favor as a result of the inevitable onset of counterterrorism fatigue.[12]

The attacks that North America is more likely to experience approaching 2025 will be those conducted by home-grown terrorist groups that are inspired by Al Qaeda's ideology. The organization's international network may support these home-grown groups financially, technically, and physically. Attacks by these groups would probably mirror the terrorist acts launched in London and Madrid in 2005. The arrests of U.S. citizens accused of operating terrorist cells in New York City in 2007, Miami in 2006, and Buffalo in 2002 all provide some evidence of the threat of attack by home-grown terrorists in the United States. Canada's arrest of Canadian nationals planning to bomb targets across Toronto and to behead the prime minister in 2006 provides an example of the shared nature of this threat. Future attacks by similar groups are likely to be on a smaller scale, possibly involving suicide bombers or improvised explosive devices designed to cripple public transportation or the placement of roadside bombs across critical choke points. If attempts by home-grown groups are successful, it is likely that Al Qaeda will announce its support of their operation; however, if the attacks fail, the organization will claim no knowledge of these groups' activities. In the short term and looking toward 2025, it is essential for all three governments to take all necessary steps to ensure that home-grown terrorism cannot flourish in their countries. Canada, Mexico, and the United States must examine immigration activities, policing and intelligence practices, and the ways in which each country engages with different cultural groups and communities within its borders in order to find the solutions that will protect its residents from these threats.

Although Al Qaeda and organizations inspired by Al Qaeda pose a certain direct and indirect threat to Mexico—primarily because of the level of integration between the U.S. and Mexican economies and the havoc a strategic attack would wreak on both nations—instability and unrest generated by domestic actors pose a far greater threat to Mexico's security today and will continue to do so for the foreseeable future. The two most powerful drug cartels—the Sinaloa and Gulf cartels—have claimed responsibility for much of the violence in Mexico. Moreover, it is widely believed that drug cartels in Mexico have been behind a campaign of intimidation against journalists, government officials, and the public at large; examples include targeted murders and attacks on press offices. Upon taking office in December 2006, President Felipe Calderón made the fight against organized crime his top priority and announced a highly visible national campaign to combat these groups. His administration's action steps included the extradition of 15 cartel bosses to the United States in January 2007; the deployment of 10,000 members of the armed forces to several states across Mexico; and the creation of the Federal Support Special Military Corps in May 2007, with a mandate to restore public order and security and fight against drug trafficking and organized crime. The detonation of an explosive device in Mexico City, which was carried out by the Sinaloa Cartel on February 15, 2008, in an effort to destroy the Mexico City government's Secretariat of Public Security, raises concerns given that the nation's capital had—up to that point—never been the target of cartel attacks employing such devices.

However, Mexico also has a number of minor actors who further complicate the task of ensuring a secure and stable environment throughout the country. The Popular Revolutionary Army (EPR), a far Left organization that emerged in the 1990s and has its roots in southern Mexico, is the most dangerous of several small radical groups in Mexico. Over the years, the EPR has carried out a series of sporadic bombings of either foreign banks or office buildings housing multinational corporations throughout Mexico City. The explosive devices used in the bombings, however, have always been detonated between 2:00 A.M. and 5:00 A.M. as a way to demonstrate the group's opposition to imperialism and or neoliberalism without inflicting casualties. In 2007, the EPR began what could be the start of a sustained bombing campaign meant to apply more direct pressure on the government. In July and again in September 2007, the EPR claimed responsibility for a series of early morning bombings on key natural gas pipelines; these attacks signify a level of organizational capacity and technical sophistication far greater than the organization has ever demonstrated.[13] The attacks came after a year of extreme political unrest in the state of Oaxaca, where, according to the EPR, the federal government arrested two EPR members, and in the wake of the disputed outcome of Mexico's 2006 presidential election. The EPR's statements represent a deep frustration among the radical Left in Mexico and also indicate that the Left is disillusioned with the current economic and political system. The EPR has stated that it would continue a campaign against the "interests of the oligarchy" and the country's "illegitimate government." Even though the bombings caused no loss of life, they did lead to a significant fall in Mexico's energy revenues and also shut down hundreds of manufacturing sites for several days. Despite the government's apparent ability to respond to the EPR's actions, the threat the group poses distracts from the security risks arising from the activities of drug cartels and criminal organizations. If anything, Mexico has always had an underlying concern about the possible linkage between radical groups and organized crime—a link that cannot be discounted in the future.

ENERGY

The world had a glimpse of the detrimental effects of disruptions to the energy supply during the oil shortages of 1973–1974 and 1979–1980, and the economy of the United States in 2008 is even more vulnerable to significant long-term disruptions in the global oil supply. Even though Canada and Mexico are net exporters of oil, depending on the ramifications to the global economy and the impact of higher energy prices in their own societies, the costs resulting from a new set of global oil shocks are likely to outweigh any benefits these two countries would gain from higher oil prices.

The current North American economic model is based on a vast supply of petroleum. North American industries—including the airline, automobile, transportation, petrochemical, agriculture, construction, and tourism industries—are all highly reliant on a secure supply of fossil fuels. Constant energy disruptions would halt the operational capacity of key industries and negatively affect the North American population's way of life. The United States is vulnerable to energy disruptions caused by intentional state actions and dramatic interruptions of operations in major oil-producing states; depending on the magnitude of the disruption and its ripple effects, Canada and Mexico are vulnerable as well.

To insulate against disruption in oil supplies, the three North American countries have become members of the International Energy Agency, which was established by treaty in 1974 to institutionalize effective systems for managing shocks to the global oil supply. Under the framework, the United States, as a net oil importer, is required to maintain a petroleum stock equivalent to 90 days of the volume consumed the previous year; Mexico and Canada, as net oil exporters, are exempt from this requirement. In the event of disruption in oil supplies, the International Energy Agency could coordinate a variety of response measures aimed at increasing the supply of energy and reducing the demand. The United States has also undertaken measures to insulate itself against supply shocks in the natural gas market. The emergency measures could mitigate the effects of a small-scale disruption, but they serve only as a Band-Aid in the event of a larger disturbance. In the case of a prolonged crisis, oil prices would continue to rise in response to future expectations—even with the release of strategic reserves. Measures to decrease energy consumption would still need to be implemented, and the scarcity of oil—coupled with the government regulations required to respond to the situation—would have a serious impact on North Americans' way of life, which could conceivably trigger undesirable ripple effects.

As discussed in the chapter on the outlook for energy in North America, U.S. demand for energy is expected to rise and domestic resources are expected to decline. Absent a major shift in supply or consumption patterns, the United States will grow more reliant on foreign energy sources. A rise in the global demand for energy will further strain the global supply, resulting in higher fuel prices. The potential for global energy disruptions will increase as supply becomes ever more concentrated in the Middle East, Africa, Russia, and the area around the Caspian Sea. Threats to energy security include vulnerabilities in the global transportation network, such as the shipping lane choke points in the Strait of Hormuz and the Straits of Malacca. Critical infrastructure in oil-producing and energy-consuming countries represents another key area of concern. Finally, as interdependence in the global energy market deepens, geopolitical threats to oil production will be of even greater international concern.

Increased development of the oil sands has allowed Canada's oil production to grow faster than its oil consumption. Eastern Canada will continue to import crude oil and refined products, while exports of bitumen and synthetic crude from western Canada will grow.

In the case of Mexico, a lack of sufficient public and private investment in the country's energy infrastructure may lead to a dramatic fall in production capacity. The Mexican government has made it a priority to provide the state-run oil company, Petroleos Mexicanos (PEMEX) with greater resources for exploration and development. As explained in the chapters on the outlook for North American energy, competitiveness, and infrastructure, private investment could be an effective solution to the general decline in the development of resources. However, the Mexican Constitution prohibits private investment in PEMEX; therefore, the executive and legislative branches of the Mexican government would have to achieve the necessary political consensus to amend the Constitution and push through sorely needed energy reforms. The debate over energy reform has made great strides over the past 10 years, and—at least today—reform appears to be within the realm of political possibility; this would put Mexico in a better position over the long term in terms of its own energy security. The EPR's recent attacks on natural gas pipelines present a more immediate concern for the security of Mexico's energy market. Mexico's ability to protect its critical infrastructure from future attacks may have implications for the reliability of its production of oil and natural gas. In fact, energy reform, which would allow for some form of national and/or foreign private investment and thereby help solve the problem of Mexico's diminishing oil supply, could itself elevate the country's risk of attack—be it by the EPR or some other domestic radical group that could emerge in the wake of a highly contentious debate over energy reform or by foreign groups merely seeking to strike at facilities in which U.S. companies have invested. Such an attack, particularly if it were to affect production over a period of time, would have ramifications for the United States and, to a lesser extent, for Canada. Consequently, it is even more important to strengthen the protection provided for the infrastructure that is critical to Mexico's energy sector.

The governments of the three nations have developed an appreciation for the importance of working together and, for the moment, have initiated cooperative efforts to address the problem posed by the diminishing energy supply. In July 2007, the energy ministers of the North American countries gathered in Victoria, British Columbia, and signed a trilateral framework for sharing technology and coordinating campaigns aimed at reducing energy consumption. At a press conference following the meeting, Gary Lunn, Canada's minister of natural resources, made the following statement:

> By putting in place a framework for pooling our knowledge, for working together more closely, we can move forward faster and more efficiently than any one of us can move forward alone. This trilateral agreement opens the door to that kind of cooperation. It opens the door for all three of our nations to increase the potential returns on our investments in energy science and technology. It opens the door to the sustainable, affordable, secure energy future for North America we seek—the energy future we need to fuel our economic growth.[14]

As North America moves forward, the challenge will be to use the collaborative framework effectively to address whatever energy challenges may be looming on the horizon.

CLIMATE CHANGE

As the year 2025 approaches, environmental pressures have the potential to have a detrimental impact on North American security.

The effects of these pressures will be felt both directly, when the three countries respond to future natural disasters inside their own borders, and indirectly because of political and economic ripple effects brought about by disasters and changing conditions in the rest of the world.

Climate change is occurring and the consensus of the scientific community is that, if the pace and nature of climate change do not slow down, the consequences will be severe. (These consequences are described in detail in the chapter on the environment.) Despite the uncertainty about the projected extent of climate change, the clarity of the trends should provide the impetus for strategic thinking on how to limit the extent of future climate change, how to mitigate some of the worst effects the change may have both globally and regionally, and how to best prepare for and coordinate responses to severe and frequent natural disasters.

The United Nations Intergovernmental Panel on Climate Change (IPCC) represents the broad scientific community in its assertion that the earth is warming at a rate that is inconsistent with historical levels. The IPCC argues that over the last 50 years this rate was almost double that of the past century (a change of $0.13°C \pm 0.03°C$ per decade today compared with $0.07°C \pm 0.02°C$ in the past). According to the UN panel, "for the globe as a whole, surface air temperatures over land have risen at about double the ocean rate after 1979 (more than $0.27°C$ per decade vs. $0.13°C$ per decade)."[15] Chapter 2 explains how greenhouse gases (GHGs), which are made up primarily of carbon dioxide emissions, are the principal cause of the accelerated rate of climate change. It seems unlikely that serious efforts will be undertaken to curtail the overall production of GHGs, and, even if governments could take action to reduce GHGs, the carbon cycle and the sheer size of the earth's oceans and its atmosphere make it likely that it would take decades or more for the process to stabilize.[16]

Climate change could have the most severe and immediate impact on tropical and polar regions, including areas in Asia, Africa, the Middle East, and Central America. The strain on government institutions and resources could cause regional instability and have global economic and political consequences. In 2007, a panel of 11 senior retired U.S. admirals and generals released a study that evaluated the implications of climate change on U.S. and global security.[17] The study warns that climate change could put in motion a series of multiplier effects that will place stress on governance, stability, and international security. Among the greatest concerns is the availability of freshwater resources, particularly in the Middle East and Africa. The International Water Management Institute predicts that, by 2025, 1.8 billion people will live in countries or regions experiencing absolute water scarcity. The widespread scarcity of water will strain food production and have ripple effects throughout the economy.[18] Frequent or severe natural disasters could have the same repercussions.

In countries with weak institutions, the devastation could trigger massive migrations, increased tensions along borders, economic and political instability, and even conflicts over essential resources. The economic ripple effects are likely to be felt on an international scale, particularly if the afflicted states are energy producers or economic powers. The consequences may also be seen if international terrorist groups or other nonstate actors are able to exploit the failures of governance, thereby increasing their access to resources, widening their sphere of operations, and perhaps expanding their base of support.

Global climate change may present the most unique threat to security in North America. The effects of climate change extend far beyond temperature increases and bring about fundamental changes in ecosystems that can cause severe alterations in traditional weather patterns. Although the pace of climate change is debatable, there is little doubt that the world—and North America—will see an increase in the intensity, duration, frequency (which in turn reduces recovery times), and geographical extent of violent weather in the twenty-first century.[19] Heat waves will occur more often, which will increase rates of evaporation and result in a rise in droughts and wildfires. The increase in sea surface temperatures will also bring with it an upsurge in hurricane activity. Land may be lost because of permanent flooding or rising sea levels. Climate change is likely to exacerbate drought and water scarcity and could be the cause of massive food shortages across large populations. Scientists believe that, as glaciers melt and relieve pressure from the earth's crust, the tectonic plates may be in danger of slipping, causing severe earthquakes and tidal waves. The breadth, complexity, and uncertainty surrounding the implications of climate change make it hard to create the political will to address the issue. Nevertheless, the difficulty of addressing the problem does not excuse inaction.

Mexico, the United States, and Canada will not be exempt from facing some of the same tensions that climate change and its repercussions will unleash on the rest of the world. Not only will each of the three nations run the risk of having to contend with tensions between provinces and states and/or municipalities, as each vies for a greater share of dwindling resources, but one can also anticipate transnational tensions. The U.S. and Mexican public already had a glimpse into the future during the recent tensions between the United States and Mexico over the Rio Grande/Rio Bravo River and over the Colorado River.

In the case of the Rio Grande/Rio Bravo River, the state of Texas was recently pitted against the Mexican states of Chihuahua, Coahuila, Nuevo Leon, and Tamaulipas over Mexico's mounting water debt tied to the Rio Grande/Rio Bravo, as per the water sharing arrangements set out under the terms of the 1944 Water Treaty. This water debt—which at one point had amounted to 1.5 million acre-feet as a result of the "extraordinary drought" that Mexico had experienced—affected the relationship between the United States and Mexico, and these tensions dominated the bilateral relationship during President George W. Bush's first term. The strain resulted from the intense political pressure that the White House came under from the president's former constituents, who had supported him politically and contributed financially to his campaigns for governor and president, thus making him highly susceptible and receptive to their grievances, which, in turn, became *the* priority issue for the White House among all the issues that the U.S.-Mexican bilateral relationship encompasses. Ultimately, Mother Nature came to Mexico's rescue by providing abundant precipitation, thus enabling the government of Mexico to pay back this contentious water debt in September 2005. However, looking at 2025 and beyond, depending on Mother Nature to solve a problem may not be a viable option. What's more, if the White House were to be occupied in 2025 and beyond by a president from a state that shares a border with either Canada or Mexico, the result could conceivably be heightened tensions in future bilateral relations between the United States and the affected neighbor.

The other contentious issue in the U.S.-Mexican relationship that hints at the sort of environmental tensions with which future governments may have to contend involves the lining of the All-American Canal. The dispute has pitted the Mexican state of Baja California against the U.S. state of California over the invaluable water seepage from the Colorado River that has been trickling for years and has replenished groundwater aquifers on the Mexican side of the border to the benefit of fresh produce farmers and communities in Baja California. The lining of the canal now ensures that the water will remain in the United

States, thus depriving communities and farmers on the Mexican side of the border of the groundwater on which they have come to depend. Despite this short-term remedy—at least for agricultural communities in the United States—a study of water management in the Colorado River Basin conducted by the National Research Council in 2007 predicts substantial decreases in river flows as a result of the effects of larger populations coupled with climate change.[20]

It is also likely that climate change will have implications for the transboundary agreements between the United States and Canada. One such impact will probably involve the management of the Columbia River and its tributaries—which form the dominant water system of the Pacific Northwest. Even though 30 percent of the Columbia River Basin is located in Canada, approximately 50 percent of the river's stream flow in the late summer originates in Canada.[21] Nonetheless, the 1964 Columbia River Treaty has provided for the successful management of the river. Over time, however, climate change is likely to reduce the availability of water in the summer because of changes in snowpack and the seasonal nature of natural stream flows, resulting in heightened tensions between the two countries.

Even though the International Water Boundary and Water Commission, which manages all the various water treaties between the United States and Mexico, and the International Joint Commission, which does the same for Canada and the United States, have done an exemplary job in transboundary water management, these agencies will be subject to unprecedented levels of political pressure as the stress on the availability of water mounts. Hence, the need to strengthen these institutions will become increasingly important in the future.

The failure of governments throughout the world to effectively address some of the challenges raised by environmental change and depletion of natural resources that loom on the horizon—at least as their respective populations perceive these problems—could conceivably result in the sprouting of radical environmental groups or nonstate actors, who may be inclined to take up arms in order to protect the natural resources in the region. North America has already had to contend with such groups—which frequently opt to cross the line that separates "direct action" from criminal acts of ecoterrorism—when dealing with the actions undertaken in the United States and Canada by the Earth Liberation Front, a militant ecoterrorist group, as well as by its sister organization, the Animal Liberation Front. It is within the realm of possibility that similar groups could multiply and threaten the stability and security of the area they choose to attack.[22]

Over and above the detrimental impact on the Arctic's ecosystem, global warming—and the melting of Arctic ice caps or glaciers in particular—will also introduce an element of geopolitics into the region. The Arctic and the Arctic passageway have long had geostrategic importance, dating back to the World War II and the ensuing Cold War. With the Arctic ice caps melting at an alarming rate, making the navigation of ships and submarines—not to mention exploration and transport of resources—an even more plausible option in the future, the sovereignty of the Arctic passageway acquires added relevance. Despite differences over Canadian sovereignty claims regarding the Northwest Passage, Canada and the United States have been able to resolve their differences over the waterway through the agreements signed by former Prime Minister Brian Mulroney and former President Ronald Reagan in the late 1980s. One of the differences—the U.S. view that the Northwest Passage is an international passageway and the Canadian claim that it is Canadian territory—has been mitigated by the United States' decision not to question Canadian sovereignty over its Arctic islands and to support the Canadian investments that have been made to exercise Canada's sovereignty.[23] Nonetheless, in his October 2007 Speech from the Throne, Canada's prime minister Stephen Harper noted that

> the Arctic is an essential part of Canada's history . . . [requiring] new attention. New opportunities are emerging across the Arctic, and new challenges from other shores. Our Government will bring forward an integrated northern strategy focused on strengthening Canada's sovereignty, protecting our environmental heritage, promoting economic and social development, and improving and devolving governance, so that northerners have greater control over their destinies . . . . Defending our sovereignty in the North also demands that we maintain the capacity to act. New Arctic patrol ships and expanded aerial surveillance will guard Canada's Far North and the Northwest Passage. As well, the size and capabilities of the Arctic Rangers will be expanded to better patrol our vast Arctic territory.[24]

Despite their past differences, Canada and the United States have a common interest in presenting a united front, particularly in light of Russia's strategic interest in the Arctic passageway, which is clearly shaping up to be an issue that will require utmost diplomacy in the future, especially if the U.S. Senate fails to ratify the United Nations' Law of the Sea Treaty, which would provide the regulatory framework with which to govern those northern waters, thwart future claims, and resolve navigational disputes.[25]

When all is said and done, global climate change is a daunting challenge that will reveal the deficiencies or limitations of a nation-centric, stovepipe approach to a transnational problem that will have truly catastrophic consequences. Environmental change will challenge current government structures and their ability to mitigate severe problems effectively. Nevertheless, dealing with climate change could conceivably be the very first *real* opportunity for North American governments to think transnationally in terms of policy formulation and implementation. The Intergovernmental Panel on Climate Change proved to be successful from the standpoint of analytical research and the panel's ability to arrive at a baseline consensus. Mexico, the United States, and Canada can strengthen their track record in cooperative ventures on the international stage not only from the standpoint of mitigating problems but also from the standpoint of contending with some of the ramifications stemming from climate change. Be it through the Commission for Environmental Cooperation or some other trilateral or multilateral mechanism, North America can set an example that the rest of the world can follow and also assume a leadership role globally.

NATURAL DISASTERS

U.S. government agencies' poor response to the disaster caused by Hurricane Katrina and the ensuing collapse of the region's levee system in 2005 is clearly documented. The hurricane caused loss of life, massive human displacement, and economic devastation—all of which could have been mitigated by better preparation and more effective response on the part of the government. The U.S. government's lack of preparedness to respond to a foreseeable disaster is a matter of great concern, particularly because the country was considered to be affluent enough to do so. The tragedy should serve as a reminder to governments at all levels of the importance of strengthening their disaster preparedness through investment, training, material support, and strategic planning. In the last decade alone, the world has seen the consequences of a massive tsunami, Category 5 hurricanes, tornadoes, and seismically powerful earthquakes. All these natural disasters have revealed the need to improve preparation and response mechanisms. Logistical and bureaucratic hurdles hinder response efforts, and resources typically fail to reach the affected populations in a manner that is most efficient. As North America and the world confront the possibility of more frequent and more devastating natural disasters, the need for better planning and improved coordination between local, state, and national governments—as well as the private and voluntary sectors—is even more pressing.

Mexico, the United States, and Canada have an opportunity to reinforce their cooperation in efforts to mitigate the threat caused by environmental change and to prepare for its most likely consequences—including the need to provide disaster relief. Formalized coordination of relief and response mechanisms could aid in the case of not only hurricanes on Mexico's Yucatan Peninsula and the United States' gulf coast but also tornadoes that devastate the central U.S.-Canadian border region known as "tornado alley," forest fires in the San Diego-Tijuana region,[26] and floods that affect the Mississippi delta.

The Canadian and Mexican governments' responses to Hurricane Katrina's devastation in the United States serve as an example of North American cooperation in providing disaster relief and point to several opportunities for improving coordination. The government of Canada provided support by deploying a destroyer, two frigates, three Sea King helicopters, and about 35 rescue and engineer divers to assist the work of the U.S. Navy's Second Fleet. Canada's air force also transported 27 Canadian Red Cross workers as well as Canadian government officials to support the relief efforts. In addition, Canada's air force sent two CH-146 Griffin helicopters to help the U.S. Coast Guard in the Northeast, when the Coast Guard's resources were strained because of the assistance it was providing for flood relief efforts in New Orleans. In all, more than a thousand personnel from Canadian forces contributed to the relief efforts after Hurricane Katrina hit the United States.[27]

The government of Mexico also provided support in the wake of the hurricane, when the Ministry of National Defense deployed 184 military officers and 45 vehicles to New Orleans. During their 18-day deployment, the officers served 160,735 hot meals; provided 1,106 medical and dental consultations; distributed 1,118 boxes of bottled water, 398 boxes of applesauce, and 148 blankets; and delivered 184.161 metric tons of supplies that had been donated by *Diconsa*, a quasi-governmental agency that is involved in social development.[28]

The Mexican navy deployed the *Papaloapan* A-411 battleship—the same ship that the Mexican government had sent to provide disaster relief following the tsunami that devastated Indonesia in December 2004—to transport about 385 naval personnel, including search-and-rescue teams, engineers, and divers. The ship also transported eight land vehicles, seven amphibious vehicles, two tanker trucks, one ambulance, five Zodiac inflatable rescue boats, and two MI-17 helicopters to assist in various types of missions.[29]

The trilateral cooperation in these missions was impressive, but the effort had serious shortcomings. Aid money intended for the victims went unclaimed by the U.S. government, and bureaucratic entanglements hindered international donors' shipments to the United States. Ultimately, Canadian and Mexican doctors were unable to provide medical support because they lacked U.S. certification to practice medicine on U.S. soil.

Clearly, the one area that has experienced the lowest level of cooperation between the three nations of North America to date has been disaster relief—be it in response to natural or man-made disasters. By 2025, when North America—along with the rest of the world—will be contending with an increase in the frequency and intensity of natural disasters, the nations that are best positioned to respond will be the nations that can minimize the negative secondary effects of the shocks and sustain a relatively uninterrupted level of subnational, national, or transnational economic growth. Moving forward, the three federal governments of North America would benefit from having representatives of the U.S. Federal Emergency Management Administration and its Canadian and Mexican counterparts, Public Safety Canada and *Protección Civil*, respectively, at their respective embassies in all three countries so that, when faced with a natural disaster, these representative could commence working in a more concerted and coordinated fashion. In addition, it may be in the best interest of all three nations to develop an overall North American strategy that extends strengthening the capability to provide disaster relief to the Caribbean region and Central America.

At the state level, governors from the border states of the United States and Mexico have begun to realize the importance of cooperating on disaster relief measures and coordinating their efforts. At the Fifteenth Border Governors' Conference, which was held in Puerto Peñasco, Sonora, in October 2007, one of the secondary working group meetings dealt with disaster relief and emergency response. The relegation of this topic to the second tier might be indicative of the lower level of importance that the issue has traditionally received. At this meeting, the heads of the state-level emergency response agencies from U.S. and Mexican border states met to discuss ways to improve their cooperation. Officials from the Federal Emergency Management Administration and *Protección Civil* were invited to observe the discussion as special guests. It is worth noting, however, that at the Sixteenth Border Governors' Conference to be held in Hollywood, California, in 2008, the meeting of the working group set to address disaster relief and emergency response will ascend to a spot as one of the primary working group sessions. One would assume that theses initial steps reflect the greater importance that the three governments will be placing on these issues in the years ahead.

Regardless of North America's progress in implementing federal or state-level measures to improve emergency preparedness, some believe that society will have to come to terms with the reality that the state will not always be able to respond effectively to some of the threats that its citizens will face in the future—whether they come from natural disasters or man-made ones. This school of thought contends that the state has traditionally been seen as a paternalistic organ, leading societies to expect that the government will protect them and improve their living conditions following a disaster. As society witnessed with Hurricane Katrina, however, the state does not always have the capability to respond effectively; and this is why they believe that this shift in the conceptual framework is one that should evolve further as the region moves closer to 2025 and beyond.

PUBLIC HEALTH AND WELL-BEING

Vulnerability of the Food Supply

Tainted consumer products imported from China to the United States—such as the recent contamination of animal feed by *melamine* as well as the recall of California-raised meat or California-grown spinach contaminated by *E. coli* and Georgia-produced peanut butter contaminated by *salmonella*—have drawn public attention to health regulations and vulnerabilities of the food supply. Although these outbreaks have been isolated and in large part contained, they are reminders of the vital importance of securing the food supply for the public welfare of the population of North America. Ensuring the security of North America's food supply requires a comprehensive strategy focused on health and safety standards, production capacity and sustainability, diversification, and an efficient and alert system that rapidly identifies hazards and shares information across borders.

North America's raw and processed food trade has increased steadily over the last decade. Agricultural trade between Mexico and Canada was valued at just under US$2 billion in 2006;[30] two-way agricultural trade between Mexico and the United States was valued at less than US$19 billion and less than US$24 billion between Canada and the United States for the same year.[31] Interdependence in the North American food market will further increase as 2025 approaches, as will the global trade of processed and nonprocessed food. The volume of North American trade and the geographic proximity of production areas give reason for the region's three governments to approach the security of the food supply as a challenge that the entire hemisphere faces together, not just one that is confined to each nation's borders.

The most important challenge for the three countries in ensuring the security of the food supply in the decades to come will be to establish a resilient and geographically diverse agricultural supply that meets the needs of North America's population. In the past, droughts, hurricanes, insects, and diseases have devastated individual crop harvests. For example, a current threat to the broad agricultural sector has emerged in the United States and parts of Canada with the mysterious and dramatic collapse of bee populations over the past year. Bee pollination adds billions of dollars to the agricultural businesses responsible for greater yields and a higher quality of agricultural products. In the United States, the phenomenon is known as Colony Collapse Disorder, and it is unclear if the bee collapse in Canada is related to the one in the United States. As another example, most scientists predict significant regional shifts in growing seasons as a result of climate change. These shifts will force new and sometimes disruptive changes in crop choices and will create the need to develop crops that can grow in higher or lower temperatures than those to which they are naturally accustomed, grow in soil with a high salt content, and perhaps grow while submerged in water. Moreover, policymakers do not yet fully comprehend the full extent of the ramifications that production of genetically modified foods will have—particularly in rural areas in all corners of the world.

A more immediate concern is the need to protect the food supply from contamination. Canada, Mexico, and the United States have their respective government organizations that are charged with enforcing the array of regulations governing this expansive field. The concerns range from assuring safe growing practices and safe food handling techniques to preventing the contamination of food by terrorists at distribution centers. The United States has recently given increased attention to the security of imported consumer products and food items, particularly products from China. Although creating mechanisms to ensure the health and safety of the public is critical, future regulatory measures must also strive to be as minimally disruptive as possible in order to facilitate the critical trade networks in place.

At the ministerial meeting of the Security and Prosperity Partnership (SPP) held in Washington, D.C., in 2005, the three nations pledged to "enhance the stewardship of our environment, create a safer and more reliable food supply while facilitating agricultural trade, and protect our people from disease." Canada and Mexico have bilaterally pledged to cooperate with the United States in sharing information about contaminated agricultural and processed foods that affect their neighbor. Canada and the United States will undoubtedly draw from the numerous lessons learned from the spread of bovine spongiform encephalopathy or Mad Cow Disease in 2003. Efficient mechanisms for early detection, effective measures to trace the source of contamination, and rapid and thorough dissemination of information are critical to this partnership. It will also be important to consider the impact of policy choices on the agricultural supply and on prices—for example, the pursuit of ethanol fuel produced from corn as an alternative source of energy. A reliable food supply in the coming decades must be geographically diverse and use more resilient and productive crops. The countries of North America should take full advantage of the vast geographic space they occupy and jointly consider policies that would encourage a more reliable, productive, and secure food supply.

Influenza Pandemic

An influenza pandemic can occur when a new influenza virus emerges that has not been previously transmitted from person to person. Although the incidence of flu pandemics is relatively rare, they have appeared at various intervals up through the twentieth century. The consequences of a pandemic can be devastating because most human immune systems have no preexisting protection against these viruses. Previous pandemics included the Spanish flu in 1918, the Asian flu in 1957, and the Hong Kong flu in 1968, killing 40–50 million people, 2 million, and 1 million, respectively. The highly pathogenic Avian Influenza A—more commonly referred to as Avian flu—is a virus with certain characteristics that has many experts concerned that a new pandemic may be imminent. Today's high level of global travel and extremely urbanized societies provide conditions for the fastest global transmission of a virus that has occurred in human history.

Concern over Avian flu grew after the world witnessed humans' severe vulnerability to infection in 2003. That year, Severe Acute Respiratory Syndrome (SARS), a highly contagious virus, spread to 29 countries in a matter of months, killing 10 percent of those infected. The full-fledged pandemic that was originally feared was averted thanks to the relatively slow spread of the SARS virus, which made it possible to implement centuries-old techniques of quarantine and good hygiene. However, the emergence of SARS provided a stark warning that a more virulent strain could evolve—one that could be easily transmitted from human to human.

Such a pandemic would have severe economic and social costs as a result of soaring levels of illness and a high mortality rate. Health care systems and medical supplies would be inadequate to contain the spread of disease. High rates of worker absenteeism because of illness would cripple the nation's economy and could result in disruptions in basic services, such as providing power, water, transportation, communications, and emergency response. Because society is highly globalized today—and will become even more so in the future—these disruptions will be magnified in individual countries, with a real possibility that a global recession would ensue. International health officials agree that current quarantine methods would prove ineffective at preventing a global pandemic unless they are put in place in the earliest stages of human infection. Early warning systems will be critical. According to a study conducted by Harvard University, if 80 percent of the population that is originally infected could be treated with a mix of strong antiretroviral drugs, there is the chance that a global catastrophe caused by a pandemic could be averted.[32]

The Avian flu virus has infected poultry populations across Asia, the Middle East, Africa, and Europe. Massive die-offs among wild birds have been recorded and outbreaks continue, despite preventive culling measures taken by many governments. In 2007, the Avian flu appeared in domestic poultry populations in 19 countries around the globe.[33] As of September 2007, the number of humans infected by the virus totaled 325—200 of which resulted in fatalities. Although the virus has yet to achieve sustained human-to-human transmission, its constant evolution and endemic spread among bird populations poses a high risk of a global pandemic in the foreseeable future.

Mexico, Canada, and the United States attempted to address this issue—and many others—in March 2005, when the North American leaders signed the Security and Prosperity Partnership of North America, discussed in detail later in this report. The SPP includes several points that can guide collaboration among the three countries in managing various stages of an influenza pandemic. Under the SPP, the United States, Canada, and Mexico created a trilateral committee responsible for the conservation and management of the region's wildlife and ecosystems, and this committee is responsible for coordinating surveillance that will lead to early detection of the Avian flu in North America's wild birds.

In August 2007, the SPP also developed a North American Pandemic Response Strategy, which in essence outlines a broad framework. Even so, the three governments of North America have yet to develop an actual operational work plan. More progress would have been expected, as scientists firmly believe that a pandemic is a matter of when, not if, and know that its severity depends on the intensity of the virus. In October 2008, the government of Canada will host a tabletop exercise focused on advancing a trilateral communications strategy. Coordinating trilateral communications effectively will be of paramount importance if the three governments are to issue consistent strategic messaging and convey an awareness of each governments' response measures (along with the justification)—measures that, after all, may be disparate depending on each nation's viral circumstances. Such coordination will maximize the prospects for social distancing and reduce the migration of panic-stricken individuals from county-to-county, state-to-state, province-to-province, or even across borders—from one border community to another—as they seek refuge from the pandemic and search for more effective health care.

Although these steps are certainly in the right direction, it is vital to implement more widespread measures—such as regular tabletop exercises and simulations to include border state and municipal governments as well as civil-military and military-to-military exercises to strengthen and coordinate surveillance systems, stockpiling, rapid-response strategies and communications.

NORTH AMERICAN SECURITY ARCHITECTURE

Having laid out in detail a series of global trends that may very well evolve into security threats in the year 2025 and beyond, it is helpful to review the security architecture that is currently in place in the region. This section will briefly trace how the security relationship between the three North American nations has evolved, particularly since September 11, 2001. The aim of the discussion is to bring about a better understanding of the current state of North American security relations and to encourage the three governments not only to assess the relevance of these relations in light of potential security threats in the year 2025 but also to identify shortcomings and improvement opportunities.

North America would be in the best position to combat the looming security threats through a comprehensive security architecture—perhaps even one that is linked with hemispheric initiatives—that would respect each country's sovereignty and ensure its national security. Such an arrangement would be a reaction to the realities of a changing world and the need for each country to adapt its own security apparatus and would also allow Canada, Mexico, and the United States to continue to pursue and implement unilateral, bilateral, trilateral, and even multilateral security measures, depending on each country's individual security needs.

SECURITY RELATIONS BETWEEN CANADA AND THE UNITED STATES

Canada's long-standing security relationship with the United States dates back to the 1940 Ogdensburg Declaration, which established that North American security was indivisible and also created the Permanent Joint Board on Defense.[34] Canada and the United States—the only two North American countries that are members of the North Atlantic Treaty Organization (NATO)—are committed to fulfilling the goals of the North Atlantic Treaty that was signed in April 4, 1949. In essence, the treaty resolved to unite the efforts undertaken by all 26 member countries to provide for collective defense and the preservation of peace and security.[35]

The principle of collective security was underscored again in 1958, when the United States and Canada established the North American

Aerospace Defense Command (NORAD) to monitor and defend U.S. and Canadian air space. Canada sought to amend the NORAD agreement in August 2004, thus reaffirming its commitment to the bilateral command and to making NORAD's missile warning capabilities available to the U.S. commands that are responsible for missile defense.

The terrorist attacks of September 11, 2001, set in motion the transformation of the U.S.-Canadian security relationship away from its Cold War origins and into a relationship that places almost an absolute focus on the war against terrorism. This outright shift in paradigm was propelled by the United States' preoccupation with securing its homeland—after all, the terrorist attacks evoked the U.S. public's memories of the preemptive Japanese bombing of the U.S. Pacific Fleet based in Pearl Harbor on December 1941 and prompted a comparable pledge not to allow a future attack on U.S. soil.

As part of the swift and wide-ranging response to the perceived threat, the governments of the United States and Canada signed the 30-point United States-Canada Smart Border Declaration and Action Plan on December 21, 2001, to secure the U.S. border with Canada. The aim of the agreement was to create a border that continued to facilitate the legitimate flow of goods and people while also securing the border against potential entry by terrorists. The swiftness of making this agreement was partly based on concerns over the existence of possible terrorist cells in Canada—a concern rooted in the apprehension of Ahmed Ressam, an Al Qaeda-trained Algerian national, as he attempted to enter the United States through Port Angeles, Washington, in December 1999 in order to bomb Los Angeles International Airport. The upcoming 2002 Winter Olympic Games in Salt Lake City also played a part in rapidly reaching the agreement.

In the wake of the terrorist attacks, the United States proceeded to orchestrate one of its boldest institutional reorganizations of security agencies since the 1949 amendment to the National Security Act of 1947, which consolidated the U.S. Army, Navy, and Air Force under a civilian secretary of what today is known as the U.S. Department of Defense. After the attacks of September 11, however, the reorganization merged more than 22 government agencies under the newly created U.S. Department of Homeland Security (DHS) on March 1, 2003—a clear response to the attacks.

Recognizing the implications of the attacks—as well as the ramifications stemming from the creation of the Department of Homeland

Security—in 2003, the government of Canada also decided to undergo an institutional reorganization of its own by creating Public Safety and Emergency Preparedness Canada—now known as Public Safety Canada—to ensure coordination across all federal departments and agencies responsible for national security and for the safety of Canadians. Public Safety Canada integrated the core activities of the previous Department of the Solicitor General, Office of Critical Infrastructure Protection and Emergency Preparedness, and National Crime Prevention Center—all under one minister.[36] The department provides policy advice and support to the Ministry of Public Safety, which is also responsible for a portfolio of six agencies:

- Canada Border Services Agency,

- Canada Firearms Centre,

- Canadian Security Intelligence Service,

- Correctional Service of Canada,

- National Parole Board, and

- Royal Canadian Mounted Police.

Apart from realizing the merit of merging all the security-oriented ministries and agencies under a single ministry, the Canadian government was well aware that its own reorganization would also serve as a counterweight to its colossus U.S. counterpart—the Department of Homeland Security, the U.S. department to which Public Safety Canada is most analogous.

The U.S. Department of Defense also undertook its own internal reorganization by creating the U.S. Northern Command (NORTHCOM) on October 1, 2002.[37] Headquartered at Peterson Air Force Base in Colorado Springs, Colorado, NORTHCOM was created to provide "command and control of Department of Defense homeland defense efforts and to coordinate defense support of civil authorities."[38] The command's assigned area of responsibility includes the air, land, and sea within the borders of continental United States, Alaska, Canada, and Mexico, as well as the surrounding water out to approximately 500 nautical miles. The commander of NORTHCOM also commands NORAD and is responsible for "theater security coordination" with Canada and Mexico.

In an attempt to continue to strengthen the level of military-to-military cooperation between the United States and Canada—particularly in light of the creation of NORTHCOM—in December 2002 the two countries opted to create a Binational Planning Group for what was originally intended to be a two-year period but was extended until May 2006. In the interim, the government of Canada undertook two major policy steps: (1) In 2004, Ottawa published its National Security Policy, which called for closer cooperation with the United States in the protection of both countries' coasts and territorial waters. (2) In June 2005, the Canadian government announced the creation of Canada Command as part of its transformation of Canadian armed forces in response to "the new international security environment and a commitment to place greater emphasis on the defense of Canada and North America."[39] Canada Command provides a unified and integrated chain of command for the deployment of maritime, land, and air assets in support of Canadian domestic operations and is also consistent with Canada's commitments and obligations under the NORAD agreement.

In April 2006, a month before it was dismantled, the Binational Planning Group released its list of accomplishments, which essentially conceptualized the manner in which the Canadian and U.S. militaries would interact with each other and coordinate their attempts to prevent, mitigate, and—if need be—respond to attacks on either country by terrorists or other parties.[40] Some of the group's specific accomplishments include helping to define the relationship between NORAD, NORTHCOM, and Canada Command; introducing a Canadian presence in the NORTHCOM Joint Operations Center; and developing and participating in binational military training and exercises.

From an intelligence standpoint, Canada's intelligence agency—the Canadian Security Intelligence Service—created the Integrated Threat Assessment Centre to enable Canada to collect, analyze, and disseminate intelligence more effectively. This new center would be comparable to the Terrorist Threat Information Center, which was created in the United States in May 2003 and was transformed into the National Counterterrorist Center in August 2004.

The relationship between Canadian and U.S. law enforcement agencies did not undergo the same type of restructuring or reorganization as did the security establishment. Nonetheless, the relationship between the Royal Canadian Mounted Police and the U.S. Federal Bureau of Investigation is healthy; the two have worked together effectively in counterterrorist interdiction.

SECURITY RELATIONS BETWEEN CANADA AND MEXICO

By and large, the security relationship between Canada and Mexico has seen little activity, which may be a result of insufficient appreciation for the strategic importance of Mexico's security to Canadian national interests. For its part, the government of Mexico has not recognized the strategic importance of Canada's security to Mexican national security interests. Neither country has the geographical proximity or the linkages that would warrant such a relationship. Moreover, the United States has been serving as a buffer zone as far as the security of either country is concerned.

The government of Canada, however, has recently come to the realization that it is in Canada's best interest to ensure that Mexico modernizes its security apparatus, primarily because the U.S. government—and particularly the U.S. Congress—tends to bundle Canada along with Mexico when it comes to border security. Therefore, as long as the U.S. Congress perceives the southern border with Mexico as a vulnerable area, legislators will continue to call for more stringent measures to enforce border security, including those on the northern border with Canada. This perception was again reinforced on September 27, 2007, with the release of the U.S. Government Accountability Office's testimony before the Senate Finance Committee, entitled "Border Security: Security Vulnerabilities at Unmanned and Unmonitored U.S. Border Locations." The scope and tenor of the report partially explain why, on August 21, 2007, the government of Canada announced a new initiative—"Canada-Mexico: A Joint Action Plan 2007–2008"—that includes the creation of the Working Group on Canada-Mexico Security. The working group's activities are intended to complement the political-military talks established in 2006 between Canada and Mexico. According to the Canadian government, the aim of the Working Group on Canada-Mexico Security is to "enhance cooperation under the security agenda of the SPP in areas such as law enforcement, border administration, emergency management and critical infrastructure protection" to be spearheaded by Public Safety Canada and Mexico's Center for Investigation and National Security (CISEN).[41]

SECURITY RELATIONS BETWEEN MEXICO AND THE UNITED STATES

The security relationship between the United States and Mexico is by no means as established as the one between the United States and Canada.

The weaker relationship is largely attributed to the conceptual divide that has traditionally existed between the United States and Mexico in terms of how each country views security. Mexico has not faced any serious external threat since the late nineteenth century; hence, the country has not been called upon to define its own national security, much less develop a national security doctrine.[42] In fact, it was not until January 31, 2005, that Mexico's very first National Security Law (*Ley de Seguridad Nacional*) went into effect. Ironically, it was the absence of legislation covering national security that gave the government of Mexico the latitude to cooperate with the U.S. government to the extent that Mexico did between September 11, 2001, and January 31, 2005. Prior to the passage of its National Security Law, Mexico had no legal framework for regulating the activities of the country's Center for Investigation and National Security—which turned out to be the principal Mexican counterpart to the U.S. Department of Homeland Security—nor any congressional oversight to speak of. Thus, the absence of a regulatory regime in the area of security made it possible for the Mexican government to proceed with and announce the 22-point United States-Mexico Smart Border Partnership and Action Plan that the two countries signed on March 22, 2002.

The Bush administration's concerns over the perceived threat posed by terrorism and the vulnerabilities along the U.S. border with Mexico continued through 2004. The concerns were based on a "stream of reporting [that] told [the CIA] of al-Qa'ida plans to smuggle operatives through Mexico to conduct suicide operations inside the United States"—regardless of the accuracy of the reports.[43] Unlike Canada, which used the September 11 attacks and the ensuing major restructuring within the U.S. government as a catalyst for Ottawa's own organizational restructuring and formulation of new security policies, Mexico did not undertake a similar reform. The government chose not to reorganize its security apparatus despite a debate within Mexican national security circles as to whether it was in Mexico's interest to restructure its civilian security institutions as well—much as the United States did in creating the Department of Homeland Security and Canada did with Public Safety Canada.

As far as relations between U.S. and Mexican military forces are concerned, the Mexican Ministry of Defense (SEDENA) was averse to collaborating with NORTHCOM, despite the concerted effort by Gen. Richard Myers, the chairman of the Joint Chiefs of Staff at the time, who visited Mexico numerous times—while the Iraq war was going on—in an attempt to persuade the Mexican secretary of defense at the time, Gen. Gerardo C.R. Vega, to join the Northern Command. One of the principal objections was that SEDENA wanted to interact exclusively with the U.S. secretary of defense and the chairman of the Joint Chiefs of Staff, not with a regional command. In addition, SEDENA objected to the need to undergo restructuring that would have created a Mexico Command-type structure. In 2006, SEDENA even declined an invitation to assign one of its officers as a liaison to NORTHCOM.

In contrast, the Mexican navy (SEMAR) has been much more receptive to adapting to the twenty-first-century security context and becoming mission-ready. SEMAR accepted an invitation to assign one of its naval officers as a liaison officer to NORTHCOM in February 2007 and assigned a commander to serve a two-year commission as SEMAR's first liaison officer to the command.[44] Although SEMAR did not undergo a major restructuring akin to a Mexico Command-type structure, it assigned its International Affairs Office (*Comisión de Estudios Especiales*) the responsibility of overseeing the relationship with NORTHCOM.

Mexico's Ministry of Defense has been less receptive to undergoing its own transformation. It is hoped that SEDENA's hermetic culture will have changed by 2025, largely because of the generational change among high-ranking officers and because of influence from the transformation of its sister institution, SEMAR.[45] In fact, the apparent receptiveness of President Calderón's secretary of defense, Gen. Guillermo Galvan Galvan, to assigning SEDENA's first liaison officer to NORTHCOM bodes well for such a transformation in the future.

The U.S. Department of Defense has been diligently trying to engage the Mexican military and, in so doing, has even proposed that Mexico join the Permanent Joint Defense Board. This effort has been met with reticence on the part of the Canadian government, which would rather preserve the Joint Defense Board as an exclusive forum for discussion of issues related to NORAD. In its place, the government of Canada has suggested the creation of an alternative trilateral mechanism, and the U.S. Department of Defense has responded favorably to this recommendation; but the suggestion has yet to progress beyond a conceptual phase.

The U.S. Department of Defense also considered the possibility of extending to Mexico status as a Permanent Non-NATO Ally, which would be more of a symbolic overture, but the offer did not materialize partly because of wavering on the part of the U.S. Department of State as well as uncertainty as to whether Mexico would even accept such an offer. It is worth noting that Permanent Non-NATO Ally status is a designation made by the United States, as opposed to an official designation bestowed by NATO; nonetheless, this status has been granted to strategically important nations, such as Israel, Australia, and Japan.[46]

The Mexican government's success in strengthening the capacity of the country's security apparatus so that it can confront the security threats of 2025 and beyond will largely depend on how successful President Felipe Calderón is in working with the Mexican Congress to implement many of the objectives that his administration has laid out in the National Development Plan 2006–2012. Mexico's success in this area is also tied to the extent to which Mexico's next two presidents— irrespective of their political parties—can ensure a certain level of continuity in implementing reforms and strengthening the nation's security institutions.

The Calderón administration's National Development Plan lays out 18 overarching objectives, together with more specific strategies to be used for achieving those objectives. A summary of the strategies that are aimed at strengthening Mexico's security apparatus includes the following specific measures:

- interconnecting the various criminal databases that make up the Criminal Information System belonging to the National Public Security System as a way to ensure more effective use of these resources;[47]

- strengthening Mexico's intelligence gathering and analytical capability by standardizing and integrating databases in an effort to facilitate the sharing of information—be it audio, video, or data files—thereby enabling instant criminal background checks nationwide as well as the maintenance of a national registry of law enforcement officers who have been terminated for cause or have resigned with disciplinary actions pending;[48]

- professionalizing approximately 350,000 police officers who serve in Mexico's 1,661 law enforcement agencies—including federal, state, and municipal agencies;[49]

- providing the funds necessary to modernize the military and the navy technologically and to bring them into the digital age, with the goal of enabling them to more effectively carry out their responsibilities as the defenders of Mexican sovereignty, protectors of national interests, and guarantors of domestic security—all of which entails combating organized crime;[50] and

- protecting Mexico's southern border against the criminal elements that take advantage of the porous border.[51]

If President Calderón succeeds in achieving security reform, the outcome will have implications for both Mexico's future national security and the collective security of North America in 2025 and beyond.

In an attempt to support President Calderón's leadership on security issues and to help strengthen the Mexican government's capacity to combat the growing threat posed to both nations by transnational organized crime, on October 22, 2007, President Bush announced that his administration, together with the Calderón administration, had conceptualized the framework for an unprecedented U.S.-Mexico security cooperation program referred to as the Mérida Initiative. This initiative is aimed at combating the threat posed by drug trafficking, arms smuggling, human trafficking, money laundering, and contraband. President Bush requested US$1.4 billion over a three-year period for this initiative as part of his US$46 billion request for supplemental funding for the wars in Iraq and Afghanistan. The financing of the Mérida Initiative is therefore subject to approval by the U.S. Congress.

If approved, the support package will address some of the institutional asymmetries that exist between Mexican security agencies and their U.S. (and Canadian) counterparts by providing the Mexican government eight transport helicopters, two surveillance airplanes, secure communications technology, database technology and document verification systems to be used for immigration control, expansion of an ongoing initiative to identify and prosecute smugglers of human beings, nonintrusive inspection equipment, prosecutorial case management systems, modern forensics capability, and training aimed at professionalizing personnel throughout the various stages of the process of administering justice—for example, police officers, forensic scientists, court clerks, prosecutors, judges, and prison management personnel.[52] The proposed support is a substantial increase over the estimated US$40 million that Mexico currently receives from the United States each year.[53] The Mérida Initiative is consistent with the objectives outlined in President Calderón's National Development Plan and also underscores the

Mexican Congress's own concerns over security, as evidenced by the 24 percent increase in funding for these agencies allocated in Mexico's FY 2007 federal budget—an amount that brings the annual security-oriented appropriations total to about US$2.5 million.[54]

The support package included in the Mérida Initiative also includes an estimated US$500 million over a three-year period for Central America to provide funding for technologies and the professionalization of personnel comparable to the type of assistance earmarked for Mexico. During the past five years, the United States and Mexico have come to realize that lack of security in Central America has implications well beyond the region and therefore warrants much greater attention from both nations.

If the U.S. Congress approves the Mérida Initiative, the program would have a high degree of influence over the future of security cooperation between the United States and Mexico as well cooperative efforts they undertake with the nations of Central America. Although the Mérida Initiative does not address many other pressing needs facing both Mexico and the United States, the program may cement the security relationship between the two countries and lead to cooperation that is not only deeper but also wider because of the inclusion of Central America, thereby perhaps even serving as a framework for regional security agreements.

NORTH AMERICAN SECURITY RELATIONS

From a policy standpoint, the decision to pursue a North American security paradigm evolved from the notion of harmonizing the various bilateral initiatives that had been brokered between the executive branches of the governments of the United States, Canada, and Mexico. These include the following:

- United States-Mexico Partnership for Prosperity (September 2001),

- United States-Canada Smart Border Declaration and Action Plan (December 2001),

- United States-Mexico Smart Border Partnership and Action Plan (March 2002), and

- Canada-Mexico Partnership (October 2004).

With Paul Martin succeeding Jean Chrétien as Canada's prime minister in December 2003 and George W. Bush's reelection for a second term in November 2004, the political conditions in both Canada and the United States became conducive to moving forward with a trilateral framework. President George Bush, then Mexican President Vicente Fox, and then Prime Minister Paul Martin agreed to sign the Security and Prosperity Partnership of North America in Waco, Texas, on March 23, 2005.

In the June 2005 report—the first Leaders' Report that was compiled just three months after the creation of the SPP—the trilateral security working groups outlined 33 bilateral and trilateral action items, which fell under three overarching themes:

1. securing North America against external threats,

2. preventing and responding to threats within North America, and

3. further streamlining the secure movement of low-risk traffic across shared borders.

Many of the 33 collaborative action items, however, were items that were simply carried over from the previous border agreements.

On March 31, 2006, Mexican president Vicente Fox hosted President George Bush and newly elected Canadian prime minister Stephen Harper for the second SPP Leaders' Meeting held in Cancun, Mexico. Prime Minister Harper's participation was significant, because it marked the continued support of the SPP by the Canadian government, despite a change in government—particularly from a Liberal Party government to a Conservative Party government. Further underscoring Prime Minister Harper's commitment was his offer to host the next SPP Leaders' Meeting.

The second SPP Leaders' Report was released in August 2006.[55] By then the trilateral security working groups had outlined 25 initiatives and 102 specific action items to be taken under the three overarching themes and nine subthemes:

1. securing North America against external threats:

- travelers' security

- cargo security

- bio-protection

2. preventing and responding to threats within North America:

- aviation security
- maritime security
- cooperation among law enforcement agencies
- cooperation on intelligence gathering and sharing
- protection of critical infrastructure

3. further streamlining the secure movement of low-risk traffic across shared borders

- facilitation of the crossing of documented goods and people at the borders.

In August 2007, Prime Minister Stephen Harper hosted President George Bush and newly elected Mexican president Felipe Calderón for the third SPP Leaders' Meeting, which was held in Montebello, Canada. President Calderón's support demonstrated that the SPP had survived another succession of power—this one in Mexico. At this meeting, the three North American leaders instructed their respective ministers to focus on the following five priority areas for the following year:

- enhancing the global competitiveness of North America,
- ensuring the safety of food and products,
- developing sustainable energy and environment,
- establishing smart and secure borders, and
- preparing emergency management and preparedness plans.

The last two priorities are more security-oriented, and they allude to the specific action items in the report.

Addressing the need to ensure smart and secure borders, the three leaders underscored the following:

Effective border strategies minimize security risks, while facilitating the efficient and safe movement of goods, services and people, as trade and cross-border travel increase in North America. These strategies will draw on risk-based border management, innovative use of new technologies, coordinated border infrastructure development, and by moving, where possible, inspection and screening away from the land border.[56]

The leaders also instructed their respective ministers (1) to develop mutually acceptable inspection protocols to detect threats to the region's security, such as those from incoming travelers during a pandemic and from radiological devices on general aviation; and (2) to further cooperate on law enforcement, screening, and facilitation of legitimate trade and travelers across the borders.

In the case of emergency management and preparedness, the three leaders acknowledged that "the consequences of catastrophic events often transcend national borders, hence, preparation and planning can mitigate the impact of such events on people and our economies."[57] They also directed their respective ministers (1) to address any obstacles preventing critical equipment, supplies, and personnel from being deployed expeditiously to those parts of North America where they are needed; and (2) to develop procedures for managing the movement of goods and people across shared borders during and following an emergency.

The viability of the Security and Prosperity Partnership was recently reinforced. In an effort to guarantee the continuity of the SPP, despite a succession of power in the United States following the November 2008 presidential election, President Bush offered to host the fourth Leaders' Meeting in New Orleans in April 2008. The venue is symbolic of the spirit of North American partnership; the location is the site of the unprecedented disaster relief support provided by the governments and peoples of both Canada and Mexico in the aftermath of Hurricane Katrina, which devastated the city.

The Security and Prosperity Partnership has been the target of a variety of criticism by civil society and some members of the nations' legislatures, but the agreement is perhaps best viewed as an effort by the three governments to explore ways in which to optimize the integration that has already taken place since the North American Free Trade Agreement (NAFTA) went into effect more than 14 years ago—on January 1, 1994. From that day until the formulation of the SPP, the three governments had assumed that their work was done, and they ceased exploring innovative ways to further optimize the economic integration that had steadily been taking place all those years between a host of stakeholders in all three nations. The SPP encourages the emergence of a new security model while addressing the need for Canada,

Table 6.1. Assessment of the Security and Prosperity Partnership of North America

Strengths	Deficiencies
Presidential/prime ministerial-level commitment	Exclusion of Congress and Parliament
Policy formulation in a North American context	Exclusion of civil society
Public-private participation	Overly broad scope
Implementation despite the leadership of minority governments	Failure to communicate its mission succinctly

the United States, and Mexico to strengthen their respective and collective economies in order to remain competitive in a changing global economy.

The SPP does have critical shortcomings, however, and these are listed in table 6.1. The initiative was driven solely by the executive branches of the three nations and excluded their three legislatures. Excluding national legislatures from involvement in the SPP was a significant oversight, given that many of the programs emanating from the SPP would ultimately require either appropriations or legislation—both of which are the responsibility of each country's legislative branch. Officials from each government's executive branch maintain that they regularly brief their respective legislatures on the progress of the SPP; in Canada's parliamentary system, doing so is facilitated by the fact that prime ministers and cabinet ministers also preside as members of Parliament. Nevertheless, criticism by members of all the three legislatures over having been overlooked has not ceased, leading one to question if the legislators have used the SPP as a wedge issue in relations between their executive and legislative branches.

In addition, the participation of members of civil society within all three nations was omitted from the SPP process—the same critical oversight that occurred in the NAFTA process, which led in part to the strident opposition the agreement has been receiving among certain sectors. The Bush administration also missed a valuable opportunity to harness the SPP and catapult the relationship of the United States with Canada and Mexico by almost exclusively promoting the security component of the SPP, despite repeated requests by the governments of both Canada and Mexico to advance an agenda in which there was a better balance between security and prosperity.

The three North American governments have obviously been quite busy implementing various cooperative measures to ensure the security of all three nations. Their efforts, however, appear to be more of a reaction to particular events and an undertaking done in an ad hoc fashion versus one that is based on a clearer vision as to where the three countries want to be in terms of security in the year 2025.

POLICY RECOMMENDATIONS

As detailed in the first part of this chapter, North America will need to prepare for a variety of severe challenges coming from diverse sources—natural and man-made. This section offers recommendations for policies that should be adopted as well as an effective North American security architecture that can help prevent or at least mitigate the effects of the security threats facing the continent in 2025 and thereafter.

Policymakers in Canada, Mexico, and the United States must begin to implement measures that take into account and respond effectively to threats that will define the region's security context in 2025. Specific areas that need to be addressed are border security, immigration controls, customs procedures, intelligence gathering, and law enforcement, the energy supply, and economic security. Attention to each of these policy areas can have an effect on the various types of threats—from terrorist attacks to natural disasters and environmental change, energy shortages, and economic crises—that can be expected to threaten North America's security in the years to come.

MEETING FUTURE CHALLENGES

Anticipating and preparing for the threats that North America will face in 2025 poses a challenge for individual countries and international institutions alike. To ensure a peaceful and economically prosperous transition to the emerging multipolar system, the three governments of North America should work together to achieve the following overarching objectives:

- Fuller integration of international markets: Reinvigorating global trade talks either through the Doha round or through new initiatives will be critical. Encouraging trade and mutually beneficial relations is an important strategy for creating incentives to arrive at peaceful resolution of disputes. A true reduction in global trade barriers will also promote growth and opportunity in the developing world.

- Reform of international institutions to reflect the changing global environment and the threat it poses: If the United Nations power structure continues to reflect the post–World War II era, this body will no longer be a legitimate actor in world affairs. Reforming the United Nations Security Council lies at the heart of this task.

- Strengthening of democratic institutions and the rule of law in the Western Hemisphere, particularly in Central America and the Caribbean region: Preventing the emergence of a failed state in the Western Hemisphere is one of the most important priorities for all three North American countries.

- Prevention of state failure whenever possible: Protecting regional stability and international security will often require states to take actions that will prevent the failure of fundamental governing institutions over territorial areas. State failure can lead to humanitarian disasters and gross human rights violations and can also provide fertile operational territory for terrorist groups and transnational criminal organizations.

- Strengthening of the nuclear nonproliferation regime and implementation of more stringent international regulations governing lethal technologies: Even though there is no challenge to the current nonproliferation regime by a vast majority of states, the key concern is to prevent the world's most dangerous states and actors from acquiring the world's most dangerous weapons. To do this, the economic and political powers in the international community must unite in a sustained disarmament and counterproliferation campaign.

- Incorporation of immigrant populations into their new cultures: The challenge of countering the emergence of home-grown terrorism that is now manifest in North America—a threat that is likely to increase in the future—will be to ensure that each country can adequately integrate immigrants into their new communities. Securing strategic border points will continue to be important as will having effective law enforcement and intelligence gathering capacity to intervene when home-grown terrorist activities are detected, but it is equally important for the three governments to engage with new immigrants in order to attune them to their new home country's cultural values, including tolerance, diversity, and the rule of law.

Gathering and Sharing Intelligence

The recent successes of counterterrorism operations in Europe—such as the responses to the incidents in London, Spain, the Netherlands, and Denmark—clearly demonstrate that even governments on a continent with seamless borders, such as those in Europe, are able to combat both home-grown and foreign terrorists. As the year 2025 approaches, with failed states and nonstate actors posing an increasing threat to global security—not just to North America's security—it will be imperative for Canada, Mexico, and the United States to continue to strengthen their intelligence gathering capability and to create a mechanism by which intelligence can increasingly be shared fully and effectively.

In the case of North America, the intelligence capability of the United States and Canada is at an adequate level—albeit clearly in need of constant adaptation. Both countries need to strengthen this capability and preserve its autonomy as the region approaches 2025 and other enemies emerge. The mechanism for intelligence sharing between the nations of North America is deficient and must be improved. In order to foster greater collaboration between the intelligence agencies of North America, the three governments must agree on a common agenda and work toward advancing it. One would hope that small-scale confidence building exercises would help establish the level of mutual trust that is essential for the region's success. However, intelligence sharing between North American agencies cannot be intensified further if there is no improvement in the integrity of Mexico's intelligence agencies, where corruption has impeded intelligence sharing among the Mexican agencies themselves, let alone with their U.S. and Canadian counterparts.

Even though one can appreciate the inherent limitation of coordinating the gathering and sharing of intelligence with a neighboring nation—which some would fear could conceivably threaten one's own national sovereignty one day, particularly if there is a certain level of mistrust—there is no reason to fail to achieve a mutually agreed-upon agenda for such cooperative efforts. The United States and Canada should aspire to establish the type of cooperation in intelligence gathering and sharing that they both enjoy with Great Britain and Australia or that Mexico enjoys with Spain.

Mexico's intelligence gathering capability, however, is in need of further institutional strengthening, particularly if North America puts itself in a position to even consider gravitating toward the possibility of seamless borders. Improving Mexico's capability in this sphere will require, among other things, a reconfiguration of the organizational structure of the country's intelligence apparatus. Currently, Mexico's Ministry of Government has two distinct missions. One mission is political: to serve as the president's political arm in relations with the various national political actors. The second mission is to oversee a host of government agencies, including the Center for Investigation and National Security, the National Migration Institute, and the country's emergency management agency system (*Protección Civil*). For the government of Mexico to be better positioned to meet the challenges that lie in 2025 and beyond, the ministry's dual missions need to be eliminated, so that it may be able to concentrate exclusively on a single mission—whichever one that may be—and do so effectively.

In the United States and Canada, it took a compelling event—the September 11 terrorist attacks and the need to take rapid simultaneous action in a wide range of areas, including intelligence, border security, and so forth—to create the necessary political impetus to undertake major organizational overhauls. Despite observers' confidence that Mexico will have transformed its security structure by 2025, it remains to be seen whether Mexico will need to experience a compelling event of its own in order to create the necessary political impetus to undergo its own organizational restructuring and to eliminate some of the current organizational challenges that impede its security-oriented agencies' optimal performance.

The United States has recently had firsthand experience with the detrimental impact that a lack of autonomy can have on ensuring that national security objectives remain apolitical. Mexico's Center for Investigation and National Security would clearly benefit from achieving a greater degree of autonomy from the country's executive branch—particularly in light of the agency's politicized past. Restructuring the CISEN would not only enable it to focus on threats to Mexico's national security but also remove the agency from the appropriations crosshairs of the Mexican Congress—particularly if that body is politically divided—which tends to bundle the CISEN with the Ministry of Government.

Increased funding for the CISEN would also reduce some of the operational asymmetries that currently exist vis-à-vis its North American counterparts; this problem also limits the ability of the three governments' agencies that are responsible for security to engage with one another. Moreover, the importance of further strengthening Mexico's intelligence gathering capability is underscored by the need to mitigate some of the international illicit flow of drugs and weapons, as well as their negative influences, that are already streaming into Mexico from Central America or the United States—whether these flows are intended to remain in Mexico or to pass through to another market.

Law Enforcement

It is imperative to recognize the transnational nature of the threat that North America will face in the future. In order to counter the transnational threats effectively and to address the risk posed by home-grown threats to security that are anticipated in 2025 and beyond, Canada, the United States, and Mexico need to acknowledge that the first line of defense against security threats may end up being the law enforcement apparatus, rather than the military, which has had that responsibility when it comes to the conventional threats to which the region has become accustomed. Canada, the United States, and Mexico have already had to contend with separate terrorist threats emerging from within their own countries. Therefore, North America must place greater emphasis on the institutional strengthening of law enforcement operations in all three countries.

North America will have to break away from the conventional, twentieth-century nation-centric, stovepipe approach to combating transnational threats that operate seamlessly and effectively across political borders. Policymakers will need to adapt to what appears to be an extremely challenging security scenario for 2025 and beyond. The shift in the paradigm will require the three governments to develop transnational strategies and perhaps even construct a transnational mechanism with an investigative and operational capability that will complement the work that is already being done by the three countries at the national, state or provincial, and local level.

It is unclear whether there is a need to create a truly trilateral law enforcement control and command center or an intelligence center for North America, or whether it is possible to harness some of the transnational benefits that the International Criminal Police Organization (INTERPOL) already offers. Until the recently announced Mérida Initiative as well as Canada's own proposed initiative to support cooperation between Canada and Mexico in measures designed to protect each nation's security, there had been relatively little support from either neighbor to help Mexico address some of the law enforcement asymmetries that exist in that country.

Eventually, Canada, the United States, and Mexico will also have to shift their focus to strengthening the law enforcement capability of their closest—if not most strategically pertinent—regional and international neighbors and work outward. The U.S., Canadian, and Mexican governments have gradually come to this realization and have begun to undertake certain measures that move them in that direction. The announcement of the US$500 million support package for Central American security—as part of the Mérida Initiative—is indicative of the shift in paradigm, as is the fact that in June 2007 Mexico hosted the very first meeting of attorneys general from Mexico, the United States, Central America, and Colombia—a meeting in which the government of Canada should have participated.

Border Security

By 2025, the three governments will have to strike an appropriate balance between security and the efficient flow of documented goods and people. Ever since the terrorist attacks of September 11, the U.S. government has been resolute in its almost singular focus on enforcing border controls, despite the official pronouncement about "further streamlining the secure movement of low-risk traffic across our shared borders." The United States has fallen short of striking a healthy balance between ensuring border security while at the same time facilitating the efficient flow of documented goods and people.

This security-centric approach to managing borders can be attributed to a number of developments that set certain measures in motion. These can be broken down into three distinct stages:

Stage 1. The first stage took place between September 2001 and 2003, when the governments of Canada, Mexico, and the United States reacted to the September 11 terrorist attacks and undertook whatever security measures were deemed necessary to protect the continent. Washington and Ottawa initiated a series of stringent and coordinated measures to secure both countries' borders, despite the fact that all the perpetrators of the three separate September 11 attacks had been residing in the United States, as opposed to having sneaked in across either its northern or southern border.

Stage 2. The second stage took place from 2002 through 2003, the period during which a sustained focus on border security was triggered by the streaming of intelligence reports—substantiated or not—indicating that Al Qaeda was considering using the border as a way to bypass security measures and enter the United States. All three countries' heightened awareness of this risk brought greater attention to the integrity of North America's borders.

Stage 3. The third stage commenced on January 7, 2004, when President Bush proposed a new temporary worker program. With that announcement, the concept of border security became entwined with the very heated debate within the United States over immigration reform. As a result of the symbiotic relationship between security and electoral politics, security—including border security—again became a focal point for both the administration and Congress. These security concerns, coupled with the dynamics of electoral politics, also may help to explain the strong influence that the Department of Homeland Security has been able to wield within the U.S. interagency policymaking process.

The media's intense focus on issues related to the border has heightened the public's concern about the risks—real or perceived—confronting North America. These stages may also be converging into a phase that is marked by what appears to be growing support for protectionist policies in the United States, and some might argue that the United States has perhaps already entered this stage. Nevertheless, it is important to recognize that reducing barriers and deepening economic integration remain the most effective paths to achieving collective security and peace. Thus, looking to 2025 and beyond, it is clear that the United States, Mexico, and Canada must continue to work cooperatively to strike the right balance between national security and the efficient flow of documented goods and people that are so vital to the integrated economies of North America.

Immigration Controls

Looking at the demographic projections for North America and the rest of the world in 2025, it is obvious that the flow of immigration and labor mobility will be extensive. Therefore, all three nations need to continue to strengthen entry and exit immigration controls, preferably through the use of leading-edge technologies that will have the least adverse impact on the efficient and legal flow of trade and people.

In Canada, immigration accounts for about two-thirds of the country's population growth today. After 2030, all of Canada's population growth will come from immigration as a result of the nation's low fertility rate (1.5 per person annually) as well as the aging of a large segment of the population (by 2031, one in four Canadians will be more than 65 years of age). What's more, even before reaching the year 2030, it is estimated that Canada's population will experience more deaths than births. The demographic face of Canada will also undergo a further transformation. Currently, about 75 percent of Canada's immigrants come from Asia and the Middle East, and about 45 percent do not speak either of Canada's two official languages—English and French. In fact, China currently accounts for the most migrants to Canada, which partly explains why the Chinese are Canada's largest minority group.[58] This demographic future will clearly bring with it a series of security challenges for the Canadian government, which will obviously need to further bolster its own ability to screen foreign nationals who want to migrate to Canada or to conduct due diligence on these immigrants after they enter the country.

The Mexican government has, for the most part, focused on migration from the standpoint of being the principal source of migrants to the United States and ensuring that the rights of Mexican nationals are respected north of the border. (It should come as no surprise that even the Mexican government's agency responsible for immigration issues is called the National Migration Institute.) However, as Mexico approaches 2025, the country will have to increasingly contend with the migration of Central Americans and South Americans, as well as those from other corners of the world, into Mexico. In fact, it is anticipated that, commencing in 2008, the government of Mexico will begin to incrementally implement and enforce more stringent entry controls at the land ports of entry, putting an end to the current situation in which anyone can enter undetected, unless they are randomly selected and stopped at secondary inspection stations. The institutional strengthening and professionalization of the National Migration Institute—and perhaps even the renaming of the agency to reflect its mandate more accurately—will have to be a priority. Mexico will also need to address that agency's integrity as well as the implementation of greater internal controls. By the year 2025, the government of Mexico is expected to have fully completed the implementation of the Integral Migratory Operation System, which will even include land ports of entry, as well as the biometric digitalization of its National Population Registry, which will give the Mexican government the capability to know who is residing in or transiting through Mexico.

Clearly, the United States has invested heavily in improvements to its immigration controls by implementing the various security measures that were legislatively mandated by the Intelligence Reform and Terrorist Prevention Act of 2004. Presumably, by 2025, the United States will have fully implemented the biometric-based U.S.-VISIT Program as well as the Western Hemisphere Travel Initiative, which requires travelers from certain countries to show their passports in order to enter the United States. Clearly, the future focus will have to increasingly be on detecting fraudulent documents both within the United States, Canada, and Mexico and as presented by foreign nationals who attempt to enter North America.

In addition, in order to shore up security *between* the ports of entry, the U.S. government has begun to implement the Secure Border Initiative, which uses detection technology and infrastructure to detect, monitor, and classify—on a real time basis—individuals approaching the border. One would expect the Secure Border Initiative to be fully operational by 2025. If anything, the enhanced, next-generation, detection system will undoubtedly lead not only to an increase in the number of individuals detected but also to violent skirmishes between Border Patrol and felons perpetrating illicit activities between the ports of entry. To avert a possible escalation of tensions stemming from a cross-border incident, the U.S., Mexican, and Canadian governments will have to improve cross-border communications and agree on clearly defined protocols of engagement.

North America will need to do more than adopt effective immigration policies and implement the security measures that are required. To meet the challenge facing the continent, each of the three nations will have to strengthen and culturally adapt its own domestic law enforcement systems and enhance its domestic intelligence gathering capabilities, at the same time being careful to avoid infringing on individuals' civil liberties.

A related challenge facing countries to which foreign nationals emigrate—such as the United States, Canada, and to a lesser extent Mexico—will be the need for these immigrants to embrace the values of their new country, including its culture of the rule of law, because some immigrants will be entering from nations that have less stringent cultures of the rule of law and less effective judicial systems. Immigrants' failure to adapt to the requirements of their new culture could lead to increased criminal activity in their new home countries and a gradual eroding of North America's own culture of the rule of law.

Customs Procedures

Currently, the flow of legitimate goods that cross North American borders is unprecedented. Indeed, today Canada is the United States' number-one trading partner—a standing it has held since 1992, when it surpassed Japan. Bilateral two-way trade between the United States and Canada has more than tripled since the implementation of the United States-Canada Free Trade Agreement in January 1988. Trade between the two countries has grown from US$153 billion in 1988 to US$539.1 billion in 2006—an increase of 348 percent. To be more specific, between 1988 and 2006, U.S. exports to Canada increased exponentially—from US$71.6 billion to US$230.6 billion—whereas, in the same period, Canadian exports to the United States have increased from US$81.4 billion to US$302 billion.[59]

At this time, Mexico is the third largest trading partner of the United States, having lost its second-place ranking to China in 2003. Bilateral two-way trade between the United States and Mexico has quadrupled since the implementation of the North American Free Trade Agreement, growing from US$81.5 billion in 1993 to US$332.5 billion in 2006—an increase of 408 percent. More precisely, between 1993 and 2006, U.S. exports to Mexico increased exponentially—from US$41.6 billion to US$134 billion—whereas Mexican exports to the United States increased from US$39.9 billion to US$198.3 over the same period.[60]

These trade figures represent an enormous movement of legitimate goods across North American borders. In 2006, an estimated 61.6 percent of the value of goods trade between the United States and its NAFTA partners was transported by freight trucks, an estimated 14.9 percent by rail, an estimated 8.1 percent by sea/water, and an estimated 4.1 percent by air.

Because freight trucks are the primary mode of transportation sustaining the robust trading relationship between these three nations, the land ports of entry assume notable importance; a total of 85 land ports of entry—the most important of which are at the Detroit-Windsor border, the Buffalo-Niagara corridor, and the Port Huron-Sarnia border—are located between the United States and Canada. In 2006, 10 ports of entry handled 92 percent of the truck freight flows in 2006, which were worth an estimated US$288 billion. Along the border between the United States and Mexico there are 25 land ports of entry; in 2006, 10 handled 97 percent of the truck freight flows, which were worth an estimated US$214 billion. The most important ports of entry between Mexico and the United States are Laredo-Nuevo Laredo, El Paso-Ciudad Juarez, and Otay Mesa-Tijuana.[61]

Despite the less significant use of rail as a mode of transportation, rail transport has nonetheless increased since the implementation of NAFTA. Currently, an estimated 35 percent of U.S.-Canadian trade—along with an estimated 17 percent of U.S.-Mexican trade—use rail to transport goods. Moreover, use of rail is likely to increase further as gasoline prices continue to rise and rail transport is seen as a more viable alternative to freight trucks—a mode that suffers from costly bottlenecks in the absence of much needed investments in infrastructure. Moreover, rail may also end up handling much of the transshipment of heavy exports that originate from overseas. Therefore, a greater emphasis will have to be placed on rail security in anticipation of the projected increase in rail use.

Given the projected shift in the economic balance of power toward Asia, it is quite likely that the maritime ports in all three countries will see increased activity in 2025 and beyond. The surge in trade with China alone may spearhead the rise in the importance of maritime ports; China has been the fastest growing export market for the United States for the past five years, with an annual growth rate of 24 percent. It is no wonder that China's Vice Minister of Commerce Gao Hucheng predicted that China will overtake Japan as the third largest export market for the United States no later than 2008.[62]

In the case of Canada, the nation's three largest container ports—Vancouver, Montreal, and Halifax—are labeled Container Security Initiative ports; that is, ports where shipping containers bound for the United States by inland transport are inspected on-site. Nevertheless, these ports will still need to continue implementing many of the security-oriented recommendations outlined by Canada's Standing Senate Committee on National Security and Defence and also build on those measures in anticipation of the security challenges expected in 2025. Currently, about 30 percent of all containers arriving at the largest Canadian ports make their way to the United States through transshipping.[63] These three major Canadian ports will benefit from a federal infrastructure initiative costing $33 billion (in Canadian dollars) that is aimed at improving the capacity of Canadian gateway ports and transportation corridors.[64] In the case of Mexico, it is likely that the maritime ports along its western border—Lazaro Cardenas and Manzanillo—as well as the planned Punta Colonet port outside of Ensenada will also need to handle more shipments that originate in Asia.

The increased use of Canadian and Mexican maritime ports may also be driven by the saturation of U.S. maritime ports, such as the Port of Los Angeles/Long Beach and the urban sprawl that envelops them and impedes their expansion. Ultimately, all North American maritime ports will have to ensure a certain security standard throughout the supply chain—from the importers and through to the carriers, brokers, manufacturers, warehouse operators, and the maritime ports themselves. Doing so will ensure the integrity of North American trade and will build confidence during a period of increasing uncertainty.

Among other tasks, the Secure Freight Initiative, which is overseen by the U.S. Department of Homeland Security and the U.S. Department of Energy, has begun to include cooperative efforts with allies to install radiological and nuclear scanning technology at foreign ports in an attempt to prevent potential threats from entering North American ports. The security measures that are part of this initiative will have to be augmented over time.[65]

Despite the projected rise of emerging economies such as China and India, it is highly unlikely that trade between the countries of North America will decline or remain static. Therefore, ensuring an efficient—not to mention uninterrupted (by a natural or man-made disaster)—flow of commerce between the three North American nations is of crucial importance not only to the economic security of all three countries today and in the future but also to the mutual trilateral national security interests of the entire continent.

The security measures that have been implemented in North America to date reflect a rapid and essential response to the attacks of September 11, 2001. Heightened security concerns and a strong economy provided a fertile context for these changes. However, as the economy begins to cool down and economic global competition heats up, North America will need to achieve a better balance. Until now, security and ensuring the efficient flow of goods have been, to some extent, approached as separate goals. In light of the security and economic conditions that North America will be experiencing in the future, clearly both objectives will have to be advanced in an all-encompassing, integrated fashion—particularly as the three governments consider future investments in infrastructure—as opposed to simply implementing ad hoc security measures. This will require that U.S. Customs and Border Protection (CBP) receive an adequate level of appropriations to carry out its mission effectively.

Energy Supply

In light of the current problems caused by shortages in the energy supply and North America's dependence on oil—a situation that is bound to get worse unless dramatic changes are made—North America's long-term prosperity and competitiveness require the governments of all three countries to pursue policies that promote multiple energy sources in the short term and a secure and stable energy supply in the future. Eventually, when the scarcity of petroleum reaches a level that makes the price of oil no longer desirable to the average consumer, the North American market will have to establish a post-petroleum economy. Concerns over environmental pressures, security issues, and the availability of alternative technologies will push the North American economies in this direction.

More advantageous than pursuing a policy of "energy independence" would be to establish a policy of "energy insulation," whereby the three North American neighbors would work together to secure current resources, share technologies, and alter consumption patterns. To ensure the security of North America's energy supply, the three governments should adopt policies that achieve the following goals:

- Maintenance of multiple energy sources, exploration of new wells needed for future production, and construction of the infrastructure that is critical for energy transfers between the three countries: Encouraging a strong North American partnership that balances the interests of all three countries will be important to the future of each. Furthermore, even though it is important to continue to import energy supplies, the three nations also need to work collectively to encourage the development, use, and sustainability of alternative sources of energy.

- Transfer of technologies to advance more efficient use of energy, cleaner output, and renewable energy systems: Whether the emphasis is on developing cleaner and more efficient ways to use current energy systems or on developing renewable energy sources, sharing scientific and technological advances in North America is critical for achieving a more diversified energy economy and moving away from dependence on foreign petroleum reserves.

- Promotion of conservation through public awareness campaigns and regulations: Reducing North America's energy consumption—or at least slowing its rate of growth—will be extremely important. Effective public awareness campaigns could eliminate some wasteful behaviors in households and businesses. Greater regulation may be needed in the automobile and airline industries.

Economic Stability

All the scenarios detailed in the first section of this chapter—the changing world order, the threat posed by terrorists from both inside and outside each country, climate change, natural disasters, the dwindling supply of energy, and so forth—can lead to an economic crisis in each of the North American nations and the region as a whole. All three governments must take steps to prepare for economic shocks and the contagion effect they may have on public welfare and political stability in each country. Shifting demographic patterns, labor mobility, and the rise of new economic powers in other parts of the world—changes that will continue and are expected to expand significantly—can dramatically alter the economic and competitive standing that North America enjoys today. Therefore, North America's economic security depends on each country's ability to meet these challenges.

In looking to 2025 and beyond, it will be interesting to see if the United States can sustain both the level of economic prosperity to which it has become accustomed as well as its standing as a global economic power. Over the next few years and possibly even decades, the United States will be subject to mounting economic pressures stemming from the following:

- a burgeoning budget deficit;

- the aging of 30 million baby boomers and the ensuing financial demands on the Social Security system and Medicare;

- lagging U.S. competitiveness vis-à-vis rising economic powers such as China and India, to name a few; and

- the risk that the U.S. dollar will lose its standing among international monetary authorities as the world's foremost reserve currency and will be replaced by the euro or the yen.[66]

In the event that the country's prosperity begins to wane, it will be interesting to see how the U.S. government will adjust to this new world economic order and whether it will do so with humility or resort to its military prowess to sustain—if not regain—its economic standing in the world. How the U.S. government responds to this likely situation could also have security implications for both Canada and Mexico, particularly if the United States ends up with hawkish administrations in the future.

Canada's economic security will largely depend on how successful Ottawa is in tackling its demographic challenges. The question is: Will Canada rely on an aggressive immigration policy to replace its aging population, thereby acquiring the necessary labor to sustain its rate of economic growth? Observers have suggested that, even if the Canadian government were to adopt an open-door labor mobility policy, it would still be difficult for the country to achieve the rate of growth to which it has been accustomed. Mexico's economic security, on the other hand, will be heavily dependent on how successful the government is in building the necessary political consensus to advance many of the structural reforms that are needed to propel the country's economic growth.

Obviously, how well or how poorly the three governments respond to these challenges will determine the level and intensity of the potential repercussions. To ensure North America's economic security in the future, all three nations—working independently of one another but with overarching aim of achieving the continent's collective prosperity—will have to place a much greater emphasis on education, implement immigration policies that are much more centered on human capital, increase their investments in research and development, modernize their infrastructure, and diversify their economies to the extent possible to enable them to weather future economic volatility.

One of the most monumental challenges in positioning the three North American nations to contend with the security threats they are likely to face in 2025 will be for the legislatures in all three countries to think beyond their constituents and to recognize the benefit that comes from doing so. Thinking transnationally can sometimes be in the best interest of legislators' constituents as well as of the nation as a whole.

The executive branches of all three North American governments have been criticized for excluding their legislatures from participation in the Security and Prosperity Partnership of North America. The criticism is justified, and the omission will have to be corrected if the SPP or another incarnation of the trilateral initiative has any chance of being truly effective. Nevertheless, it should be noted that, beyond the normal tensions between a country's executive and legislative branches—the case in all three countries, which is as it should be—the three legislatures have not necessarily exhibited the type of foresight in terms of transnational issues that the SPP embodies.

The U.S. Congress and the Canadian Parliament meet annually under the U.S.-Canada Inter-Parliamentary Group (IPG) mechanism. Similarly, the U.S. and Mexican Congress meet annually under the U.S.-Mexico Inter-Parliamentary Group mechanism. However, the IPG structure has thus far proven to be useful only in forging bilateral friendships and dialogue among a select number of legislators from the respective nations. The IPGs have yet to include the participation of their countries' legislative leadership or to result in any significant legislative initiatives, let alone craft anything that has a bilateral or trilateral dimension. In fact, despite the interest and effort on the part of some members of the legislative branch from one of the North American nations to schedule a meeting of a Canada-U.S.-Mexico IPG in 2006, the members failed to garner the necessary trilateral support necessary to hold such a meeting.

In looking to 2025 and beyond, the security of North America will be enhanced if the role of the three legislatures evolves and adapts to current circumstances. Doing so will enable this branch of the three nations' governments to increase its effectiveness in addressing some of the challenges that loom on the 2025 horizon that are of a transnational nature.

CONCLUSION

The relationship between Canada, Mexico, and the United States must be strengthened in critical ways in order to most effectively meet the security challenges that will face North America in 2025. The events of September 11, 2001, fundamentally changed the security relationship between the three neighboring countries, as the focus of the trilateral relationship moved to border protection and prevention of future terrorist attacks. In 2005, the countries launched a trilateral framework for addressing security concerns under the Security and Prosperity Partnership for North America. The SPP was an important development meant to increase trilateral cooperation on security measures, but serious structural deficiencies limit its potential as a vehicle for cooperation.

The North American governments share a sufficient commonality of interests, and, even though the three countries maintain differing perceptions and priorities when it comes to threats to their security, the differences must not be allowed to adversely affect cooperation on measures that will ensure the security of North America as a whole. Canada, Mexico, and the United States must exhibit sensitivity to competing security concerns and focus on the need for cooperation in order to secure the North American homeland. This chapter has argued that North America's current security framework is inadequate for effective mitigation of and response to the broad spectrum of threats and challenges facing the continent in the twenty-first century. In addition, policymakers in each country must encourage and work toward organizational and cultural changes so that they can protect the welfare of their countries' citizens in the decades to come.

Any effort to enhance the common security of North America should take into account a wide array of issues and pay special attention to threats that extend beyond traditional understandings of defense. The countries of North America must leverage their position in world affairs to remain competitive in a changing global environment. Preventing the world's most dangerous states and nonstate actors from acquiring the world's most dangerous weapons—especially chemical, biological, radiological, and nuclear—is of paramount importance for global stability as well as North American security. Efforts to prevent or disrupt terrorist attacks on cities, infrastructure, electronic communication, and public health delivery systems will remain central to the three countries' trilateral and bilateral relationships.

Although critically important, combating terrorism is just one of an array of priorities North America must address in order to develop cooperative relationships that the region will need in the future. Mexico's primary security concern remains focused on organized crime, drug trafficking, and money laundering. It is in the best interest of the United States and Canada to support Mexico's efforts to maintain domestic stability and economic growth, because the support will promote security throughout the region. The three countries will also need to evaluate their strategies to prevent or mitigate the effects of economic crises, environmental catastrophes, water shortages, and the spread of disease and illness. Finally, the common security of North America depends on the ability of all three countries to respond to disasters effectively and to manage their consequences—whether the catastrophe is the result of a terrorist attack, a natural disaster, an industrial accident, or a public health crisis. Coordinating disaster response is one of the glaring deficiencies in the trilateral security relationship today.

If the North American security paradigm is to confront the variety of security threats anticipated by 2025 successfully, it will have to be advanced as a balanced approach to pursuing a mutually agreed-upon vision, as opposed to being forged haphazardly by only one of the nations without a bona fide trilateral consensus. Many of the security measures implemented after September 11, 2001, were purely reactions to the terrorist attacks and the perceived terrorist threat that might ensue, as opposed to components of a well-thought-out, coherent plan to advance a North American security paradigm. Hence, most of the security measures were driven primarily by the United States' own threat assessment and less so by the specific security threats faced by either Canada or Mexico as well as by these countries' individual needs. In fact, it can even be argued that, early on, Canada and Mexico were under a certain degree of duress to agree to the various security measures promoted or implemented by the United States, because they were well aware of the post–September 11 political climate in the United States as well as the mind-set of Washington policymakers—both of which gave the U.S. neighbors very little wiggle room. Moreover, the real possibility existed that the United States would forge ahead on security measures with or without its neighbors' support. If a North American security paradigm is to succeed, it will have to be based on a convergence of issues on which all three nations agree.

At the time this chapter was written, it appeared that the Bush administration was becoming more receptive to advancing a much more balanced agenda that addresses the mutual needs of all three nations. However, it is difficult to say whether this shift is the result of having acquired a more profound grasp of the importance of a balanced agenda for trilateral initiatives or whether it is merely a reflection of an administration more willing to concede the issue in the waning months of its final term in office. At this juncture—with the next U.S. presidential election less than a year away and an extremely close race for the Democratic Party's candidate—it is impossible to gauge the tenor of the next U.S. administration as it commences its new term in office.

One thing is certain, however: the overarching principle of the Security and Prosperity Partnership undoubtedly has policy relevance, particularly in light of the policy challenges that loom on the horizon. The next U.S. administration—be it Democratic or Republican—would be well advised to continue the implementation of the SPP. If nothing else, the change in the U.S. administration will provide an opportunity to rectify some of the initiative's shortcomings.

In order to move forward and work much closer together in shoring up the security of the North American neighborhood and its ability to face the security threats of 2025, North Americans will need to acquire a much more profound understanding of the strategic importance of one another's countries. All three nations have citizens who have yet to realize the context in which North America finds itself vis-à-vis the rest of the world. Only by getting to know one another better, by respecting one another's differences, and appreciating the global context in which the continent must operate will the three North American countries be able to work collectively on those issues that warrant a united trilateral front and go a long way toward securing their welfare and prosperity.

NOTES

1. Centro de Investigación y Docencia Económicas (CIDE) and Consejo Mexicano de Asuntos Internacionales (COMEXI), "Comparing Mexican Leaders and the Mexican Public," chapter 1 in *Mexico and the World 2006: Leaders, Public Opinion and Foreign Policy in Mexico, the United States, and Asia: A Comparative Study* (Mexico City: CIDE/COMEXI, 2006), p. 19.

2. "Up from the Bottom of the Pile," *The Economist*, August 16, 2007.

3. Economic Commission for Latin America and the Caribbean (ECLAC), Statistics and Economic Projections Division, *Statistical Yearbook 2006*, http://www.cepal.org/cgi-bin/getProd.asp?xml=/publicaciones/xml/3/28063/P28063.xml&xsl=/deype/tpl/p9f.xsl&base=/tpl/top-bottom.xsl.

4. Andres Oppenheimer, "Conference Attendees Say Latin Economies Will Grow," *Miami Herald*, September 25, 2007.

5. "Informe Latinobarometro," 2006, p. 65, http://www.latinobarometro.org/index.php?id=66.

6. For an index qualifying the extent of state collapse, see "The Failed States Index 2007," *Foreign Policy* (July/August 2007), p. 12.

7. Stockholm International Peace Research Institute, "Non-State Actors in Conflict Project," http://www.sipri.org/contents/conflict/nonstateactors.html.

8. Office of the U.S. President, *National Security Strategy of the United States of America* (Washington, D.C., 2006).

9. Although many, including President George W. Bush, have declared that the war on terror includes operations against all terrorist organizations, this broad characterization is not useful. Instead, it is more helpful to look at the congressional authorization given to the president on September 18, 2001, which authorized the president to take "all necessary and appropriate force against those nations, organizations, or persons he determines planned, authorized, committed, or aided the terrorist attacks that occurred on September 11, 2001, or harbored such organizations or persons."

10. Danielle Goldfarb, "Reaching a Tipping Point: Effects of Post-9/11 Border Security on Canada's Trade and Investment," Conference Board of Canada Report, June 2007, http://www.conferenceboard.ca/documents.asp?rnext=2028.

11. Christopher Sands, "Rising Power or Fading Power: 11 September and the Lessons of the Section 110 Experience," in *A Fading Power: Canada among Nations 2002*, ed. Maureen Appel Molot and Norm Hillmer (New York: Oxford University Press, 2002).

12. Author interview with Thomas Sanderson, deputy director, Transnational Threats Project, Center for Strategic and International Studies, Washington, D.C., March 5, 2008.

13. Rafael Rios Garcia, "Riesgos a la Seguridad Interna en el México Actual," September 11, 2006, http://www.csis.org/images/stories/Americas/060911_rios.pdf.

14. Honorable Gary Lunn, P.C., M.P., minister of natural resources, Notes for a Speech Given at the Trilateral North American Energy Ministers Meeting, Victoria, B.C., July 23, 2007, http://www.nrcan.gc.ca/media/speeches/2007/200769_e.htm.

15. S. Solomon, D. Qin, M. Manning, Z. Chen, M. Marquis, K.B. Averyt, M. Tignor, and H.L. Miller, eds., *IPCC 2007: Climate Change 2007: The Physical Science Basis.* Contribution of Working Group I to the Fourth Assessment Report of the Intergovernmental Panel on Climate Change (New York: Cambridge University Press, 2007), chap. 3, p. 237.

16. Ibid., chap. 1, p. 101.

17. CNA Corporation, Military Advisory Board, "National Security and the Threat of Climate Change," April 16, 2007.

18. Mark W. Rosegrant, Ximing Cai, and Sarah A. Cline, *World Water and Food to 2025: Dealing with Scarcity* (Washington, D.C.: International Food Policy Research Institute, 2002), http://www.ifpri.org/pubs/books/Water2025/Water2025_toc.pdf.

19. Thomas R. Karl et al., eds., *Weather and Climate Extremes in a Changing Climate, Regions of Focus: North America, Hawaii, Caribbean, and U.S. Pacific Islands,* a report by the U.S. Climate Change Science Program and the Subcommittee on Global Change Research (Washington, D.C.: Department of Commerce, NOAA's National Climatic Data Center, June 2008), http://www.climatescience.gov/Library/sap/sap3-3/final-report/default.htm.

20. National Academy of Sciences, National Research Council, Committee on the Scientific Bases of Colorado River Basin Water Management, "Colorado River Basin Water Management: Evaluating and Adjusting to Hydroclimatic Variability," Washington, D.C., 2007.

21. A.F. Hamlet, "The Role of Transboundary Agreements in the Columbia River Basin: An Integrated Assessment in the Context of Historic Development, Climate, and Evolving Water Policy," in *Climate and Water: Transboundary Challenges in the Americas,* ed. H. Diaz and B. Morehouse (New York: Springer, 2003), pp. 263–289.

22. Memorial Institute for the Prevention of Terrorism, "Terrorism Knowledge Base," http://www.tkb.org/Group.jsp?groupID=41.

23. Joint Press Availability between President Bush, Prime Minister Harper of Canada, and President Calderón of Mexico, Fairmont Le Chateau Montebello, Montebello, Canada, August 21, 2007, http://www.whitehouse.gov/news/releases/2007/08/20070821-3.html.

24. Prime Minister Stephen Harper, "Strong Leadership: A Better Canada," Speech from the Throne, Ottawa, Canada, October 16, 2007, pp. 3–4, http://www.sft-ddt.gc.ca/grfx/docs/sftddt-e.pdf.

25. Carrie E. Donovan, "The Law of the Sea Treaty," Heritage Foundation, Web Memo No. 470, Washington, D.C., April 2, 2004, http://www.heritage.org/Research/InternationalOrganizations/wm470.cfm.

26. The work done by the U.S.-Mexican multiagency group, Border Agency Fire Council (BAFC), which was formed in October 1995 and continues to operate to this day, should be recognized for this effort. The BAFC is a

consortium of public and private organizations. Information about BAFC is available at http://www.fs.fed.us/r5/cleveland/fire/bordercouncil/index .shtml.

27. See http://www.forces.gc.ca/site/newsroom/.

28. See http://www.sedena.gob.mx/index.php?id_art=395m/view_news_e .asp?id=1740.

29. Government of Mexico, Secretariat of the Navy, Press Release 092/05, September 5, 2005, http://www.semar.gob.mx/boletin/2005/bol_092_05.htm.

30. Agriculture and Agri-Food Canada, "Mexico at a Glance,"http://www .ats.agr.gc.ca/info/lac-e.htm.

31. U.S. Department of Agriculture, Economic Research Service, "Foreign Agricultural Trade of the United States (FATUS)," http://www.ers.usda .gov/data/FATUS/#fiscal.

32. Christina Mills et al. "Transmissibility of 1918 Pandemic Influenza," *Nature* 432, no. 7019 (December 2004). North Atlantic Treaty Organization, http://www.nato.int/docu/basictxt/treaty.htm.

33. The countries include Japan, Hong Kong, Thailand, Vietnam, Hungary, Russia, Pakistan, Indonesia, Turkey, Nigeria, Laos, Afghanistan, Kuwait, Myanmar, China, Bangladesh, Saudi Arabia, Cambodia, and Ghana. An updated list of infected areas can be found on the World Health Organization's Web site, http://www.who.org.

34. Canada's International Policy Statement, "A Role of Pride and Influence in the World," *Defence* (2005), p. 25.

35. North Atlantic Treaty Organization, "North Atlantic Treaty," Washington, D.C., April 4, 1949, http://www.nato.int/docu/basictxt/treaty.htm.

36. See Public Safety Canada's Web site, http://www.safecanada.ca/role_e .asp?DeptID=35.

37. The U.S. Department of Defense currently has six regional commands: U.S. Pacific Command (USPACOM, created in 1947), U.S. European Command (USEUCOM, 1952), U.S. Southern Command (USSOUTH-COM, 1963), U.S. Central Command (USCENTCOM, 1983), U.S. Northern Command (NORTHCOM, 2002), and U.S. Africa Command (USAFRICOM, 2007). The department also has four functional commands: U.S. Joint Forces Command (USJFCOM, 1947), U.S. Special Operations Command (SOCOM, 1986), U.S. Transportation Command (TRANSCOM, 1986), and U.S. Strategic Command (STRATCOM, 1992). Information about all these commands is available at www.defenselink. mil/specials/unifiedcommand/.

38. See U.S. Northern Command, http://www.northcom.mil/About/index .html.

39. Canadian Department of National Defence, "Backgrounder, Canada Command," Ottawa, June 28, 2005, http://www.forces.gc.ca/site/Newsroom/

view_news_e.asp?id=1692 or http://www.canadacom.forces.gc.ca/en/background_e.asp.

40. U.S. Embassy, Canada, "Backgrounder: The Bi-National Planning Group," Ottawa, April 2006, www.canada.usembassy.gov/content/can_usa/bpg_backgrounder_040606.pdf.

41. Foreign Affairs and International Trade Canada, News Release, no. 115, Ottawa, August 21, 2007.

42. Armand Peschard-Sverdrup, Sara Rioff, and Brian Latell, *U.S.-Mexico Border Security and the Evolving Security Relationship: Recommendations for Policymakers,* Report of the U.S.-Mexico Binational Council, co-sponsored by the Center for Strategic and International Studies and the Autonomous Technological Institute of Mexico, Washington, D.C., and Mexico City, April 2004, p. 29.

43. George Tenet with Bill Harlow, *At the Center of the Storm: My Years at the CIA* (New York: Harper Collins, 2007).

44. Commander Victor Alarcon Daowz is the very first Mexican naval officer to be assigned as a foreign liaison officer to NORTHCOM.

45. Roderic Ai Camp, *Mexico's Military on the Democratic Stage* (Westport, Conn.: Praeger/CSIS, 2005).

46. We are indebted to John (Jay) Cope from the Institute for National Strategic Studies at the National Defense University for his insights on these issues.

47. Government of Mexico, Office of the President, "National Development Plan 2006–2012," Mexico City, 2007, p. 45.

48. Ibid., p. 55.

49. Ibid., p. 71.

50. Ibid., p. 67.

51. Ibid., p. 66.

52. U.S. Department of State, "Overall Justification Document for FY2008 $500 Million Supplemental Request: Mexico ($500 Million)," Washington, D.C., October 22, 2007.

53. Alfredo Corchado, "U.S. May Send Mexico $1.4 Billion in Drug War," *Dallas Morning News*, October 2, 2007.

54. Armand Peschard-Sverdrup, "The Mérida Initiative: U.S.-Mexico-Central America Security Cooperation," Testimony Before the U.S. House of Representatives, Foreign Relations Committee, Subcommittee for Western Hemisphere Affairs, Washington, D.C., October 25, 2005.

55. Security and Prosperity Partnership of North America, Second Leaders' Report, August 2006, pp. 60–76.

56. Prime Minister Stephen Harper, President George W. Bush, and President Felipe Calderón, Joint Statement at the North American Leaders' Summit, Montebello, Quebec, August 21, 2007, p. 3.

57. Ibid., pp. 3–4.

58. Pamela White, Director, Demography Division, Statistics Canada, PowerPoint Presentation at the Center for Strategic and International Studies, Washington, D.C., March 23, 2007.

59. Data provided by the U.S. Census Bureau, Foreign Trade Statistics, http://www.census.gov/foreign-trade/balance/c1220.html#1988.

60. Data provided by the U.S. Department of Commerce, http://www.export.gov/articles/Mexico_MoM.asp.

61. Michael J. Sprung, "Increased Trade Spurs Growth in North American Freight Transportation," U.S. Department of Transportation, Bureau of Transportation Statistics, Special Report SR-001, Washington, D.C., May 2007.

62. As reported in *China Daily*, August 24, 2007, http://english.people.com.cn/90001/90778/6247219.html.

63. "Canadian Security Guide Book: Seaports," Report to the Standing Senate Committee on National Security and Defence, Ottawa, March 2007.

64. Government of Canada, "Building Canada: Modern Infrastructure for a Stronger Canada," 2007, p. 12, http://www.buildingcanada-chantierscanada.gc.ca/plandocs/bg-di/bg-di-info5-eng.html#eco2.

65. National Nuclear Security Administration, "Radiation Detection Testing Underway at Two Foreign Sea Ports," press release, April 11, 2007.

66. Alan Greenspan, *The Age of Turbulence: Adventures in a New World* (New York: Penguin Press, 2007).

APPENDIX A

Daniel Chiquiar Cikurel
Gerente de Investigación del
  Sector Real
Banco de México

Jaime Andrés de la Llanta Flores
General Director of National
  Accounts and Economic
  Statistics
INEGI

Felipe Duarte Olvera
Technical Secretary for the
  Economic Cabinet
Office of the President of Mexico

Hector Espíndola Díaz
Director de Manifestaciones de
  Impacto Regulatorio
COFEMER

Mario Iacobacci
Director of Research
Conference Board of Canada

Laura Kirkconnell
Counselor for Economic Affairs
U.S. Embassy to Mexico

Sharee Lawler
Manager, Government Affairs
E.I. duPont de Nemours and
  Co., Inc.

Carlos Alberto Martinez
Direccion
Banco de Mexico

Roberto Newell Garcia
Director General
Mexican Institute on
  Competitiveness

Armand Peschard-Sverdrup
*Director, North American Future
2025 Project*
CSIS

Maralty Ramírez
Director of Competitiveness
*Economic and Competitiveness
Cabinet at the President's Office*

Robert Rogowsky
Director of Operations
*U.S. International Trade
Commission*

Jorge Schiavon
Secretary General
CIDE

Daniel Schwanen
*Chief Operating Officer and
Director of Research*
*Centre for International
Governance Innovation*

Robert S. Shaw
Intern Scholar
Mexico Project
CSIS

Kristin Wedding
*Research Associate, North
American Future 2025 Project*
CSIS

Sidney Weintraub
*William E. Simon Chair in
Political Economy*
CSIS

APPENDIX B

Danilo Contreras
Coordinator, Americas Program
CSIS

Linda Doman
International Energy Analyst
International Energy Outlook
U.S. Energy Information
* Administration*

Virginia Doniz Gonzalez
Director of Energy Prospective
Mexican Secretariat of Energy

Joseph Dukert
Independent Energy Analyst and
* Senior Associate*
CSIS

Ian Hayhow
Assistant Director, International
* Energy Division*
Natural Resources Canada

Veronica Irastorza Trejo
General Director of Energy Planning
Mexican Secretariat of Energy

Sarah O. Ladislaw
Fellow, Energy Program
CSIS

Lauren Mayne
Operations Research Analyst
U.S. Energy Information
* Administration*

Armand B. Peschard-Sverdrup
Director, North American Future
* 2025 Project*
CSIS

Glen Sweetnam
Director, International, Economics,
* and Green House Gases*
* Division*
U.S. Energy Information
* Administration*

Frank Verrastro
Director, Energy Program
CSIS

APPENDIX C

Ian Ascher
TransCanada Pipelines

Carlota Cagigas
General Director
Electricity Restructuring Unit
Energy Regulatory Commission
(Mexico)

Chantal Line Carpentier
Head, Environment, Economy
and Trade Program
Commission for Environmental
Cooperation

Len Coad
Director, Western Office
Conference Board of Canada

Linda Doman
International Energy Analyst
International Energy Outlook
U.S. Energy Information
Administration

Virginia Doniz Gonzalez
Director of Energy Prospective
Mexican Secretariat of Energy

Elizabeth Dowdeswell
Special Adviser to the Board of
Directors
Nuclear Waste Management
Organization

Joseph Dukert
Independent Energy Analyst and
Senior Associate
CSIS

George Eynon
Vice President, Business Develop-
ment and External Relations
Canadian Energy Research
Institute

Annette Hester
Economist and Policy Strategist

Dara Hrytzak-Lieffers
Energy Policy Analyst
Centre for Energy Policy Studies
Fraser Institute

Tom Huffaker
U.S. Consul General, Calgary

Jim Hughes
Manager of Energy Analysis
Imperial Oil

Veronica Irastorza Trejo
General Director of Energy
 Planning
Mexican Secretariat of Energy

Sarah O. Ladislaw
Fellow, Energy Program
CSIS

Chappell Lawson
Professor, Department of Political
 Science
Massachusetts Institute of
 Technology

Jorge Martínez Herrera
Manager, Strategic Planning
Office of the Chief Operating
 Officer
PEMEX

John Muir
Country Executive–Canada
GE Energy

William A. Nitze
Chairman
GridPoint

Arturo Núñez
Director of Project Development,
 New Sectors
North American Development
 Bank

Armand B. Peschard-Sverdrup
Director, North American Future
 2025 Project
CSIS

Jorge Schiavon
Secretary General
CIDE

Glen Sweetnam
Director, International, Econom-
 ics, and Green House Gases
 Division
U.S. Energy Information
 Administration

Jaisel Vadgama
Policy Analyst and Senior Assis-
 tant to the Executive Director
Pembina Institute

Kristin Wedding
Research Associate, North
 American Future 2025 Project
CSIS

APPENDIX D
ENVIRONMENT ROUNDTABLE PARTICIPANTS
CALGARY, ALBERTA, APRIL 27, 2007

Gonzalo Bravo
Communications Manager
Border Environment
  Cooperation Commission

Chantal Line Carpentier
Head, Environment, Economy,
  and Trade Program
Commission for Environmental
  Cooperation

Len Coad
Director, Western Office
Conference Board of Canada

Carlos de la Parra
Research Professor
El Colegio de la Frontera Norte

Elizabeth Dowdeswell
Special Adviser to the Board of
  Directors
Nuclear Waste Management
  Organization

Joseph Dukert
Independent Energy Analyst and
  Senior Associate
CSIS

Tom Huffaker
U.S. Consul General, Calgary

Peter Julian
Member of Parliament
Burnaby–New Westminster,
  Canada

Chappell Lawson
Professor, Department of Political
  Science
Massachusetts Institute of
  Technology

Ignacio Loyola
Procurador Federal de Protección
  al Ambiente

Alastair Lucas
Acting Dean and Professor and
Chair of Natural Resources Law
University of Calgary

William A. Nitze
Chairman
GridPoint

Arturo Núñez
Director of Project Development,
New Sectors
North American Development
Bank

Armand B. Peschard-Sverdrup
Director, North American Future
2025 Project
CSIS

Alejandro Posadas
Minister
Ministry of Environment and Nat-
ural Resources (SEMARNAT)

Richard Revel
Professor, Faculty of Environ-
mental Design
University of Calgary

Jorge Schiavon
Secretary General
CIDE

Jaisel Vadgama
Policy Analyst and Senior Assis-
tant to the Executive Director
Pembina Institute

Kristin Wedding
Research Associate, North
American Future 2025 Project
CSIS

Gonzalo Bravo
Communications Manager
Border Environment Cooperation
  Commission

Enrique Cabrero Mendoza
Director General
CIDE

Hector Camacho Calderón
Deputy Managing Director
North American Development Bank

Daniel Chacon
General Manager
Ecological Transboundary
  Cooperation Commission
Border Environment Cooperation
  Commission

Luis de la Calle
Managing Director and Founder
De la Calle, Madrazo, Mancera,
  S.C.

Jesus Fernandez
Administrador Central para
  Asuntos Internacionales
Administracion General de
  Aduanas

Simone Heinlein
Economic Affairs
U.S. Embassy to Mexico

Mario Iacobacci
Director of Research
Conference Board of Canada

Luis Alberto Ibarra
Director General de Gabinete de
  Infraestructura
Coordinación de Gabinetes y
  Proyectos Especiales
Presidencia de la República

Patrick Maher
National Intelligence Council
Office of the Director of National
  Intelligence

Elizabeth K. Martin
Economic Section
U.S. Embassy to Mexico

Ivonne Pantoja
Director of Foreign Trade
CANAINTEX

Armand B. Peschard-Sverdrup
Director, North American Future
  2025 Project
CSIS

Alberto Ortega Venzor
Chief of Staff
Office of the Mexican Secretary of
  the Economy

Oscar Ringenbach
Under Secretary for Intermodal
  Projects
Secretaría de Communicaciones y
  Transportes

Raul Rodriguez
Chairman, North American
  Center
Arizona State University

Gordon Rogers
Deputy Director, Planning
  Director
Whatcom Council of Govern-
  ments

Jorge Schiavon
Secretary General
CIDE

Robert S. Shaw
Intern Scholar
CSIS Mexico Project

Scott Seeley
Senior Vice President, Corporate
  and Transactions Law
NBC Universal

Eduardo Sojo Garza-Adalpe
Mexican Secretary of the
  Economy

D. Rick Van Schoik
Managing Director
Southwest Consortium for Envi-
  ronmental Research and Policy
  (SCERP)

Juan Carlos Villa
Research Scientist, Economics and
  Policy
Texas Transportation Institute
  Texas A&M University

Kristin Wedding
Research Associate, North Ameri-
  can Future 2025 Project
CSIS

Sidney Weintraub
William E. Simon Chair in Politi-
  cal Economy
CSIS

Rosalind Wilson
Director, Business Development,
  Mexico
Canadian Pacific Railway

APPENDIX F

Amy Apodaca
Statistical Demographer
International Programs
U.S. Census Bureau

Howard Davis
Acting Director, Office of Analysis
  for Inter-American Affairs
U.S. Department of State

Carlos Felix
Migration Affairs
Embassy of Mexico

Silvia E. Giorguli Saucedo
Academic Coordinator
Center of Demographic Studies
El Colegio de México

Louis Grignon
Director, Workplace Unit
Labour Market Policy
Human Resources and Social
  Development
Canada

Luis Herrera-Lasso
Director General
Grupo Coppan

Paul Hewitt
Executive Director
Americans for Generational
  Equity

Raul Hinojosa-Ojeda
Associate Professor
University of California, Los
  Angeles

Mario Iacobacci
Director of Research
Conference Board of Canada

Roger Jones
Senior Analyst, Strategic
  Intelligence-Assessment Division
Canada Border Services Agency

310

Les Linklater
Director General
Immigration Branch
Citizenship and Immigration
  Canada

B. Lindsay Lowell
Director of Policy Studies
Institute for the Study of
  International Migration
Georgetown University

Patrick Maher
National Intelligence Officer for
  the Western Hemisphere
National Intelligence Council
  (NIC)

Jeffrey Passel
Senior Research Associate
Pew Hispanic Center

Armand B. Peschard-Sverdrup
Director, North American Future
  2025 Project
CSIS

Michael D. Puccetti
Senior Adviser for Global Affairs
Office of Policy Planning and
  Coordination
Bureau of Western Hemisphere
  Affairs
U.S. Department of State

Jeffrey Reitz
Professor, Department of
  Sociology
University of Toronto

Enrique Rojo
Chief of Staff
Undersecretary of North
  American Affairs
Mexican Foreign Ministry

Alejandro Villagomez
Professor
CIDE

Kristin Wedding
Research Associate, North
  American Future 2025 Project
CSIS

Sidney Weintraub
William E. Simon Chair in Politi-
  cal Economy
CSIS

Pamela White
Director, Demography Division
Statistics Canada

Ma. Elena Zúñiga
Independent Consultant
Former Secretary General of
  Mexico's National Population
  Council (CONAPO)

APPENDIX G

Sigrid Arzt
Secretaria Tecnica del Consejo de
  Seguridad Nacional
Oficina de la Presidencia

Raul Benitez
Professor
Universidad Nacional Autonoma
  de Mexico

Nabor Carrillo Flores
Attorney General's Office Attaché
Embassy of Mexico

Jorge Chabat
Professor
CIDE

Frank Cilluffo
Associate Vice President for
  Homeland Security
George Washington University

Howard Davis
Acting Director, Office of Analysis
  for Inter-American Affairs
U.S. Department of State

Craig Deare
Dean of Academic Affairs
Center for Hemispheric Defense
  Studies
National Defense University

Juan Carlos Delgadillo Salas
Staff Director (Secretario Tecnico)
Committee on National Defense
Mexican Senate

Richard Downie
Director
Center for Hemispheric Defense
  Studies
National Defense University

Jacques Duchesneau
President and CEO
Canadian Air Transport Security
  Authority

Carol Dumaine
Founding Director
Global Futures Partnership
Central Intelligence Agency

Daniel Flynn
Director, Long-Range Military-
  Security Program
Office of the Director of National
  Intelligence

Rolando Garcia
Director, International Affairs
Instituto Nacional de Migracion

Vice Admiral Moises Gomez
Cabrera
President
Mexican Naval War College

Maj. Gen. Pedro F. Gurrola
Defense, Military and Air Attaché
Embassy of Mexico

Paul Herman
Director, Long-Range Policy
  Program
Office of the Director of National
  Intelligence

Luis Herrera-Lasso
Director General
Grupo Coppan

David Heyman
Director and Senior Fellow
Homeland Security Program
CSIS

Mauricio Ibarrra
Special Affairs and Human Rights
Embassy of Mexico

Roger Jones
Senior Analyst, Strategic
  Intelligence-Assessment Division
Canada Border Services Agency

Patrick Maher
National Intelligence Officer for
  the Western Hemisphere
National Intelligence Council
  (NIC)

Michelle Malenfant
Research Officer
Canadian Air Transport Security
  Authority

Javier Medina
Director, Legislative Affairs
TV Azteca

Trefor Munn-Venn
Associate Director
Conference Board of Canada

Gerardo Olmos
Director de Analisis
CISEN

Kevin O'Reilly
Director
Latin American Affairs
Office of International Affairs
Department of Homeland Security

Armand B. Peschard-Sverdrup
Director, North American Future
  2025 Project
CSIS

Michael D. Puccetti
Senior Adviser for Global Affairs
Office of Policy Planning and
  Coordination, Bureau of
  Western Hemisphere Affairs
U.S. Department of State

Enrique Rojo
Chief of Staff
Undersecretary of North
  American Affairs
Mexican Foreign Ministry

Chris Sands
Senior Associate
CSIS

Charles Swett
Senior Adviser for Defense
  Planning Scenarios
Office of the Secretary of Defense

Mario Verduzco
Assistant Defense Attaché
Embassy of Mexico

Kristin Wedding
Research Associate, North
  American Future 2025 Project
CSIS

Dave Whiddon
NORAD USNORTHCOM

INDEX

Page numbers followed by the letters b, f, *and* t *refer to boxes, figures, and tables, respectively. Page numbers followed by the letter* n *refer to chapter endnotes.*

ABOUT THE EDITOR AND AUTHORS

Norman F. Anderson is president and chief executive officer of CG/LA Infrastructure, LLC, a firm that focuses on developing infrastructure projects globally and provides strategy assessment for the public and private sector through databases and diagnostic models of strategic infrastructure. Anderson provides services aimed at increasing the level of investment in infrastructure as well as the performance of existing infrastructure stocks in developed and developing countries alike and manages events associated with major projects, including the Global Infrastructure Leadership Forum and the Latin American Leadership Forum. He holds a graduate degree from Harvard University's Kennedy School of Government and an undergraduate degree from the University of Virginia. He continues to write and speak about infrastructure issues broadly, both publicly and privately, and has lectured at Harvard University, Mexico's Universidad Iberoamericana, Spain's Universidad Politécnica, and in Russia as part of a London School of Economics team.

José Carlos Fernández Ugalde is program manager for the Office of Environment, Economy, and Trade at the Commission for Environmental Cooperation. His responsibilities include assessing the environmental impacts of trade liberalization, promoting trade in green goods and services, fostering green procurement, and working with the private financial services sector on strengthening links between investment and the environment. Fernández Ugalde joined the CEC in July 2007, after six years as director of environmental economics at Mexico's National Institute of Ecology, where his primary responsibility was to provide technical and policy advice to the Ministry of the Environment in areas related to environmental and resource economics. Earlier he spent two years as national coordinator of environmental policy at Pronatura A.C., one of Mexico's largest nongovernmental organizations dedicated to environmental issues. Other experience includes conducting research at El Colegio de la Frontera Sur in Mexico, studying sustainable use of wildlife at the World Conservation Monitoring Centre, and assessing environmental projects at the Instituto Tecnológico Autónomo de México. Fernández Ugalde received a degree in economics from the Autonomous Technological Institute of Mexico and a M.Phil. in economics (with honors) from Cambridge University in England.

Hans Herrmann is head of the Biodiversity Conservation Program of the North American Commission for Environmental Cooperation (CEC) and a marine ecologist with more than 23 years of experience in the fields of phytoplankton ecology, biodiversity conservation, and natural resource policy. At CEC, he has led efforts to develop and implement a North American strategy for the conservation of biodiversity, the North American Network of Marine Protected Areas, and the continental conservation plans for marine and terrestrial species of common continental concern. He has authored and coauthored several books and scientific publications, including *Marine Ecoregions of North America*; "Marine Coastal Management in Mexico: International Cooperation"; "Maize and Biodiversity: The Effects of Transgenic Maize in Mexico"; and "Priority Conservation Areas in the Baja California to Bering Region." Before joining the CEC, Herrmann was the general director of Pronatura, the largest nongovernmental organization devoted to the conservation of biodiversity in Mexico. Earlier he was the science director of the Scientific Research Center of Quintana Roo in the Yucatan Peninsula, where he was responsible for managing and coordinating scientific research in the Sian Ka'an Biosphere Reserve. Herrmann is a member of board of the Canadian Healthy Oceans Network, Pronatura, Sea Watch, and the Mexican Institute for Renewable Resources; he is also a member of the International Union for Conservation of Nature (IUCN) World Commission for Protected Areas.

Sarah O. Ladislaw is a fellow in the Energy and National Security Program at CSIS, where she concentrates on the geopolitical implications of energy production and use, energy security, energy technology, sustainable development, and climate change. She has been involved with CSIS's work on the geopolitics portion of studies conducted by the National Petroleum Council and the Smart Power Commission, for which she focused particularly on energy security and climate issues. Ladislaw has also worked on the implications of global energy trends, prospects for greater energy integration, U.S. leadership on climate change, and carbon management strategies and technologies. She joined the Department of Energy in 2003 as a presidential management fellow; from 2003 to 2006, she worked in the Office of the Americas in the department's Office of Policy and International Affairs, where she covered a range of economic, political, and energy issues in North America, the Andean region, and Brazil. At the Department of Energy, she also worked on comparative investment frameworks and trade issues as well as the development and use of biofuels both in the Western Hemisphere and around the world. Ladislaw received a bachelor's degree in international affairs/East Asian studies and Japanese from George Washington University in 2001 and a master's degree in international affairs/international security from George Washington University in 2003 as part of the Presidential Administrative Fellows Program.

B. Lindsay Lowell is director of policy studies for the Institute for the Study of International Migration at Georgetown University. Previously he was director of research at the congressionally appointed U.S. Commission on Immigration Reform, where he was also assistant director for the Mexico-U.S. Binational Study on Migration. Dr. Lowell has served as research director at the Pew Hispanic Center at the University of Southern California, worked as a labor analyst at the U.S. Department of Labor, and taught at Princeton University and the University of Texas at Austin. He coedited *Sending Money Home: Hispanic Remittances and Community Development* and has published more than 150 articles and reports on his research interests in immigration policy, labor force issues, economic development, and the global mobility of highly skilled workers. He received a doctoral degree in sociology, specializing in demographics, from Brown University.

William A. Nitze is a CSIS adjunct fellow and chairman of Oceana Energy Company, a corporation that is developing a new technology for converting tidal energy into electricity, and Clear Path Technologies, a corporation that designs and manufactures neutron beam devices that detect and identify explosives and other dangerous substances in containers. He was cofounder and former chairman of GridPoint, Inc., a corporation that designs, produces and markets intelligent energy management systems for homes and small businesses, and cofounder and president of the Gemstar Group, a nonprofit corporation that was dedicated to developing and implementing market-based solutions to environmental problems. His work on water issues focuses primarily on the border region between the United States and Mexico. Prior to establishing GridPoint and Gemstar, from 1994 to 2001, Nitze served as assistant administrator for international activities at the U.S. Environmental Protection Agency, where he was the U.S. environmental border coordinator for the U.S.-Mexican border region and represented the agency's administrator on the boards of the Border Environmental Cooperation Commission and the North American Development Bank. Nitze is president of the Committee for the Republic and chairman of the Board of Advisors of the European Institute, the Galapagos Conservancy, and the Climate Institute. He is a member of the Council on Foreign Relations and of the Board of Directors of several institutions, including the Aspen Institute and the Krasnow Institute at George Mason University. Nitze holds degrees from Harvard College, Wadham College, Oxford University, and Harvard Law School.

Armand B. Peschard-Sverdrup is president and chief executive officer of Peschard-Sverdrup & Associates, a consulting firm that serves governments, Fortune 500 companies, investment firms, think tanks, and universities with research and analysis specific to Mexico's political, economic, and security environments as well as issues impacting U.S.-Mexican bilateral relations. In 14 years at CSIS, he served as director of the Mexico Project (1999–2007), assistant director (1996–1999), and research associate (1994–1996), and remains a CSIS senior associate. Peschard-Sverdrup directed the CSIS North American Futures 2025 Project (2006–2008). Earlier he was a senior consultant with Econolynx International in Ottawa, Canada, and a research fellow with the UN Economic Commission for Latin America and the Caribbean in Mexico City. Peschard-Sverdrup, a recognized opinion leader on Mexican issues, regularly briefs government officials and corporate officers on developments in Mexico. His recent publications include *U.S.-Mexico Ports of Entry: A Capacity Analysis and Recommendations for Increased Efficiency* (Colegio de la Frontera Norte Press, 2008); "The Merida Initiative," Testimony before the U.S. House of Representatives, 2007; *The Merida Inititative: Why It Must Succeed* (AEI, 2008), *Mexican Governance: From Single-Party Rule to Divided Government,* coeditor (CSIS, 2005); *U.S.-Mexico Border Security and the Evolving Security Relationship* (CSIS, 2004). Peschard-Sverdrup received a bachelor's degree in political science and economics from Carleton University in Ottawa, Canada, in 1988 and pursued graduate studies in government at the Center for Latin American Studies at Georgetown University's School of Foreign Service.

Jamie K. Reaser is the founder and president of Eco Systems Institute, an organization that builds the capacity of individuals and organizations that are dedicated to environmental conservation and sustainable development. She has worked around the world as a biologist, international policy negotiator, environmental educator, and trainer for such organizations as the Smithsonian Institution, U.S. Department of State, National Invasive Species Council, and the Global Invasive Species Programme, where she served as executive director. Reaser is a conservation ecologist and ecopsychologist. She serves on the *Newsweek* Global Leadership and Environment Advisory Committee, Conservation Value Advisory Committee, and the IUCN-World Conservation Union's Species Survival Commission and Commission for Education and Communication. Reaser was awarded science and policy fellowships by the American Association for the Advancement of Science in 1998 and 2003; in 2004 she received the NLP World Community Award for her contributions to environmental conservation. She is the author or editor of more than 100 publications, including *Bring Back the Birds: What You Can Do to Save Threatened Species.* Her photographs, illustrations, and poems appear in books, magazines, and calendars. Reaser received a Ph.D. in biology from Stanford University and a B.S. in field biology from the College of William and Mary.

Robert S. Shaw received an M.A. from The Fletcher School of Law and Diplomacy at Tufts University in May 2008. He has spent more than two years studying, researching, and working in Mexico. In 2004, he received a research grant from Dickinson College to study

U.S.-Mexican migration and remittances and in 2008 was awarded a fellowship from the Jebsen Center for Counter-Terrorism Studies to evaluate U.S. border security and cooperation with Mexico. During summer 2007, he worked as an intern scholar with the CSIS Mexico Project, providing analytical support on Mexico as well as for the North American Futures, 2025, Project.

Jaisel Vadgama has been a senior policy analyst at the Pembina Institute since 2006, where he first worked in 2002–2003 as a technical analyst, investigating the life cycle impacts of different electricity generation options and supporting community energy planning. Between 2003 and 2006, he worked on sustainable development policy for Natural Resources Canada, studied urban water and sanitation issues for the Water Utility Partnership in Senegal, and as a project evaluator in Madagascar. Vadgama holds bachelor's degrees in chemical engineering and in urban studies and planning from MIT and a master's degree in anthropology from the University of Sussex in England.

Sidney Weintraub holds the William E. Simon Chair in Political Economy at CSIS. He is also professor emeritus at the Lyndon B. Johnson School of Public Affairs at the University of Texas at Austin, where he was Dean Rusk Professor from 1976 to 1994, when he then joined CSIS. A member of the U.S. Foreign Service from 1949 to 1975, Weintraub held the post of deputy assistant secretary of state for international finance and development from 1969 to 1974 and served as assistant administrator of the U.S. Agency for International Development in 1975. He was also a senior fellow at the Brookings Institution. Weintraub's many publications include *Energy Cooperation in the Western Hemisphere: Benefits and Impediments* (CSIS, 2007); *NAFTA's Impact on North America: The First Decade* (CSIS, 2004); *Issues in International Political Economy: Constructive Irreverence* (CSIS, 2004); *Free Trade in the Americas: Economic and Political Issues for Governance and Firms* (Edward Elgar, 2004); *Financial Decision-Making in Mexico: To Bet a Nation* (Pittsburgh, 2000), and *Development and Democracy in the Southern Cone: Imperatives for U.S. Policy in South America* (CSIS, 2000). Weintraub has also published numerous articles in newspapers and journals. He received a Ph.D. in economics from American University and an M.A. in economics from Yale University.